the new

Labrador Retriever

Ch. Agber Daisy of Campbellcroft, CD, WC (left) with her great-granddaughter, Ch. Amaretto of Campbellcroft, CDX, JH, WC (Ch. Coalcreek Perish of Char-Don ex Campbellcroft's Bardot); behind them is the Labrador Retriever Club of Southern California Best of Opposite Sex trophy which they both won—nine years apart!

the new

Labrador Retriever

janet i. churchill

HOWELL
BOOK
HOUSE

Macmillan General Reference
A Simon & Schuster Macmillan Company
15 Columbus Circle
New York, NY 10023

Howell Book House
MACMILLAN is a registered trademark of Macmillan, Inc.

Library of Congress Cataloging-in-Publication Data

Churchill, Janet I.
The new Labrador retriever/ Janet I. Churchill.
p.   cm.
Includes bibliographical references
ISBN 0-87605-206-5
1. Labrador retriever. I. Title.
SF429.L3C48   1995
636.7'52—dc20

Manufactured in the United States of America
10 9 8 7 6 5 4 3 2 1

To Joan Macan
She was a true heroine in World War II
as a young woman working on dangerous,
secret missions. After the war, she was devoted
to Labradors at her Timspring Kennels in England.

Blueprint
of the Labrador Retriever

Skull

Neck

Stop

Croup

Withers

Cheek

Muzzle
or Jaw

Thigh

Second
Thigh

Brisket

Hock

Elbow

Shoulder

Loin

Stifle

Pastern

Contents

the new

Labrador Retriever

Am., Can. Ch. Campbellcroft's Angus, CD, WC, winning BOB at the Golden Gate Labrador Retriever Club Specialty in 1985 under Mrs. Helen Warwick. At seven and one-half years of age, "Gus" retired the Golden Gate Labrador Retriever Club BOB Memorial Trophy. *Fox & Cook*

Foreword

Jim and Helen Warwick loved and appreciated Labrador Retrievers, and they were generous in sharing their knowledge with newcomers to the breed. The legacy they left includes numerous sound, good working dogs, and the book on the Labrador written by Helen, *The Complete Labrador Retriever*. Many present-day Labrador owners have bloodlines from the Warwicks' Lockerbie breeding stock that are successfully running in AKC Hunting Retriever Tests or being shown in conformation. In addition, the Labrador Retriever Club, Inc. National Specialty show and Working Certificate program were supported by the Warwicks' volunteer efforts at a time when few people were interested in organizing these events. While some of their club work is now considered controversial (inevitable with this kind of effort), it is sad and disappointing to find that their positive contributions have been forgotten or ignored by those critics.

—Marianne Foote*

Marianne Foote has been a Labrador breeder and exhibitor for more than 35 years, producing bench and field champions. She is a Director of the Labrador Retriever Club, Inc.; Judges' Education Coordinator for the Labrador Retriever Club; and Yearbook Editor for the Labrador Retriever Club, Inc. For 10 years, she was Editor of Retriever International.

Three yellow Labradors, owned by Lorraine Taylor, were used in the filming of *Reversal of Fortune* with Glenn Close. Pictured are: (l. to r.) Ambleside Killingworth Robin, Toynton's Killingworth Katie, and Killingworth Kelt O' Hanover.

Acknowledgments

In writing this book, I have tried to describe the Labrador Retriever and its many accomplishments. Details on training and breeding dogs are subjects for separate treatises. However, there are many things specific to Labradors that are mentioned herein.

I would like to thank all the Labrador fanciers who were kind enough to submit pictures for the book. Thanks also to those who took their time to tell me about their dogs and experiences. These include Debby Kay, Lisa Agresta, Colonel Jerry Weiss, Bill Hadden, Pat Valdata, Enid Bloome, Joan Read, Mary Swan, and Chief John Farrell.

We are also indebted to Dr. Autumn Davidson, Dr. George Lust, Dr. Gustavo D. Aguirre, the University of Pennsylvania School of Veterinary Medicine's *Bellwether* magazine, and the Del Bay Retriever Club.

The Labrador's proverbial willingness to work has never been limited to his peerless abilities in field and marsh. Here Int. Ch. Spenrock's Banner, WC and Ch. Lewisfield Spenrock Ballot, WC prepare to show their abilities in harness for the author's daughter and her friends. *Jan Churchill*

chapter 1

Why Own a Labrador Retriever?

When I moved to the Eastern Shore of Maryland in the 1960s, I soon learned that the local sport was waterfowl hunting. Realizing that I would need to choose a retriever breed to hunt waterfowl, I studied the three major retrieving breeds—Labradors, Goldens, and Chesapeakes. It seemed to me that the Labrador was the best all-around choice for a family dog and hunting companion. I never gave a thought to showing a Lab. I had won top honors many times with Foxhounds in both AKC shows and hound shows, and my German Shepherds all had obedience degrees, so there was no challenge in trying to make a champion out of a retriever. I just wanted a dog to be part of the family and to be my hunting companion.

I looked in the Sunday *Baltimore Sun* and answered an ad about Labradors for sale. I made an appointment and drove to a farm near Washington, D.C. The man (he never said who he was) showed me some very young puppies. Since I had a large number of dogs at home, the little pups seemed like more than I could handle, and they couldn't hunt for another year. I think the man was supposed to sell these first, because when he sensed my reluctance, he said he had an older male puppy—would I like to see him? He brought out a black Lab about four months old. I had never seen a Lab puppy before, but this was a good specimen no matter what breed. I said, "I'll take him."

The man said, "I don't have his papers yet, but the owner will mail them to you." Then he said, "Do you want to see the pup's sister?" To be polite, I said "Sure," and out came a lively bitch who raced over and started tugging on my knee socks. She literally begged me to take her, too. I wasn't sure about taking two dogs home, so I said, "I'll have to think this over—I'll call you tomorrow."

Janet Churchill with
Ch. Lewisfield Spenrock
Ballot, WC and Int.
Ch. Spenrock's Banner,
WC when they were
eight months old.

I couldn't get that bitch out of my mind as I drove home, and as soon as I could get to the phone, I called the man and said I'd be back for the bitch tomorrow. The rest, thankfully, is Labrador history, because this bitch and her offspring have had a tremendous influence on Labrador Retrievers in America.

When the pedigrees came in the mail, I was surprised to see lots of champions, and line breeding of English champions. As a breeder, I recognized a thoughtfully structured pedigree.

When the puppies reached about nine months of age I entered Spenrock Banner and Lewisfield Spenrock Ballot in a Virginia dog show. By then I knew the breeder was James F. Lewis III of the famous Lewisfield kennel. When I got to the show, he rushed up to see what he had told his kennel manager to sell. Thinking I was a novice in the show ring, Mr. Lewis said, "Let me show your dogs for you," which he did. It was rather embarrassing because Banner just stood there when it was time to move the dogs. She was stagestruck, as she had never had any training for the show ring. In spite of this, she was Reserve Winners Bitch that day.

I went home and gave the dogs some training, and at the suggestion of Mr. Lewis, we entered the large shows on Long Island. Mr. Lewis was so pleased with Banner that he continued to show her for me. She finished her championship very quickly and became a real showgirl. Later in her career she was professionally handled by Bob and Jane Forsyth. I handled her myself on many occasions, including at the Westchester Kennel Club, where she won Best of Breed and went on to get a Group placement the following week.

It took Ballot longer to get his title, as the show ring did not interest him at all.

The Labrador Retriever Club (LRC) had a rule that for a dog to use the title "Champion," it had to have a working certificate or a field trial title. Helen and Jim Warwick, who owned the sire of my two Labs, became my good friends and urged me to join the LRC. At prestigious shows at that time,

Int. Ch. Spenrock's Banner, WC, handled by owner, winning BOS under English judge, Mrs. Dora Lee in 1968. *Gilbert*

Int. Ch. Spenrock's Banner, WC, retrieving a live mallard duck at Janet Churchill's Maryland farm.

the Club awarded a very nice silver cup with the club seal to champions with a working certificate. I decided to train my dogs with this in mind. I purchased two dozen mallards, kept them in poultry pens on my farm, and used them for training. My two Labs, with me reading a book on how to train retrievers, learned what to do.

I took the two dogs, along with two ducks in their own crate, up to northern New Jersey where the Warwicks lived. Jim Warwick administered the tests, which the dogs passed with flying colors. This project being complete, I liberated the ducks in the marsh on the farm.

Now I had two well-trained gun dogs and they were both my hunting companions for many years. I had good friends who owned Perry Cabin Farm in St. Michaels, Maryland. They took out commercial gunning parties and needed a dog to retrieve what the clients shot. Ballot liked these people and it was agreed that he would stay with them during the gunning season.

Later Banner's son, Ch. Spenrock Cardigan Bay, became my chief gun dog. Cardigan Bay did well in the show ring, too. He was placed in groups and handled only by his owner. Cardigan was an extremely intelligent gun dog. He would sit in the blind with me at the riverbank and watch for ducks and geese one way while I watched the other direction. They flew by at top speed, leaving no time for hesitation on the part of the gunner. Cardigan figured out whether or not they were in gun range. If they were too high, he merely watched. If they were within shooting range, he came to attention and expected the gunner to shoot them.

Cardigan Bay was a dog I could send out with my guest gunners. I was always impressed that he would work for people he had just met. My cousin used to come and hunt with a friend and told me that many times Cardigan's ability to find a cripple saved the day. Cardigan Bay was a large dog, so clumping around in the marsh was an effort, but he was tireless in his quest for cripples.

Banner and Ballot also did well on upland game, both quail and pheasants. We hunted quail in some very rough country in Virginia. These dogs were better than Pointers because they hunted closer to me while I was on foot rather than on horseback. Labradors don't point, but they stop and freeze looking at the spot. They don't have to point to get their message across. Pheasants require different hunting techniques; my Labs excelled at this, too.

Back then, the Lab world for competition was either field trials, which took constant training and sorting through many dogs to find suitable prospects; or bench shows, which were interesting for showing off one's stock, but not much of a challenge to a trainer. Dual champions were, and still are, rare. The same dogs were seldom found both at field trials and in the show ring.

I knew from my experience with Foxhounds that you could have good sport with animals that excelled in conformation and breed type. You didn't have to breed just for speed, nose, or tail carriage. Actually, the reason for good conformation is for better performance in the hunting field. Proper conformation enables a dog to stay sound while doing a hard day's work, day after day. The dog will stride more efficiently and not tire as easily as a dog of poor conformation.

Banner's first litter produced a National Specialty winner. This was quite an honor for a young bitch. Ch. Spenrock Sans Souci was sold to a man who hunted with her along the rugged New England coastline. He was an avid hunter and would never consent to having her bred.

Obviously there is no reason why "show type" dogs can't perform creditably in the field. The instinct is always there, and given a chance it will provide one with a great hunting dog.

Another of Banner's pups was purchased by a New York Lab breeder for a friend in Texas. The pup was shipped down and put with a field trial trainer. It did very well in field trials, and eventually the new owners acquired an extended pedigree. Imagine their surprise when they saw all the English and American show champions and no American field trial breeding!

Banner went on to have a great impact on American breeding. Margery Brainard of Briary Kennels sent a bitch, Ch. Briary Floradora (by Ch. Lockerbie Brian Boru, WC) to Banner's son, Ch. Spenrock Anthony Adverse. This produced two daughters, Briary Allegra and Briary Abbey Road, now found behind many lines. Ch. Briary Bonnie Briana (by Ch. Lockerbie Brian Boru, WC) mated to Ch. Spenrock Anthony Adverse produced Ch. Briary Bustle, the yellow foundation bitch for Marilyn Reynold's Finchingfield Kennels. Anthony sired only a few litters prior to his untimely death.

Ch. Spenrock Ambassador, Ch. Spenrock Anthony Adverse, and Spenrock Argonaut, littermates at three months of age, with Jenny Churchill Reynolds. Sire: Ch. Lockerbie Stanwood Granada, dam: Int. Ch. Spenrock's Banner, WC.

Ch. Spenrock Brown Bess (Ch. Spenrock Heatheredge Mariner ex Ch. Wayward of Old Forge) at 9 weeks old retrieving a bird. *Jan Churchill*

Agnes Cartier sent Ch. Whiskey Creek Lisa to Ch. Spenrock Cardigan Bay, and this breeding produced Ch. Agber's Daisy of Campbellcroft, CD, WC, who was the foundation for Virginia Campbell's Campbellcroft Labradors in California, among others. This breeding also produced the nice yellow dog Ch. Agber's Daniel Aloysius.

When I first started breeding Labradors, I made many trips to England to learn about the dogs in my pedigrees. It was soon obvious to me that the best dogs were still in England. There was a two-inch difference in height in the American and English breed Standards, with the result that many larger Labs were sent to the United States.

Over the years I imported a number of Labradors from England. The first stud dog I brought over was Ch. Spenrock Heatheredge Mariner. I went to visit his breeder, Miss Margaret Ward, in Yorkshire. She was a very knowledgeable lady who told me she only kept bitches and sent them out to the best available dogs. Mariner was the thirteenth generation of her breeding. He did well at stud and his name is found in the pedigrees of dogs that win in the show ring, in the field, and in the obedience ring, and best of all, are guide dogs for the blind. Mariner surprised me by siring three colors in his first litter, being bred to Madge Dempster's nice yellow Wayward of Old Forge, an English import.

Ch. Spenrock Brown Bess was the chocolate from this litter, and she went on to do well in the show ring. She was very typey, but problems with false pregnancies kept her from winning top honors. Notwithstanding, she was one of the best hunting dogs I ever shot over. Of medium size, she could expertly skim herself over the marshes seeking crippled ducks. She was also a great family companion, as were all the Spenrock Labradors.

Importing English and later American Ch. Lawnwoods Hot Chocolate was a real adventure. An airline pilot carried the money and a crate to England and met the Satterthwaites and Hot Chocolate at London's Heathrow Airport. The officials insisted that Hot Chocolate get into the crate and be carried out to the cargo plane. Hot Chocolate, a headstrong dog, objected strenuously. Once on the airplane, he was allowed to ride loose in the crew quarters at the front of the plane.

The Satterthwaites had written to me about this dog they had sold to a policeman. He was more dog than the man could handle, so he was returned to his breeders. Knowing I was looking for another male, Marjorie Satterthwaite told me she had a dog sired by Ch. Follytower Merrybrook Black Stormer. She had shown him a few times, winning some Reserve Challenge Certificates. His chocolate color counted against him (it was not popular in England), as did the unruly behavior that he occasionally demonstrated in the show ring.

I went to England to meet Chock and take a close look at his hip x-ray. I sat watching him at a dog show with Mary Roslin-Williams. It was nice to hear her say, "Chock will make it," even though she didn't know I had

Eng. and Am. Ch.
Lawnwoods Hot Chocolate
(Ch. Follytower
Merrybrook Black Stormer
ex Lawnwood's Tapestry)
photographed in England.

purchased him. I left Chock in England to be shown for his English championship. He was qualified in the field and therefore eligible to become a full champion. He won nine Challenge Certificates in England and Ireland before flying to the United States in the cockpit of a TWA cargo plane.

By breeding Labradors for over 20 years, we found that breeding carefully for soundness and good breed type can result in great hunting companions and wonderful family dogs. Banner always slept on my bed and it never kept her from retrieving well. I also used her as a sled dog! Sometimes I drove just two Labs. When she was harnessed with Ch. Spenrock Rivermist Tweed, the male would lag and sniff at certain snowbanks; and when he stopped pulling, Banner would reach over and nip his flanks until he started to pull properly.

Labradors are truly dual-purpose dogs in the broadest sense. Their excellent memory, acute sense of smell, and high intelligence make them superb retrievers. Their trainability and desire to please make them useful in many areas besides hunting, such as guide dogs, therapy dogs, arson detectors, and water searchers. If you learn just a little about the breed, you will be able to select a nice Labrador for your family. Unfortunately, when a breed becomes popular enough to be number one in registrations, some breeders don't know what they are doing. If everyone involved with these wonderful dogs would just take a little time to learn about the breed, the good qualities would be preserved for many generations.

chapter 2

The Early Labrador

The Labrador Retriever as we know it today descended from the "water dogs" of Newfoundland. These dogs first arrived in England in the early 1800s. The name Labrador was seen in 1823 under a painting of a Labrador bitch, Cora, by Edwin Landseer. Cora, owned by L. Allsopp, Esq., was black with medium-long hair and white paws, white chest, white tip of the tail, and a tiny stripe on her nose. The retrievers from Newfoundland were called various names such as the St. John's dog, the little Newfoundlander, and the Labrador. The name Labrador was given to the breed by the third Earl of Malmesbury around 1840 to differentiate the water dog from the larger Newfoundland dogs. The fifth Duke of Buccleuch used the name Labrador about the same time, writing in his diary that he took his Labrador, Drake, with him on his yacht to Naples, accompanied by Lord Home with his Labrador, Moss.

Early books on sporting dogs had pictures of retrievers, mostly with smooth-lying coats and feathered tails. There was more similarity in coat to today's Flat-coated Retrievers, while the heads were much like some modern Labradors. One early woodcut illustration shows a deep-bodied black dog with a heavy, thickly feathered coat, calling it the St. John's dog or Labrador.

In 1832 another illustration depicted a black-and-white or tricolored dog with feathering. This was an imported "Labrador" that was purchased at Poole Harbor and given to Mr. John Cotes. In 1905 Col. J.C. Cotes' winning Flat-coated Retriever was a direct descendant of this dog.

During the 1800s a retriever type began to emerge, but there were no well-defined varieties as we know them today. Stud books did not exist and the landed gentry guarded their own strains closely. Gamekeepers were in

A St. John's Labrador. *G. Earl*

charge of matings. Crosses were made with water spaniels, setters, Pointers, and Newfoundlands. The gamekeepers bred for working ability. Shooting people were not interested in uniformity of type or breed Standards.

ORIGINS

Dogs resembling Labradors were seen in paintings as early as 1552 when Titian painted *Giovanni dell' Acquaviva*. This painting shows a dog resembling a yellow Labrador with ears slightly darker than the overall coat color. The dog has a Labrador-type head, but a somewhat thin rather than otter-like tail.

The Labrador traces its roots back to the Molossians—hunting dogs with excellent noses. The ancestors of our Labradors traveled across Europe to Portugal, where they were known as the *Cão de Castro Laboriero* (cattle dog) and the *Cão de Agua* (water dog).

Portuguese ships sailed to Newfoundland for fishing off that coast around 1500, taking these utility dogs along. Clifford Hubbard writes:

> From about the early fourteenth century Portugal has had its special breed of dog which has been bred and trained for service with the fishing community. In the Middle Ages dogs of this type were spread along the entire

Portuguese coastline and were renowned for their remarkable swimming powers. . . . It is almost certain that the larger vessels of the Great Armada which sailed from Lisbon on the 18th of May, 1588 (that is, quite half of the 130 ships which made up the fleet) carried Portuguese Water Dogs specially selected for sea rescue work. . . . Its job of work is unique. The dogs are taken out in the fishing vessels and work as retrievers of fish which have jumped the nets, and of tackle which is washed overboard. . . . So useful are these dogs in fact that they are let out on hire by retired fishermen in the areas where the breed is in short supply. Ashore the dogs guard the boats and nets during the night and prove themselves extremely capable guard dogs. . . . There are two varieties of the breed, the long coated and the curly coated. . . . The long coated variety is certainly better known of the two.[1]

Mr. Hubbard goes on to describe this dog:

The head is fairly large . . . slightly domed across the top and showing a pronounced stop. The eyes are medium, round and coloured dark brown or black; the ears are set fairly high, medium, nearly triangular, and carried folded close to the sides of the head; the muzzle tapers from the foreface to the nose but without snipiness, having every indication of strength of jaws which carry powerful level teeth. The neck is relatively short and well muscled, and although showing a slight arch holds the head rather high. The body is exceptionally well knit together with a rather short level back, a broad and deep chest, a moderately tucked up loin and powerful couplings; the legs are straight, strong and well boned with rather large round feet which invariably possess the inter-digital webs found in some other swimming breeds of dogs; the tail is set in line with the back, of full natural length, rather thick at the base but tapering to the end, which reaches to a little above the hocks . . . and carried low in repose but carried over the back when excited. The coat is abundant and rather open and shaggy with a fair gloss. . . . Colours are black, black and white, dark grey, chocolate and white, pearl and grey and whole white. . . . The height is 20 to 22 inches and the weight about 46 pounds. In general appearance the Portuguese Water Dog is an exceedingly active dog of medium, rather square build and attractive appearance.

This description of the Portuguese Water Dog, except for weight, color, and coat texture, certainly describes the modern Labrador, and indeed, many of the words are found in the original British Standard. The "powerful level teeth" refer to a tight scissors bite rather than an overshot or undershot jaw.

In the Portuguese language the word *lavrador* means laborer or workman, so the dogs that traveled to Newfoundland were called Labradors. They

---

[1]The Book of the Dog, *edited by Brian Vesey-Fitzgerald, Nicholson & Watson, 1948.*

were crossed with Newfoundland's St. John's dog and called either Labradors, lesser Newfoundlands, or St. John's dogs. The resulting water dogs were valued for their retrieving ability and coats that were water-repellent and did not hold ice, as well as their sword-like tails that steered their stoutly made bodies through the rough ocean waves found along the shores of Newfoundland.

The Portuguese cattle or sheep dog had a short body with a level back, a strong loin, and full-size tail. The tail was of medium length and bushy, without fringe, thick at the base, and slightly curved. Ears were held close to a wide head with a rather flat skull. There was a slightly pronounced stop and a strong muzzle that was shorter than the back skull. The eyes were almond-shaped and colored from dark to light brown, giving an intelligent appearance. Their coats were described as thick, rough, and short, being shorter on head and legs. Colors were black, wolf-gray or yellow, brindle, dark fawn, and brown. Today, one of the native breeds of Portugal is a yellow dog, the Perdigeiro, which looks very much like a Labrador Retriever.

Parts of Newfoundland are accessible only by boat, making it possible for dogs to remain "pure" as described by Lady Barlow of St. John's, Newfoundland. In 1974 Lady Barlow was able to travel by boat to Grand Bruit on the south coast of Newfoundland. Here she found true "water dogs" with "a great deal more white on them than one imagines, which accounts for the white spot allowed in our Labrador Standards, and which reappears especially in the original and older strains of Labradors today." Lady Barlow also saw several mixed colors as well as dark yellow and black water dogs.

Lady Barlow tells of the diaries of W.E. Cormack of St. John's, who had traveled across Newfoundland on foot in 1822, more than a hundred years before her exploration of the South Coast. He took a boat from St. George's Bay on the West Coast and reported that he saw "small water dogs, admirably trained as retrievers in fowling and otherwise useful. . . . The smooth short haired dog is preferred because in frosty weather, the long haired kind becomes encumbered with ice on coming out of the water." Cormack noted that these dogs were mostly black.

THE WATER DOG GOES TO GREAT BRITAIN

The Newfoundland fishing fleet usually had at least one dog on board that was a natural water retriever. In the early 1800s, these dogs were arriving at Poole Harbor in Dorset, England, where they attracted the notice of local sportsmen. Many dogs missed the boat going back and hung about the waterfront.

The early importers of Labradors included the second and third Earls of Malmesbury, the fifth Duke of Buccleuch, and the eleventh Earl of Home. The second Earl of Malmesbury (1778–1841) rode over to Poole and saw these dogs playing in the sea, picking up fish that had been thrown away as

"Bennie" with Lady Jacqueline Audley Barlow in 1929. Bennie was bred in 1929 by Countess Howe at her Banchory Kennels. A dog with true Labrador temperament and intelligence, he was Lady Barlow's constant companion.

unsuitable for market. He bought four dogs that he bred for many years to use for wildfowling at his estate, Hurn Court. The third Earl (1807–1889) also imported the retrievers and built kennels for a serious breeding program. As early as 1809 dogs from Newfoundland were used for shooting at Hurn Court by the second Earl of Malmesbury. These dogs were cared for by the estate's gamekeepers, and until the end of the nineteenth century the Labradors were kept in relative obscurity in private shooting kennels belonging to the Earls and their aristocratic friends. The only place where the Labrador was kept pure was in the Malmesbury family kennels at Hurn Court.

The third Earl of Malmesbury was the largest importer from Newfoundland. He gave some of his dogs to the Duke of Buccleuch and the eleventh Earl of Home, as they were impressed with the work of Lord Malmesbury's dogs, especially in water. The Duke of Buccleuch had previously purchased a pair of retrievers from a Newfoundland fishing vessel which had sailed into the River Clyde in Scotland. Unfortunately the strain subsequently died out.

In 1885 Lord Malmesbury bred Avon (Malmesbury Tramp ex Malmesbury Juno) a few years after he got Ned, also a good dog. Most English Labradors can be traced back to these two dogs. Ned stood about 19 inches high while Avon, a slightly larger dog, was about 20 inches high. Avon was one of the most important stud dogs in Labrador history. He had a splendid wide head with excellent expression, a decently wide muzzle, great bone, heavy coat, and a superb otter tail. Avon was the ancestor in direct tail-male (offspring from one male to the next over many generations) line of a famous Labrador, known for his typical head and expression, Dual Ch. Banchory Bolo. These early Labradors had the true Labrador head and expression, which is not seen often enough at the present time.

Some years later the seventh Duke of Buccleuch and his brother, Lord George Scott, wrote to their friend Sir John Middleton, the Governor of Newfoundland, asking him to find a water dog to ship to England. They were eager to find out if any dogs had survived after the 1885 duty imposed on all dogs in Newfoundland (which the fishermen couldn't afford), as well as the ban on all dogs in 130 Newfoundland districts, which caused the end of breeding these dogs. The Navy captains patrolling the more remote parts of Newfoundland, armed with photographs of the type of dog to look for, did find several dogs.

In England the little Newfoundlanders, or St. John's Labradors as they were also called, were crossed with setters and spaniels, a cross that entered into the background of the Flat-coated Retriever as well as the Labrador Retriever. Many years later, after both had been recognized as breeds, Flat-coats were bred to Labradors to improve the eye color from yellow to dark brown. Some Labradors also had a Flat-coat type of coat as a result of these crosses. Field Ch. Gun of Arden was an example.

The earliest printed reference to the "Labrador Breed" was in Col. Peter Hawker's classic of 1814, entitled *Instructions to Young Sportsmen in All*

That Relates to the Guns and Shooting. In describing the difference between the two types of Newfoundland dogs, he talks about the St. John's dog:

> The other, *by far the best for every kind of shooting,* is oftener *black* than of other colour, and scarcely bigger than a Pointer. He is made rather long in the head and nose; pretty deep in the chest; very fine in the legs; has *short* or smooth hair; does not carry his tail so much curled as the other; and is extremely quick and active in running, swimming or fighting. . . .
>
> The St. John's Breed of these dogs is chiefly used on their native coast by fishermen. Their sense of smell is scarcely to be credited. Their discrimination of scent, in following a wounded pheasant through a whole covert full of game, or a pinioned wild fowl through a furzebrake, or warren of rabbits, appears almost impossible. The real Newfoundland may be broken in to any kind of shooting; and without additional instruction, is generally under such command that he may be safely kept, if required to be taken out with Pointers. For *finding wounded game of every description there is not his equal in the canine race:* and he is *sine qua non* in the general pursuit of waterfowl.[2]

Major Maurice Portal in *Guns at Home and Abroad* mentions that Blaine in his *Encyclopaedia of Rural Sports,* written in 1852, refers both to the Newfoundland *retriever* and the St. John's breed, which latter dog, Blaine says, is preferred by sportsmen on every account, being smaller, more easily managed, and sagacious in the extreme, his scenting powers being also very great. "Probably this latter," writes Major Portal, "is the ancestor of the Labrador as we know him today. How the breed was evolved is hard to say, but the probabilities are that the fishermen of Newfoundland wanted a good, strong water dog, since they are reported to have found them useful in cases of wrecks and wreckage on that coast, and crossed the heavy coated, strong, black Newfoundland retriever with a black Pointer, and evolved in time a hard, short coated dog with great staying powers. That this is probably the origin is borne out by the fact that if Labradors are inbred, the result is often a light-made dog, long on the leg, light of bone, with a thin tail and Pointer-like ears."[3]

Elsewhere, the British bred the St. John's dog out of existence through myriad crosses. Many dogs, called by some the English Retriever, were bred solely for their ability to retrieve.

Many years went by between the arrival of the first Labradors in England and their great national popularity as we know it today. The Earls of Malmesbury and the Radclyffe family had been breeding Labradors for many years, but even so, many of the original strains died out.

---

[2] *Warwick, Helen.* The New Complete Labrador Retriever, *1968, p. 21.*
[3] *Warwick, Helen.* The New Complete Labrador Retriever, *1968, p. 18.*

Hyde Ben, also known as Ben of Hyde, whelped 1899 (Major Radclyffe's Neptune ex Mr. Tapper's Duchess, both blacks), was the first yellow registered Labrador Retriever. He traces back to C. J. Radclyffe's Turk, imported from Newfoundland in 1871. From Ben descend many famous families including Knaith, Zelstone, Folkingham, Boghurst, Hawkesbury, Kettledean, and Braeroy. *W.A. Rouch*

In 1885 England passed a Quarantine Act requiring all imported dogs to spend six months in a quarantine kennel. That same year Newfoundland had passed for the second time (the first was in 1780) anti-dog laws to promote sheep raising by placing a very high tax on bitches.

At this time in Great Britain, the methods of hunting influenced the type of dog needed. Most shooting was for upland game, with spaniels searching for the game and then retrieving after birds were shot. A specialized retriever was not called for, the working dogs being Pointers, spaniels, and setters. The exceptions were the water retrievers used by the Earls of Malmesbury and Colonel Radclyffe. Their land was on a flood plain, and in the winter the Stour River would flood large areas, including Hurn. There were vast areas of marshland bordering the rivers Stour and Avon which provided breeding grounds for innumerable waterfowl. Landowners dug channels to control some of the water. In one section there was a 40-acre lake about four feet deep. There were plenty of ducks to shoot, and since they fell in the water most of the time, a swimming retriever was a great asset.

On the big estates, shoots were organized and Labradors allowed to "pick up" the shot game. Shooters were gathered together and briefed on their shooting stands as they moved from one spot to another. Beaters walked the terrain scaring up the birds so that they would fly in front of the shooting stands. After the shooting, the retrievers were sent to bring back the shot birds.

In some sections Labradors were used to hunt the birds, and since they hunted a closer pattern, more game stayed on the ground. Eventually the above-average Labrador set the standard for other dogs. By the first World War Labradors came to be fully appreciated.

It was in the hunting field that the Labrador first achieved popularity. The founding of the Gun Dog League in 1895 was the beginning of serious field competition in England. Many retriever people (in those days all retrievers were classified under one heading) felt that field tests would not prove the merits of a retriever doing real work. Nevertheless, some dedicated people

Dual Ch. Staindrop Saighdear (center) with his son, FT Ch. Staindrop Ray (left) and daughter, FT Ch. Hiwood Peggy (right).

Glenhead Jimmie, the sire of Dual Ch. Staindrop Saighdear (bred and owned by John Annand). Ch. Inglestone Ben was his great-great-grandsire on both sides of his pedigree.

organized field trials as a way for hunting people to get together and compare the merits of their dogs. The first trial for retrievers took place in 1889.

By 1900 the Labrador breed was established in Great Britain. Fortunately enough Labradors had survived which could be traced back to the Malmesbury, Home, and Buccleuch lines.

FT Ch. Zelstone Darter (Darley Bracken ex Glenmorag of Podington). *Harry Allen*

Ch. Zelstone Leap Year Lass, daughter of FT Ch. Zelstone Darter, and sired by Braedrop Bruce, a son of Dual Ch. Staindrop Saighdear. Winner of 9 CCs and many field trial awards, she won BOB over an entry of 98 Labradors at age 10. *Thomas Fall*

Munden Single, a five-year-old black bitch owned by the Honorable A. Holland-Hibbert, was the first Labrador to enter a field trial in England in 1904. Running in the International Gun Dog Trials at Sherborne, she earned a Certificate of Merit. Single placed in other trials as well and so impressed people that when she died, her body was mounted and presented to the British Museum for all to see what a Labrador should look like. In many opinions justice was scarcely done "this beautiful and intelligent creature. Her gentle and sagacious countenance was a joy to behold and her methods at work unusually interesting." After World War II Single was removed to a museum at Tring.[4]

During her lifetime Single produced outstanding progeny with beauty and brains, true dual-purpose Labradors that could win in the field and at dog shows.

---

[4]*Warwick, Helen*. The New Complete Labrador Retriever, *1986, p. 44.*

Until the early 1900s, Flat-coated Retrievers dominated the trials. By 1910 Labradors were the leading contenders in field trials, a position they have not relinquished.

Major Portal's Flapper went on to be a great sire of field-trial-winning dogs. Six years after Flapper was whelped, Captain Archibald Butter's Peter of Faskally was born and, in addition to a fantastic record in the field, became one of the greatest sires on record. The *Stud Book and Record of Field Trials for Retrievers, 1899–1922,* published by the Labrador Retriever Club (of England) says of Flapper and Peter of Faskally:

> Not only did these two great dogs prove winners themselves but when reading the list of dogs whose progeny have won at trials, one is struck by the fact that their progeny to win at trials is three times as numerous as that of any other retriever, the next on the list being another Labrador, Champion Ilderton Ben.

It is interesting to note that retriever trial handling methods started with the success of Peter Clutterbuck's entries, especially his dog Sarratt, sired by Flapper out of Munden Single. Mr. Clutterbuck believed it was best to leave one's dog to the business of retrieving its game with little or no interference from the handler. Some very astute comments were made by Charles Eley, who wrote:

> It was a treat indeed to see the free and independent way in which Sarratt went about his work. He was very fast but seldom over-ran his nose and the longest day's work failed to get to the bottom of him. This invaluable quality of *tirelessness* cannot of necessity be given full credit at field trials. The impossibility of really completely testing *stamina* at a trial is very unfortunate from two points of view; it sometimes permits a dog of *indifferent stamina* to achieve high honors and also prevents a dog of *exceptional stamina* from exhibiting this great quality. A resultant injury to the breed may well ensue from this, owing to the use for breeding of animals deficient in stamina, due to this serious defect being unknown to breeders. [5]

FT Ch. Flapper was one of the most distinguished dogs in the breed. Flapper was four generations removed from Malmesbury's Sweep in male line (sired by Stag out of Brig. Gen. Loftus' Bates's Betsey). FT Ch. Flapper towered over the other field trial dogs and was regarded as a "pillar of the first magnitude in the breed's history," according to historian C. Mackay Sanderson. Flapper was the first Labrador to win a stake at field trials at the 1907 Kennel Club Trials.

---

[5] *Warwick, Helen.* The New Complete Labrador Retriever, *1986.*

Ch. Holton Joyful, 1937. The first Holton champion owned by Leila and Maurice Gilliat.

Ch. Holton Baron, 1951 (Sandyland's Bob ex Holton Whimbrel), bred and owned by Maurice C.V. Gilliat. Baron won 14 CCs and numerous field trial awards. *Thomas Fall*

In 1909 a new star at the field trials arose, and with it a style of handling directly opposite to Mr. Clutterbuck's. This dog was Peter of Faskally, handled by his owner, Archibald Butter. Peter of Faskally won the International Gundog League's Championship Stake, the highest win possible. Butter was the first man to apply sheepdog hand-signals and whistling to direct a retriever in its work. Butter was a man with great "dog sense" and knew exactly when to signal his dog. Many of his imitators did not fare as well. Butter's handling methods were not used again until 20 years later when Dave Elliot, a Scottish gamekeeper, introduced them to the United States.

In 1904 the English Kennel Club recognized the Labrador Retriever as a separate breed. Retrievers were registered as the breed they resembled. Some litters had two types of retrievers such as Labradors and Flat-coats. The dogs were identified by coat length and in some cases a litter was registered as half Labradors and half Golden Retrievers. The word "yellow" was assigned to Labradors to separate them from Golden Retrievers. The first retrievers listed in the stud books came in all colors and coat textures. The majority of

Holton Pegasus, 1953 (Ch. Holton Baron ex Holton Una). A dog with a very kind expression with correct head, eye, and muzzle, he is photographed as a veteran.

Ch. Reyan Lass (Story ex Helen), bred by Mrs. Veronica Wormald, was one of the earliest yellow bench champions descended from Ben of Hyde (aka Hyde Ben). *Thomas Fall*

Flat-coats (once called Wavy Coated in early days) were liver (later called chocolate). The early chocolate Labradors descended from FT Ch. Peter of Faskally.

In 1909 the Kennel Club passed a rule making it compulsory for all gun dogs to obtain a working certificate before they could be recognized as conformation champions. This was to prevent a retriever from being a bench champion when it had no inclination to retrieve or was hard-mouthed or gunshy. If the dog didn't become a full champion, its title was Show Champion.

In April 1916 a Labrador Club was founded in England with the Hon. A. Holland Hibbert (later Lord Knutsford) of Munden Kennels as President and Mrs. Quintin Dick (later Lorna, Countess Howe) as Secretary. Also serving on the Committee were Lord Chesterfield, Lord Lonsdale, Lord Vivian, Lord Harlech, Mr. B. Coutts, MP, Mr. A. Nichol, and Mr. R. Heaton. A Standard for the breed was written by this prestigious group of shooting people in July 1916. In setting up the breed Standard they had one basic requirement—that the Labrador should be a working dog, a retriever par excellence, an intelligent companion, and a dog which the owner would be proud to take anywhere.

The size and shape of the true Labrador has changed very little since the early days. Remember when you read the first English Labrador Standard that many comparisons were made to the Flat-coated Retriever. According to Jo Coulson, Secretary of the Labrador Retriever Club (England) in recent years,

> There is great emphasis on head and eye and it is not surprising that this should be so; the whole character can be assessed by looking at those gentle, intelligent eyes. The well-balanced skull and strong foreface provide the brain room and the ability to carry heavy retrieves from the shooting field. The neck and shoulder placement enables the dog to use his nose whilst seeking his game and then to lift and gently carry it back to his master. The strong, well sprung ribcage gives good heart and lung room and the powerful, well-angulated hindquarters provide the driving force to power the dog throughout a long and tiring day in the field. The tail is unique and the excellent description of the "otter" tail (in the Standard) places the correct emphasis on this special Labrador feature. Just as important is the texture of the coat, the combination of top coat and dense undercoat giving efficient protection against the cold rain and icy water through which the dog might have to work.
>
> In recent years there have been minor changes made to the original Standard, the eye color for example, and additional information has been added regarding size, but basically the Standard has survived intact. The new English Standard varies slightly in format, the original requirements all being retained, with extra details being included to conform with the Kennel Club's policy of standardization throughout all breed Standards.
>
> When the English Kennel Club first requested that representatives of the breed should review the Labrador breed Standard, there were fears in some quarters that our dogs would be changed and that the Labrador as we knew it might be in danger. However, as you will see from the new Standard, this has not happened. And why should it? The dog which has served us so well for so many years cannot be improved upon.[6]

Up until 1919 the Kennel Club recognized only dogs which had retrievers for parents. Pressure was applied by dog owners whose retrievers were not "purebred" or "interbred" to run them in trials. The Kennel Club met this demand by opening a register for "Outcross Retrievers," another name for retrievers, pedigree unknown. After two years this caused so much confusion that in 1921, the Kennel Club settled on three Registers:

1. All varieties of purebred Retrievers (Labrador, Curly, Golden, or Flat-coat).

---

[6]The Labrador Club Yearbook, *1985, p. 29.*

2. Interbred Retrievers (a cross between any two of the breeds mentioned above).

3. Gamefinders, for any dog whose owner wished to run it in a field trial, no matter what variety, pedigree unknown; and all dogs not eligible for registry in 1. and 2. above.

Subsequently the word Gamefinder was changed to Retriever Outcross.

FAMOUS ENGLISH KENNELS

Banchory

One of the Labrador's most dedicated fanciers ever was Lorna, Countess Howe. She excelled as breeder, judge, exhibitor, and astute purchaser. She had a keen eye and bought as many good ones as she bred, giving all of her dogs the Banchory prefix. Lady Howe won her first stake in 1919 with Banchory Queen at the Horsham Trials. She was the first person to finish a dual champion in 1922, the famous Dual Ch. Banchory Bolo, a fine specimen of the breed, and a grandson of Peter of Faskally. Her Dual Ch. Banchory Bob was Best in Show at Crufts in 1933 and 1934.

The great Banchory Bolo (born December 29, 1915, bred by Sir John Banner and originally named Caerhowell Bully), owned by Lady Howe, was a grandson of Peter of Faskally and the first Labrador to win both a bench and field trial championship.[7] When Bolo established his own greatness, it had been 40 years since the great Malmesbury Tramp had been so influential, and no other dog during those decades exerted such a tremendous influence as these two. Bolo enjoyed well-earned prestige as a competitor and at stud, after some early mishaps from which he recovered, thanks to the kindness of Lady Howe. Bolo had been abused by some men before Lady Howe got him, and then he became ill.

Lady Howe and her gifted gamekeeper, Tom Gaunt, brought together animals from all over Great Britain, which all possessed uniformity of type although they had different bloodlines. Over the years the Banchory Kennels housed four dual champions, 29 bench champions, seven field champions and countless other stake and Challenge Certificate (CC) winners. Among the famous dogs in her kennel were Dual Ch. Bramshaw Bob and his remarkable sire, Ch. Ingleston Ben; Dual Ch. Peter The Painter, and Ch. Ilderton Ben.

Lady Howe inaugurated classes for gamekeepers at the Crufts dog show and special stakes for them at trials. Her recognition of their accomplishments was an important factor in the success of the Labrador breed, not only in England, but also in the United States.

---

[7]*Connett, Eugene V. American Sporting Dogs, 1948, p. 214.*

Lady Howe's success with Banchory Bolo gives an insight into her intelligent determination. Bolo was given to Lady Howe when he was two years old after several trainers had given up on him because of his surly disposition. Lady Howe nursed Bolo through two life-threatening illnesses and made friends with the dog. Once she had gained his confidence, he began to work for her to his full potential. At the age of five, he entered competition and became a field champion. In 1922, two years later, he became a dual champion.

C. Mackay Sanderson, Secretary of the Scottish Gamekeepers' Association until his death, and keeper of The Labrador Retriever Stud Book, wrote a fine tribute to this dog's success (thanks to Lady Howe and Tom Gaunt):

In order to assess the imprint of the descent from Malmesbury's Tramp in its wholeness and right proportion, a separate feature has to be accorded in the line from Field Ch. Peter of Faskally through Scandal of Glynn which gained its fullest expression with the emergence of Dual Ch. Banchory Bolo. Between the period which had given birth to Tramp and the advent of Bolo some 40 years later, no single figure had arisen which had exercised such a great and moulding influence on progress.

Bolo's coming may be said to have breathed a spirit of new life for the breed, the prestige enjoyed by this dog as a competitive and stud force giving lasting impetus to Labrador fortunes, and subsequently his name runs like a golden thread through all the vital streams of progress. Bolo was undoubtedly triumphant and predominant during his period, his dominance being referable to qualities other than are actually wrapt up in his prestige as a stud force.

He came at a time when prestige both in a competitive and breeding sense was being put to rigorous tests. Behind the full story of remarkable expansion during the last period, lies the priceless contribution made by Bolo and his descendants. . . . The feats of this remarkable dog and his progeny give joy to the memory as one contemplates the advance which followed. The name and fame of Bolo will always be indissolubly bound up with the Banchory Kennel of Lorna, Countess Howe, of which he was such a distinguished inmate.[8]

Many dogs of the highest caliber trace their heritage to the Banchory lines. Bolo never sired any yellows, but his sons did, one of the most outstanding being Ch. Banchory Danilo, a dog bred by Lord Knutsford. Danilo had one of the most impressive show records in Labrador history, including a win at Crufts. The first American and English field champion made up in 1940 traces directly back to Danilo.

---

[8]*C. Mackey Sanderson.* Stud Book and Record of Field Trials of The Labrador Retriever Club, *England, 1949.*

Whitmore

The most famous dog from Mr. T. W. Twyford's kennel, which dates back to 1910, was Dual Ch. Titus of Whitmore, sired by Twist of Whitmore ex Teazle of Whitmore. Through the direction of John Cady, the Whitmore dogs made a great contribution to the breed over many years by combining excellent working dogs with high-quality bitches. Many honors were won by the same Labradors in the field and on the bench. The Whitmore dogs descended from Nethersby Boatswain.

Adderly

Mr. Reginald Corbett's Labradors excelled in working ability and brillance in the field. While most of the successful kennels up to this time had gamekeepers to train the dogs, Mr. Corbett had an outstanding record as owner-breeder-trainer-handler. He won his first field trial in 1923 with Field Ch. Vidi of Adderly at the Cheshire trials. From that time until World War II, Mr. Corbett won 35 stakes and placed in 31 others with his owner-bred dogs.

The most brilliant performer in his kennel was the bitch FT Ch. Adderly Trim, by FT Ch. Beningbrough Tanco, a grandson of Bolo. Trim won her first stake at nine months of age in 1927, and her last in 1935 when she was nine years old. She won a total of 13 stakes. Trim was descended from Malmesbury Tramp, and was trained and handled throughout her career by Mr. Corbett.

Mansergh

After World War II conditions were vastly changed in Great Britain. Owner-handlers came to the forefront as the day of the great estate kennels with gamekeepers and trainers faded into history.

Mary Roslin-Williams, who was to become a world-renowned international judge, marked her advent to the sport by piloting her Carry of Mansergh to victory at the Midland Counties Labrador Club meeting. Carry of Mansergh was the first lady-owned and -handled winner of the season. This bitch, sired by Jestaphome ex Jessica, tracing back in male line to Malmesbury's Tramp, became Mrs. Roslin-Williams' foundation bitch. Ch. Midnight of Mansergh, a dog with a great show record, is a great-great-great-grandson of Carry of Mansergh. Midnight sired many bench and field winners.

In the 1970s the author had the privilege of visiting Mrs. Roslin-Williams at her home in Yorkshire. When visiting her kennels, I immediately learned that her best dogs never left England. At that time a few had been exported to the United States. I also learned that Mrs. Roslin-Williams was a very knowledgeable person regarding Labrador bloodlines. She explained to me her distress with the indiscriminate breeding that had taken place after World War II, resulting in Whippety and/or Foxhound-like characteristics in Labradors. The incorrect yellows were 24-inch leggy animals with smooth, single coats of harsh texture, straight shoulders, high sterns, cat-like feet with straight pasterns knuckling over at the knees, and expressions that were houndy, denoting arrogance rather than a cooperative hunting companion. She also abhorred the influence of Boxers, Rottweilers, Great Danes, and Dobermans that had been mixed into the breed. She especially didn't like coarse heads with overshort muzzles. She stressed that the muzzle must be long enough to enable the dog to pick up a hare or a large cock pheasant.

Mrs. Roslin-Williams told me she got her first Labrador in 1939, but it went blind at four years of age and had to be put down. Then, searching for a dual-purpose Labrador, she got Carry of Mansergh. She said that Carry was not only a wonderful worker, but also good-looking. Carry was solid and deep with good bone and was rather short on leg, which fitted Mrs. Roslin-Williams' preference for a Labrador that wasn't too tall. Her head was a wonderful shape with an attractive contrasting eye color (not black or very dark brown); she had good reach with her long neck, excellent well-laid-back shoulders, a great ribcage, and a short loin (not a short back). Her hindquarters were extremely powerful with a thick-based otter tail.

In the late 1970s Mrs. Roslin-Williams came to visit Spenrock Kennels. I remember well the interest she expressed in Thoroughbred race horses. We visited my neighbors Mrs. Richard duPont and Kelso, who had some of the more famous horses in the world, and then we went to Windfields Farm, owned by Mr. Edward P. Taylor of Canada. (Mr. Taylor owned Ch. Spenrock Tweed of Windfields, a yellow Labrador). At Windfields Mary Roslin-Williams expressed delight and great satisfaction to stand in the same barn as three Derby winners—from America, France, and England. Mrs. Roslin-Williams was as much a student of horse pedigrees as of Labradors.

Mrs. Roslin-Williams has written three books: *The Dual Purpose Labrador, All About the Labrador,* and *Advanced Labrador Breeding.* Serious Labrador breeders will find a wealth of information in her books. Many of her exports have had a great influence on kennels in America as well as on the continent for those seeking dual-purpose bloodlines.

Knaith

Mrs. Veronica Wormald did a great deal to promote the yellow color. She started the Yellow Labrador Club in 1924 after her yellow Labrador was rudely mistaken for a Golden Retriever at an important show. All the early yellows were dark, which Mrs. Wormald said was the true yellow Labrador color. Acceptance for these dogs at shows was difficult in the early years of bench competition.

Mrs. Wormald's best-known dog was Dual Ch. Knaith Banjo, a dog with many CCs and show awards as well as 41 awards at field trials. When they traveled, Banjo and Mrs. Wormald always shared the hotel room, as this dog was not only a great performer in competition, but a companion to his mistress.

One of the reasons the Knaith kennel had spectacular success was the high quality of its bitches, especially Velvet and Mailie.

Zelstone

Mrs. Audrey Radclyffe was associated with the early yellows. Her husband, Major A. Radclyffe, was responsible for putting the yellows on the map through his yellow male, Hyde Ben (also known as Ben of Hyde). Virtually all yellow Labradors trace their ancestry back to Major Radclyffe's Neptune in direct male line. Neptune was sired by Mr. M. Guests' Sweep ex Nell, a bitch bred by Major Radclyffe. Yellows from these lines have excelled on the bench and in the field. Hyde Ben was the first registered yellow Labrador. His sire and dam were black.

The yellow bitch Ch. Zelstone Leap Year Lass had a great show record, including Bests In Show, as well as being a field trial winner and dam of field trial winners. She was a granddaughter of Dual Ch. Staindrop Saighdear.

Braeroy

Captain and Mrs. Macpherson were also instrumental in the development of the yellows. Mrs. May Macpherson also was responsible for the introduction of the chocolate color when her yellow bitch Braeroy Randy produced Derry of Chiltonfoliat as well as another chocolate.

The Macphersons outcrossed as little as possible, preferring to work within their own established bloodlines. They produced true field trial lines with dogs that were also good-looking. The Macphersons thought that there was a Chesapeake behind the chocolates they bred because some puppies had that type of coat and appearance.

Another source of the chocolate color was the Pointers that were kenneled alongside the Labradors on the big estates where the dogs were under the charge of the gamekeepers. Mary Roslin-Williams told me that this situation accounted for "ugly mugs, yellow eyes, and lack of pigment."

Poppleton

The kennels of Mrs. B. M. Outhwaite in Yorkshire had a great influence on yellow Labradors. Although she started with blacks, by the late 1930s she had developed a dominant type of yellow. The two most important males from her kennels were Ch. Poppleton Golden Flight and Ch. Poppleton Lieutenant, both of which go back to Ch. Poppleton Golden Major. Ch. Poppleton Golden Russet was the sire of Dual Ch. Knaith Banjo.

The Poppleton Labradors were known for their classic heads with distinctive, broad, flat skulls with a real almond-shaped eye giving a keen

FT Ch. Zelstone Moss (Beruch ex Ch. Zelstone Leap Year Lass) delivering a bird to Audrey Radclyffe.

expression. They had excellent coats and tails, but could be faulted for straight stifles or a lack of bend in the stifle.

A number of lines trace directly to the Poppleton dogs, among them Ch. Diant Swandyke Cream Cracker, the Kinleys, and the Garshangans.

Diant

Louise Wilson-Jones (of the Diant prefix) told me that Cream Cracker was not a pretty dog but had his good points, notably fantastic shoulders, coat, and otter tail. He was a rugged dog with flat skull and ample length of muzzle, a strong medium-length neck, deep brisket, and heavy, wavy coat. A dog of great spirit, Cream Cracker won two CCs in a week and then was so rambunctious as he clowned around in the show ring that it took two years to win a third CC to gain his championship.

Cream Cracker was sired by Ch. Poppleton Golden Flight, a grandson of Ch. Poppleton Golden Major, while his dam was a granddaughter of Ch. Poppleton Golden Major. Through his most famous offspring, Ch. Diant Juliet, one finds dogs of the Braeduke prefix.

Other lines tracing to Cream Cracker were Mrs. Marian Saffell's Rookwoods, with Ch. Rookwood Petergold being linebred to him; the Cornlands, whose first champion was Cornlands Peter So Gay (a son of Cream Cracker); Ch. Cornlands Westhelm Flight by Poppleton Lieutenant; the famous Cornlands bitch, My Fair Lady, an animal well up to size, but full of quality and personality; and the Nokeeners.

Foxhanger

The dogs belonging to Lady Simpson traced back to Poppleton Golden Russett and Ch. Poppleton Lieutenant. Foxhanger dogs performed well in many areas including police and guide work. Many were of the original dark red color. One truly dual-purpose dog was Foxhanger Summer Madness, owned by Barbara Starkey.

Kinley

Mr. and Mrs. Fred Wrigley based their breeding program on the Poppleton dogs. The Kinley dogs are found in the Poolstead and Sandylands pedigrees as well as many others.

Garshangan

The original dogs from this kennel owned by Lt. Col. and Mrs. Hills were by Poppleton Golden Flight. Ch. General of Garshangan, their most important male, by Poppleton Lieutenant, was the grandsire of Sandylands General, a dog found in many modern pedigrees. General was a strong, rugged dog of dark yellow color with very dark pigment, powerful but not necessarily of the quality associated with the Sandylands kennel. General is also found in the Poolstead pedigrees.

Blaircourt

Mrs. Marjorie Cairns of Glasgow, Scotland, told me that her foundation bitches were not successful in the show ring but were excellent brood bitches. With this confidence in her bitches, she bred Olivia of Blaircourt, a daughter of Craigluscar Dusk of Blaircourt, to Forbes of Blaircourt, a son of the same bitch. This mating produced the great Ch. Ruler of Blaircourt. Ruler was bred to Ch. Tessa of Blaircourt to produce Ch. Sandylands Tweed of Blaircourt. The mating was never repeated, as Tessa wouldn't let Ruler near her again after she whelped her first litter.

Sandylands

Mrs. Gwen Broadley, whose Labradors are known worldwide, started her kennel in the 1930s, carrying on the foundation laid by Lorna, Countess Howe. Her original lines came from Dual Ch. Banchory Bolo, Ch. Ilderton Ben, and FT Ch. Peter of Faskally. Her foundation bitch was Juno of Sandylands. The author's foundation bitch, Int. Ch. Spenrock Banner, WC, whose name is found in so many pedigrees, was a seventh-generation descendant of the original Sandylands bitch through her dam, Ch. Sandylands Spungold. Readers having Banner's name in their pedigrees can count back to see how many generations their dogs are removed from the original Sandylands bitch.

Mrs. Broadley came to America many years ago to judge a Labrador match near Washington, D.C., where she awarded Best Puppy in Show to Ch. Spenrock Anthony Adverse, a yellow son of Banner found behind many of today's pedigrees. Anthony sired only a few litters but had a great influence on the breed through his daughters Briary Abbey Road and Briary Allegra. Mrs. Marjorie Brainard of Briary Kennels sent a bitch to Anthony when he was young and unproven, and he produced these two influential bitches.

Ch. Ruler of Blaircourt (1956–1962), sired by Forbes of Blaircourt ex Olivia of Blaircourt, half-brother and sister out of Craigluscar Dusk of Blaircourt. Ruler was also linebred to Glenhead Jimmie, Int. Ch. Donnybrook Thunder, and Treesholme Thunder, giving him a tightly-bred pedigree.

Mrs. Broadley believed in linebreeding to establish type. Her goal was to produce dominant stock that would breed on. In 1965 she planned one of the most influential matings of all time when Ch. Sandylands Truth (Australian Ch. Sandylands Tan ex Sandylands Shadow) was bred to Ch. Reanacre Mallardhurn Thunder (Ch. Sandylands Tweed of Blaircourt ex Mallardhurn Pat by Ch. Poppleton Lieutenant) and produced Ch. Sandylands Mark, a black dog and one of the breed's most outstanding sires, and his yellow brother Ch. Sandylands Midas who came to the United States.

Ballyduff

Bridget Docking (née Acheson) established her kennel with Holton Opal, a daughter of Ch. Cheverells Ben of Banchory. Bridget trained all her dogs for the field and ran them in trials. Many times she did trials in the morning and, after brushing the mud off, took her dogs to shows in the afternoon. She did very well in both areas.

Her best lines were based on Ballyduff Hollybranch of Keithray (Ch. Sandylands Tweed of Blaircourt ex Ch. Hollybank Beauty). This dog was called Ben and became a champion at 15 months of age, not an easy feat in British shows. He was also a good worker in the field and passed this trait to his progeny.

Bridget Docking bred to improve the breed and it was important to her that dogs be good-looking and good workers. I recall visiting her home in the 1970s and during tea she introduced her great dogs, Ch. Ballyduff Marketeer, Ch. Ballyduff Marshall, and Ch. Squire of Ballyduff, among others.

Returning home and remembering the quality of the Ballyduff Labradors, and being impressed with their working ability, I decided it would be wise to purchase a Ballyduff bitch for my breeding program. Bridget Docking came to judge the Labrador Retriever Club of the Potomac Specialty in Leesburg, Virginia in 1977. While there she told me of a litter by Ch. Ballyduff Marketeer, just whelped, from which I could have a bitch puppy, but only if I waited until the puppy was old enough to x-ray. Mrs. Docking didn't want to send me a young puppy that I would have to dispose of because of hip dysplasia.

The following February I flew to England to show my new puppy, Swift of Ballyduff and Spenrock, at Crufts (the Spenrock prefix is registered in England). The plan was to spend a few days with the Dockings and get to know my new dog, but a fierce snowstorm hit London and made travel impossible for me. Bridget brought several of her dogs to Crufts and had me show one of the males in the Challenge after she had wins with more than one of her dogs. So I had a chance to go in the ring before I showed my puppy. Being in England, I had to show their way and Bridget was very clear in telling me to hold the lead with my hand down by the dog's shoulder and to let him move on a loose lead. In those days English-style handling was not well recognized in the United States. I did as I was told and the dog showed very nicely. I felt quite at home when I went in the ring with Swift in a large class. She took top honors and we were all pleased. There was an American contingent at ringside led by Agnes Cartier and her husband, with his movie camera, recording an American handling her own dog at Crufts. A month later Swift went Best of Winners in Harrisburg, Pennsylvania (handled by her owner) at 11 months; a month after that she won the open bitch class at the Labrador Specialty under Marjorie Cairns (Blaircourt).

Heatheredge

Miss Margaret Ward lived in the North Country where I went to visit her after purchasing Spenrock Heatheredge Mariner because I wanted to visit his breeder and learn more about his background. Miss Ward lived in a small cottage and it was there that I saw the best-looking bitch I had ever seen in England, a black daughter of Seashell of Heatheredge. I would have taken this one home with me had she not been Miss Ward's close companion.

Miss Ward told me that she never kept a stud dog. She took her bitches to the best stud available. She told me that my dog Mariner was the thirteenth generation of her breeding. She stressed that any number of people can use the best stud, but you must own the highest caliber bitch. Miss Ward was not pleased with fads that established undesirable trends, resulting in people winning with poor stock under judges who didn't know the difference. There were many poor yellows in England at that time, not at all typical, looking more like poor Foxhounds.

Miss Ward sent Heatheredge dogs to the venerable Squirrel Run Kennels of Mrs. S. Hallock duPont and to the Downsbragh Kennels of William Brainard.

Mrs. Dora Lee clearly enjoying the company of some of her Bonython Labradors.

FT Ch. Cornbury Regent, winner of Midland Counties, England, Two Day Open Stake in 1961, with his handler, Mr. A.C. White-Robinson. Regent was owned by Mr. O. V. Watney. *Nicholas Meyjes*

Timspring

Joan Macan bred a sound line of dogs that were good field workers and good-looking. Joan Macan was the leading proponent in England of x-raying dogs' hips, and in 1976 she paid to have a book published called *Hips*. Articles in the book explaining the disease and pedigrees of x-rayed dogs were included. When I first went to England in the late 1960s and early 1970s and visited many Labrador breeders, x-raying was not a common practice.

Joan Macan was a heroine in World War II doing very courageous spy work in France. Tragically, she was murdered in her home, a terrible loss to the breed and to her friends and family.

There are many more kennels that could be mentioned, but the breeding of most dogs will trace back to the original greats. The three root stocks were Buccleuch Avon, Nethersby Boatswain, and Lord Malmesbury's Smiler. In studying many of the old pedigrees it is interesting to note how much close breeding took place. This has several consequences: it sets type, but it also doubles up on genetic faults. Once there were no tests for genetic problems and the rules of inheritance were not understood. It was some time before breeders knew how to select stock free of hereditary disease.

After the 1909 rule requiring a Labrador to hold a working certificate to be a full champion, most British champions did qualify in the field, some becoming dual champions. In the prewar years, the competition in the upper classes at championship shows was hotly contested. Dogs in the lower classes had little merit, but those that rose to the top were good indeed.

Lady Howe represented the concerns of many breeders in her day, as well as the present time, when she said that she hoped Labradors would compete for many years on the bench and in the field and show people that "working gundogs should be so high in quality and so symmetrical in shape that they can more than hold their own amongst the best show dogs of the day." [9]

---

[9] The Labrador Club Yearbook, *1932.*

chapter 3

The Labrador in America

For more than a century a retriever type of dog was found in the Chesapeake Bay area. Breeding records were not kept; some of the strains were in very isolated locations, and dogs were bred solely for their ability to do their job. Waterfowling was an important source of food, game was plentiful, and in time market gunning became an important means of livelihood for the people of the Tidewater region. Eventually some of these retrievers were recognized as the Chesapeake Bay Retriever by the American Kennel Club. Chesapeake Bay Retrievers are not very uniform in type, probably due to their varied background.

The early retrievers ranged in color from a very dark seal brown to a light sedge. The coats varied from smooth, wavy, and short to heavy and thick, resembling a sheep's pelt. According to early historians[1] this difference in coat and color was in almost every litter.

These retrievers were fearless; they would swim through icy water, break ice to get to downed birds, and do whatever was necessary to bring the birds back. These dogs could dive six to eight feet down to get crippled ducks that went under water to avoid capture. Furthermore, these retrievers didn't depend entirely on their noses to track game. They would sight the game as it fell and mark the spot with their eye. This worked especially well with water retrieving.

ORIGINS

Historians tell of several sources of these remarkable dogs. Some say that "the species resulted from a cross between a retrieving dog and an otter... arising

---

[1]The Chesapeake Bay Country, *Thomsen-Ellis Co., Baltimore, 1924.*

Four excellent field trial Labradors owned by Louise and August Belmont.

Foxhanger Summer Madness with owner and handler Barbara Starkey placing first in a qualifying stake.

from the fact that in olden times they were known as otter water dogs from their resemblance to the otter in their form, color and habits."[2]

Another story, from 1807, tells of the ship "Canton" of Baltimore, which fell in at sea with an English brig, bound from Newfoundland to Poole, England, which was sinking. Its crew, along with two puppies, were taken aboard the "Canton" and soon landed in Baltimore. The two puppies were probably consigned to the second Earl of Malmesbury in England for his kennel at Hurn Court.

----

[2]*Ibid.*

After the shipwreck, the captain of the "Canton" purchased the puppies and put them ashore in Baltimore. These retrievers from Newfoundland were a black bitch named Canton (after the ship) and a dingy red dog named Sailor.

George Law bought the two puppies and gave Sailor to John Mercer of West River in Anne Arundel County, who sold him to Governor Edward Lloyd of Talbot County. Sailor became the progenitor of the Eastern Shore retrievers. Canton went to Dr. James Stewart of Sparrow Point on the Western Shore and started a strain of retrievers there.

According to an early historian, "these dogs obtained a great reputation as duck retrievers. While there are no stud books to trace any progeny from these two, the natural supposition is that they were the foundation of the stock of the Chesapeake Bay dog." In spite of the vastly different dogs Canton and Sailor were bred to, in separate geographic areas, the strains resembled each other for many years. Eventually the Chesapeake Bay Retriever was recognized by the American Kennel Club in 1878.

The early recognition of the Chesapeake was due to the efforts of a committee formed in 1877, on which Mr. O. D. Foulks served, at the Poultry and Fanciers Association Show in Baltimore. This committee was charged with establishing a Standard and classes for the *Chesapeake Bay Ducking Dog*. Recognizing the breed, the committee divided it into three classes: the Otter dog, a tawny, sedge-colored dog with wavy hair; the Curly dog; and the Straight-haired dog, the latter two being a red-brown color. A white spot on the chest of any of these dogs was not to be considered unusual.[3] Color was the most important factor, other than performance as a water retriever, as shooters wanted the dogs to blend in with their surroundings to make them less easily seen by wary waterfowl.

A third explanation of the origin of the bay retriever was related by Gen. Ferdinand C. Latrobe, who for 40 years supervised the dogs of the Carroll Island Club. According to Latrobe, "Many years ago a vessel from Newfoundland ran ashore near an estate called Walnut Grove, on the banks of the Chesapeake. On board the ship were two Newfoundland dogs which were given by the captain to Mr. Law, owner of the estate, in return for his kindness shown the stranded men. The beginning of the Chesapeake Bay dog was a cross between these Newfoundlands and the common yellow and tan coonhounds of that part of the country."[4] The hounds were selected for nose, running gear, endurance, and stamina.

In 1887 a ship commanded by Captain Thomas Lightfoot sailed with a cargo of ice from the freshwater ponds of Labrador to the Eastern Shore. Also

---

[3]*Latrobe, Ferdinand C.* Iron Men and Their Dogs, *1941.*

[4]The Sporting Dog, *Joseph A. Graham, Salisbury, Md.*

on board were jet-black, sturdy dogs with intelligent faces, which he sold to Eastern Shore duck hunters.

About the same time a well-known sportsman, Mr. O. D. Foulks, from Chesapeake City, Maryland, wrote about an American Retriever called the Brown Winchester or Red Chester. Mr. Foulks called the reddish-brown dog the Winchester and described how it would sit motionless in a blind, with color blending in nicely and turning only its head as it watched for the ducks. When a duck was in shooting range, the dog would tense, and after the bird was shot, it would leap into the water, bring the duck back, and put it down next to the shooter. When there was a choice of dead birds or cripples, the dog would pursue the cripples first, and even if they dove under the water, or took a twisty route through a marsh, the dog would bring them back. When waters were rough, the retriever would raise his front while swimming for a better view. Mr. Foulks said that when the ducks fell too far out for the dogs to see, the retriever would be guided by the motion of the shooter's hand, so even over 100 years ago, dogs were guided by hand signals when necessary.

Over 100 years later, the very same description fit my Ch. Spenrock Cardigan Bay, hunting along the shores of the Bohemia River. This dog could locate cripples better than any dog I ever shot over. Also of interest is the fact that until the Bay Bridge was built in the 1950s, the native water dogs were bred for function, not pedigree. Eastern Shore hunters were only interested in the ability of the dog to retrieve and swim strongly. Many local retrievers resembled the Brown Winchester or Red Chester Retriever and came from crosses with Labradors and the early retrievers.

Gunning has been the passion of the Eastern Shore peninsula ever since the first white man arrived. The universal sport in Tidewater Maryland and Virginia is duck and goose hunting. From the Susquehanna flats to Cape Charles, there were hundreds of river tributaries with an amazing number of birds: ducks, geese, swans, and shore birds. Until recent years, when they flew they were so plentiful that they blackened the sun. Eventually the numerous birds became wary of the shooters on shore. The men started to use heavily loaded swivel-guns mounted on canoes whereby scores of fowl were killed with a single shot. The birds naturally grew more timid. The swivel-gun was eventually outlawed, but it was still used for many years by pot hunters. A sinkboat, also called a "coffin boat," was used at night to kill sleeping fowl, especially canvasbacks, for the city markets.

On shore gunners started to use decoys so they could shoot birds at close range. Dogs were trained to frisk on the shore above and below the blinds to excite the birds into gunshot range. The dogs were handled by hand signals from the blinds. Sometimes a red flannel handkerchief was worn by the dog around his neck to make him more attractive to the birds flying overhead. The retriever had an important job in bringing the birds back in. Performance counted, rather than the looks of the dog.

Even today you will see old-style retrievers on the Eastern Shore. Many of the native retrievers were bred to English imports, which the owners admired when they heard the dogs could hunt and work well in water.

A very dark red Labrador was exported from England to America by Lady Simpson in 1963 at the age of two months to Barbara Starkey on Maryland's Eastern Shore. Named Foxhanger Summer Madness, he was by Foxhanger Mascot out of a good Scottish-bred bitch. This dog was only four generations removed from Lady Simpson's foundation bitch, WT Ch. Frenchcourt Ripple, who in addition to winning a Best of Breed award had three wins in championship stakes for tracking, 15 field awards (including firsts) in gun dog tests, and an obedience certificate. Foxhanger Summer Madness was bred to many Eastern Shore retrievers, and even today, his progeny, many generations later, can be seen riding around and working on the gunner's farms and waterfront shooting areas.

Another connection between the early retrievers came about 1925 through a dog named Clyde through the Braeroy and Folkingham kennels in Great Britain. Mrs. Macpherson owned this dog, of doubtful ancestry, for some time. She told C. Mackay Sanderson that "in type and general outline, Clyde was very much a replica of the Chesapeake Bay, being a powerfully-built dog with hard, wavy coat and extremely dense undercoat. He was a brilliant worker, always displaying remarkable courage, and a super water dog."[5]

One of Clyde's sons, Western Reiver ex Dunskey Jean, who carried a heavy infusion of Buccleuch blood, was exported to the United States. Before he was exported, Western Reiver sired field trial champions in England, the most notable being the excellent working bitch FT Ch. Braeroy Roe, one of the best yellow working bitches ever seen.

Many of the Eastern Shore retrievers went to other parts of the United States to hunters who had heard of the marvelous retrieving abilities of these dogs. They may have been Labrador, Chesapeake, or interbreds; all traced their heritage back to the dogs from Newfoundland, some of which went directly to England, and others to the United States. In due time, there was more recordkeeping as the breeds became clearly defined, but the main concern of those who had litters was to produce good hunting stock. Eventually dog shows became the place to see the breeds, but we must remember that Standards were written by owners of working retrievers, first in England and then in the United States. Only a very small segment of the Labrador Retriever population ever makes it into a show ring; unfortunately many lack the conformation of a sound, functional working dog. By the same token, many dogs seen at field trials exhibit poor conformation. Proper conformation is significant, because a true retriever needs it to be able do its work, day in and day out.

---

[5]Studbook and Record of Field Trials, *C. Mackay Sanderson, 1949.*

The author had a dog of English breeding (a litter brother to Int. Ch. Spenrock Banner, WC and Ch. Great Scot of Ayr) who didn't particularly care for the show ring. He loved retrieving so much that he stayed with friends who ran a commercial goose hunting operation near Easton, Maryland. He worked all day, every day during the gunning season, year after year, and was highly thought of by the Eastern shore watermen. When he was five years old, he needed only a major to finish his championship, so we tried him at a large show where he took a five-point major under the well-respected Canadian breeder-judge, Frank Evans Jones (Annwyn).

EARLY AMERICAN IMPORTS FROM GREAT BRITAIN

Mrs. Quintin Dick, who later in England became Lorna, Countess Howe, imported a Labrador to the United States in 1914 at the beginning of the war. In 1917 an imported black bitch from Scotland, Brocklehirst Floss, owned by Charles Meyer, was the first Labrador to be registered by the American Kennel Club. By 1927 only 23 retrievers of all breeds were registered by AKC. These were Chesapeakes, Labradors, Curly-coats, Flat-coats, and Goldens, all lumped together under one heading.

In the 1920s some retrievers were called "interbred," a cross between any two purebred varieties. The most popular was the cross of the Labrador dog and an interbred bitch. Labrador dogs and Golden Retriever bitches were also a well-regarded cross. Some Chesapeake Bay Retrievers had Labrador heads, probably from a cross-breeding. Some of the early Labradors had curly coats, the result of crossing Labradors with Curly-coats.

After 1916, interbreds were classed separately, and finally, after World War II, they ceased to be of importance.

In the 1920s the Labrador was the most popular retriever in Great Britain but it did not really come into focus in the United States until the 1930s.

After World War I, a group of wealthy Americans went to Scotland to shoot and were very impressed with the whole scenario. Wanting to emulate the British, they imported their whole shooting scene to an area north of New York City where they owned very large estates, and to Long Island which also became a stronghold for Labrador shooting dogs. These wealthy families recreated Scottish game preserves and built castle-like homes. They imported British gamekeepers, guns, and dogs. The gamekeepers raised hundreds of thousands of ducks and pheasants and handled the dogs.

The Scottish sport of pass shooting was duplicated by training the ducks to fly from a high tower, past the shooters, down to a pond. Hundreds of mallards were released for the tower shoots, as the ducks were trained to fly to their feeding area. It provided wonderful shooting for the estate owners and their guests. Birds were also planted for walk-up hunting. The Labradors were used there to pick up birds. After the owners and guests left to socialize, the Labradors would quarter the fields and locate any other birds left by the shooters. Log books were kept, as was the custom in Great Britain, of the number of birds shot.

New York Governor W. Averell Harriman had the Arden Kennels and was one of the first to import a Scottish gamekeeper. Tom Briggs came over from Scotland in 1913. The first Labrador imported from Great Britain to Harriman's estate was Peggy of Shipton, a great-great-granddaughter of Dual Ch. Banchory Bolo. The Arden Kennel was one of the most successful, thanks to this bitch that produced champions in every litter, especially when mated with Ch. Raffles of Earlsmoor, owned by Dr. Samuel Milbank.

Jay F. Carlisle of Wingan brought over Dave Elliot in 1934; Marshall Field of Caumsett brought over Douglas Marshall; and Robert Goelet of Glenmere Court brought over Colin MacFarlane, just to mention a few of the great gamekeepers who came to New York. There was a little hierarchy of transplanted Scots including Jim Cowie, who originally came over to work with setters, but soon went to work under Tom Briggs at Harriman's Arden Kennels. The owners and the gamekeepers did not socialize with each other.

The man who really put the Labrador on the map was Jay F. Carlisle. Percy Roberts, known as "the Squire of Handlers," who later became a great dog show judge, put Carlisle's kennel together and put him in touch with Dave Elliot at Countess Howe's. Carlisle imported Orchardton Doris and Drinkstone Peg, which were to be the foundation of much American breeding stock. In 1937 Banchory Night Light, another Carlisle import, trained by Dave Elliot, won the "Field and Stream Trophy," a major national honor.

Mr. and Mrs. Marshall Field kept two kennels, one for blacks and one for yellows. In 1929 they imported a chocolate Labrador and kenneled him with the yellows. This dog was Diver of Chiltonfoliat, bred by the Honorable Lady Ward. At one time Marshall Field encountered progressive retinal atrophy. He no sooner had his dogs trained and ready to compete than they were blind by age six years. To overcome this problem, he changed his lines and got some American-bred dogs. The yellow dogs returned to England, and Caumsett went to only black Labradors.

Douglas Marshall, a Scotsman, trained for the Fields in the early 1930s. His daughter Dolly later became the first woman professional trainer of field trial winners, working for Mrs. Junius Morgan's West Island Kennels.

Dr. Samuel Milbank went to Scotland in the late 1920s where he was given the influential dog Raffles of Earlsmoor (Thatch of Whitmore ex Task of Whitmore). Raffles became an American champion in three shows and was successful in field trials, becoming a dual champion. This dog sired numerous dual champions. The sire of Dual Ch. Raffles of Earlsmoor, however, could not be registered as a purebred Labrador Retriever because of two interbred dogs within three generations in his pedigree.

During this era of gentlemen shooting in Scotland and bringing the dogs they admired back to New York, Labradors were also imported to plantations in the Carolinas. Labradors were also used on the Eastern Shore of

Maryland and Virginia, where they were bred with their native cousins, retrievers who traced their heritage back to the same dogs from Newfoundland many years before.

Mr. and Mrs. Junius P. Morgan bred dual-purpose Labradors successfully under their West Island prefix. They were the first to import a yellow Labrador to the United States, a dog named Banchory Snow.

The first yellow American champion was Ch. Chidley Almond Crisp, bred by Joan Redmond Read. This bitch was a granddaughter of a litter sister to Joan Read's Ch. Hugger Mugger. One of today's most respected Labrador judges, Joan Read was a pioneer Labrador breeder in the United States. A student of bloodlines, she used inbreeding with success, her Hugger Mugger being bred to his dam, daughter, and granddaughters. Ch. Hugger Mugger was sired by Ch. Bancstone Bob of Wingan, a son of Dual Ch. Bramshaw Bob ex Marsh by Ch. Earlsmoor Moor of Arden. Ch. Hugger Mugger's son, Ch. Wildfield Mickey Finn, was a grand-looking dog. Trained by Ann Carpenter of Long Island, he won many field trial awards in addition to eight Bests of Breed in the conformation ring, a true dual-purpose Labrador.

Joan Read started her Chidley kennels with a bitch from Jay Carlisle. She mated this bitch to the imported Ch. Bancstone Bob of Wingan, producing a lovely litter. Bancstone Bob of Wingan was Mrs. Read's first champion; among his many accomplishments, he won Winners Dog at the Westminster Kennel Club show.

Chidley dogs will be found in the pedigrees of Helen Ginnel's well-known Whygin dogs, as well as Kurt Unkelbach's Walden dogs (Mr. Unkelbach wrote the marvelous Labrador story, *Love on a Leash*), the very successful Shamrock Acres Kennel owned by Sally McCarthy Munson, Barbara Barty-King's Aldenholme Kennels, and Mary Swan's Chebacco Kennels.

Dorothy Howe, author of *This Is the Labrador Retriever,* which was published in 1972, started her Rupert Kennel with a bitch that goes back to Dual Ch. Banchory Bolo on both sides. She bred her to a son of Dual Ch. Shed of Arden, getting working ability and type. She then bred to Dauntless of Deer Creek, another good field dog, and these puppies became the ancestors of Whygin, Shamrock Acres, and some of the Harrowby dogs (owned by Grace Lambert). Mrs. Howe's book contains the pedigrees of 25 English dogs going back to the original dogs, which is interesting as one can see how much linebreeding was done in the early days.

Helen and Jim Warwick began their Lockerbie Kennels in the 1940s with a great deal of good advice from Joan Read, from whom they purchased their first champion Labrador. They obtained their first imported yellow Labrador, Ballyduff Candy, from Bridget Docking's Ballyduff Kennel in England. Joan Read's Labs had good working backgrounds, as did Bridget Docking's dogs. The Warwicks successfully bred their bitches to the imported Ballyduff Reilly and Ballyduff Treesholme Terryboy at Mrs. S. Hallock duPont's Squirrel Run Kennels in Delaware.

In 1961 the Warwicks purchased two puppies from Gwen Broadley's famous Sandylands Kennels, Lockerbie Sandylands Tarquin and Lockerbie Sandylands Tidy (their Lockerbie prefix was registered in England, as well as the United States). These dogs were used with great success in the United States—Tarquin as a stud and Tidy as dam of Ch. Lockerbie Kismet. The Warwicks imported quite a few males as stud prospects, the most successful being Ch. Lockerbie Goldentone Jensen, Ch. Lockerbie Stanwood Grenada, and Ch. Lockerbie Sandylands Markwell.

THE LABRADOR RETRIEVER CLUB

The American Kennel Club (AKC) was founded in 1884 by a group of sportsmen interested in establishing rules for holding dog shows. Its activities expanded into maintaining a registry of purebred dogs. The scope of activities has increased tremendously over the years to include thousands of competitive and non-competitive events such as dog shows, obedience trials, field trials, canine good citizen tests, and other performance competitions. Membership in the AKC is limited to recognized all-breed clubs and individual breed clubs.

The Labrador Retriever Club, Inc., was organized in 1931 by a group of sportsmen and women in the Eastern United States who had become familiar with the breed while shooting over Labradors in Scotland and Europe. The members wanted to encourage the breeding of Labradors and to hold

Jane Bragaw Perry with an early winner, Ch. Wheaton's Piper in 1964. *Brown*

Ch. Harris Tweed of Ide
(Ch. Sandylands Tweed of
Blaircourt ex Cindy Sue of
Ide) with owner-handler
James F. Lewis III. *Brown*

Norsk Ch. Royal Oak
Shamrock Acre Thyme,
bred by Sally McCarthy.

field trials patterned after the trials they enjoyed in England and Scotland.
Mrs. Audrey James Field (Caumsett) was the first President of the Club. She
served in that capacity until 1935 when Jay F. Carlisle (Wingan) became
President. The first Vice-President was Robert Goelet, and Wilton Lloyd-Smith
was Secretary-Treasurer.

The custom of using distinctive kennel names appealed to Labrador breeders. Established, qualified breeders can have these names registered by the
American Kennel Club or by the Kennel Club in England. These names help
students of pedigrees to identify the origin of the dogs named, usually
the breeder, but in some cases the kennel that owned the dog. Among

the earliest prefixes were Blake (The Hon. Franklin P. Lord), Arden (The Hon. W. Averell Harriman), Glenmere (Robert Goelet), Earlsmoor (Dr. Samuel Milbank), Meadow Farm (C.L. Lawrence), and Barrington (T.M. Howell).

A parent club is the national club for a breed recognized by the American Kennel Club. It has the unique and vital responsibility of being custodian of the breed Standard. Only the parent club has the authority to submit any changes to the breed Standard to the AKC Board of Directors for approval.

In 1931 the American Kennel Club registered all retriever breeds as one group under the title of Retrievers. Forty retrievers were registered in 1931 without specifying a particular breed. By 1933 the retriever breeds were separated and 84 Labradors were registered. From this humble beginning the Labrador Retriever has, at this writing, attained the number one spot in registrations of all breeds currently recognized by the American Kennel Club.

The Labrador Retriever Club held its first field trial on December 21, 1931, at Robert Goelet's 8000-acre Glenmere estate in Chester, New York. The judges were Dr. Samuel Milbank and David Wagstaff. Unlike present-day trials, the event was patterned after the British-style "walk up" shoot. There were no specific tests. The dogs advanced in a line with the handlers and guns, while the gallery followed behind. It was several years before birds were thrown for the dogs. The Open Stake at the first trial had 16 starters; all except one were imported. The winner was Audrey Field's yellow dog Carl of

Ch. Whygin Julia of Avec, bred by Helen Ginnel and owned by Sally McCarthy. A top producing dam of 13 champions.

Ch. Shamrock Acres Light Brigade, owned by Sally McCarthy and Mrs. James R. Getz, was BIS at Palm Beach, Florida. He was handled by Dick Cooper. One of the top producing stud dogs, he sired 93 American champions, one Canadian champion, and he won 12 Bests in Show. *Shafer*

Boghurst (by Corona of Boghurst ex Hayler's Linda), bred by S. Watson. With an equally creditable performance, the rangy black Odds On, handled by Marshall Field, placed second.

The first Specialty show organized by the LRC was held in 1933 in New York City in Marshall Field's garage in the basement of his townhouse. Thirty-four Labradors, all working dogs, were entered under judge Audrey Field. Dogs and bitches were shown together in the Puppy, Novice, and Limit classes. Best of Breed was won by an import, Ch. Boli of Blake.

The LRC has a very small membership, considering the number of Labradors registered with the American Kennel Club. For years since its inception, the interests of the field trial segment were at the center of the LRC's focus. In the early years, the same dogs were seen in both field and conformation events. The founders of the LRC were committed to a dual-purpose retriever, but even so, only 13 dual champions were recorded in the first 25 years of the LRC's existence.

In addition to the parent LRC, regional breed clubs have been organized. One of the first was the Labrador Retriever Club of the Potomac, which has held a regional Specialty every spring near Washington, D.C., with record entries, usually larger than those of the National Specialty.

As regional breed clubs were organized, it became possible to rotate the National Specialty to the different time zones, thus making it easier for people throughout the United States and Canada to attend a National in their region. The host clubs also provide an area for Working Certificate tests in conjunction with the National Specialty. Local Specialty clubs serve a geographic area, providing not only matches and regular shows, but also working events and other activities for Labrador enthusiasts.

chapter 4

What Is a Labrador?

The Labrador Retriever was developed primarily as a hunting or shooting dog in Great Britain. Temperament is as important as physical features. Along with a great willingness to please, the Labrador demonstrates courage and independence, as well as persistence. These qualities that make up a good gun dog, along with good scenting ability, also make the Labrador valuable in today's world for search and rescue and as guide dogs, bomb detectors, drug sniffers, and other such activities.

The Labrador's specialized hunting ability is retrieving. In Great Britain it picks up shot birds and hares that have been flushed out by spaniels or beaters (helpers walking through the cover ahead of the guns to scare up game). In the United States, Labradors are used for retrieving ducks and geese or upland game such as quail or pheasants.

To protect the interests of the breed they loved, the founding members of the Labrador Retriever Club (England), who were hunting people, produced the first official Standard of the breed in 1916. The size, shape, and overall type has hardly changed in England, the breed's homeland, since those early days. Foreign countries which register the Labrador Retriever have adopted the British Standard. Only in the United States have breeders made changes.

A breed Standard is a means for a breeder, owner, or judge to evaluate that breed within certain specified limits. The Standard should be descriptive enough to give a general picture of the appearance of the dog and detailed so as to define the limits. The Standard emphasizes those items that come under "type," thus distinguishing the Labrador from some other kind of retriever. Disqualifications are really unnecessary as it is obvious that if the dog does not fall within the specified limits, it is not a proper specimen of the breed.

Canadian Triple Ch. (show, field, and obedience) Whistlewings Kitty McGee, WCX, five years old (Am., Can. Ch. Monarch's Black Arrogance, CD, WC, ex Can. Triple Ch. Kenosee Jim Dandy, WCX), owned by Lori Curran.

Many of the items in the Labrador Standard were worded so as to distinguish this retriever from the Flat-coated Retriever, which had reigned supreme for many years until Labradors started to outperform them in field trials. Great emphasis was placed on the shape of the head, texture of the coat, and shape of the Labrador's "otter" tail, a unique feature.

When the Labrador Standard was first prepared by the American parent club, the main difference from the English Standard was to allow an inch more in height for dogs and bitches. This was arrived at by measuring all the Club members' dogs and then taking the average height. One reason for the increase in size was because most of the dogs had been imported from England and in many cases they were too tall for the English Standard.

The description of color from the English Standard was clarified in 1956 when many Americans thought yellows were being discriminated against as an allowable, but undesirable, color. According to Helen Warwick, "One prominent judge frankly admitted a feeling of insecurity in putting up yellows that were not 'solid' shades." A lack of familiarity with yellows prevented judges from knowing about the shadings in the yellow coats.

Breeders and owners should keep in mind that the Labrador evolved specifically as a dual-purpose gun dog. Type and working ability must go hand in hand as the loss of either would lead to the degeneration of the breed. Helen Warwick, in *The New Complete Labrador Retriever,* said, "The Standard, analyzed with clarity and insight, should leave no doubt in anyone's mind that it is not discussing the animal with any 'show' intent, but as a working dog of a type distinctive and recognizable from all other varieties."

Commenting on the standard, Mrs. Warwick correctly said:

> A perfect Standard for any breed has yet to be written, and the shorter and more to the point it is, the better it proves to be. The best way to learn about a dog is to breed it and have a thorough grounding and apprenticeship with breeders who know what they are doing. Twisting a Standard's meaning to suit one's own output is not only the line of least resistance, but brings to the surface one of the most virulent forms of eye trouble . . . kennel blindness. If people are dissatisfied with the way a breed is going the fault lies with the breeders' inability to fulfill their obligations . . . it is not because a Standard is obsolete, or old fashioned, or irksome to follow.

The field and show people are breeding dogs under the same Standard, but even so there is a tremendous variation in type. For many years Midwestern dogs were tall and lanky. Other fads in the show ring have departed from the norm; in the late eighties and early nineties this is seen with some short-legged, dumpy-looking Labradors, albeit with lovely heads and tails. Breeders looking for more speed for trials bred a light, racy-looking, galloping dog. This sort of breeding also lost the proper "otter" tail as the tail became too thin, and the head lacked sufficient stop and proper ear set, thus destroying the typical Labrador expression. A great deal of type was sacrificed in the quest for speed. A few brilliant dashes at a field trial may win a bet or a title, but the goal in breeding a good Labrador is to produce a dog with enough substance and soundness to do a day's work, no matter what the type of game or conditions of the countryside or water.

When type is lost, it is not easily regained. During World War II some indiscriminate breeding took place in England, bringing undesirable traits into the breed as owners disregarded type and quality. Some 50 years later, there are still many Labradors being bred without any regard to improving the quality of the breed. If people haven't seen a top-quality Labrador, then they may not realize there is a difference between a pet-quality animal and a properly typical Labrador.

Breeders who enjoy shows or hunt tests and field trials must be careful to assess the stud dogs they use, not just on how much they have won, but on their own basic structure, that of their littermates and offspring, and the genetic background of their parents and ancestors. Wins alone do not make a good stud dog. There are no shortcuts to being a good breeder. One must understand genetics and conformation and have an innate ability to put the information to good use; all this must be accompanied by good luck as well.

GENERAL APPEARANCE

The three characteristics that distinguish the Labrador Retriever are head, coat, and tail. The correctly-shaped head will exude intelligence and a gentle expression. The tail will be of medium length and rounded (without feathering) and very thick at the root, tapering to the end. The coat will be dense and weather-resistant.

In general appearance the Labrador is a strongly built, athletic dog with sufficient substance to function as a working retriever. The dog must be well balanced, showing style and quality. At first glance, a Lab should have a typical head with expressive brows and eyes, a well-developed chest, strong back and loins, good spring of rib, and a correct otter tail. It should have an ample body with legs and neck of correct proportions. It must be able to stand freely, nicely balanced on good feet with properly proportioned forequarters and hindquarters. Stable temperament and an expression of intelligence are important.

Type is what makes a Labrador look like a Labrador, and not resemble some other breed. Type (breed characteristics) and conformation (body structure) are two entirely different things; a poor type may have good conformation and move very soundly or vice versa. The ideal Labrador will have type or breed character, good conformation, and sound movement.

SIZE, PROPORTION, AND SUBSTANCE

A Labrador is *not* well-proportioned if it is light and lacking in substance, nor is it correct if it is cloddy or lumbering. If one breeds for excess speed, the Labrador will be too light in body. The Lab should be a medium-sized, powerful dog, built for endurance rather than speed.

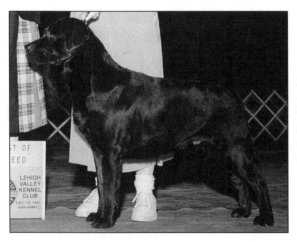

Am., Can. Ch. Strathmore The Natural, JH, WC, NAHRASC (Ch. Cranspire The Equalizer ex Scrimshaw Saving Grace), owned by Ginger Burr and Aaron Bloomfield. *Ashbey*

Am., Can. Ch. Strathmore The Natural, JH, WC, is as comfortable hunting as winning.

Proportions are very important for soundness and type. The dog must have enough length of leg for its body, not be standing on shortened leg bones. The flow of the head and neck to the shoulders is also very important. There should be enough flexion at the poll (top of the head) and reach of neck to allow the dog to reach forward to pick up game efficiently.

A Labrador should be short-coupled, which is not the same as short-backed. A dog's "coupling" is measured by feeling the distance from the last rib to the hips. Extra length here would throw a dog out of proportion. Breeding for short backs is incorrect as it also shortens the length of the dog's neck in proportion to the rest of the dog's body. A dog is not well balanced with a short, stuffy-looking neck attached to an upright shoulder.

A dog can have a good head and tail and wear a great coat, but if the body in between is too short and squat, the dog will be lacking in proportion.

Ch. Lobuff's Bare Necessities (Ch. Dickendall's Ruffy, JH ex Second Sight Brandie), bred by the Guide Dog Foundation; his littermates are all working guide dogs for the blind. This dog is a great-great-great-grandson of Int. Ch. Spenrock's Banner, WC. *Kernan*

The proportion of the hindquarters to the forequarters is extremely important. There must be good muscling and enough second thigh so that at first glance there is no impression of "not enough hindquarters."

Size in the conformation ring is dictated by the Labrador Standard. For hunting and other purposes, the activity may require a smaller or larger animal, but for the most part the Labrador is a medium-sized dog with an average height of 22 to 23 inches.

Substance means having good bone of dense quality and with correct circumference when measured around the leg, so that the animal does not look as though its legs are too thin for its body. Substance is also created by good muscling and muscle tone, not body fat.

HEAD

A correct, typical Labrador head is one of the hallmarks of the breed. Understanding head proportions is critical to recognizing the proper head. Starting at the top of the head, the skull must be broad between the ears, carrying this width down to the side of the eyes, without being apple-cheeked. There should be good width between the eyes and nice chiseling above the eyebrows. Viewed from the side, there is some roundness where the head is attached to the top of the neck, and where the skull slopes gently toward the area above the eyes.

Stop

The stop (the amount of angle between the two planes of the foreface and back skull) must be moderate and well-defined. If the stop is too high or long, the plane of the skull will tilt back at such an angle that the head will resemble that of a Flat-coated Retriever. Lack of stop gives the head an untypical expression as it also affects the placement of the eyes. If the stop is too pronounced and upright, the head will have the dish-faced appearance of a Pointer.

If the planes of the skull and muzzle are parallel with only a slight stop, the eye set will be too high on the head and the proportions between the amount of head from the eye up will be too small when compared to the amount of head from the eye to the bottom of the jowl.

Lack of stop creates a wedge-shaped head and in many cases the head loses the correct, full, Labrador gaze. Small eyes set too close together will also ruin a Labrador's expression.

Eyes

There will be a slightly concave area from between the eyes back towards the top of the head. This, along with some chiseling around the eyebrows, helps to produce a Labrador's kind expression. The eyes should be diamond-shaped, rather than round or oval, and they should be protected by a good brow.

They should be set fairly well apart, and neither full nor deepset. The eyes must suggest kindness, intelligence, and good temper.

In a black Labrador, round, very dark eyes give no expression, leaving the dog with a blank look. The preferred eye color is brown, although hazel (not yellow) is allowed in chocolates. A droopy lower lid with red showing below the eye (haw) is undesirable. Entropion (inversion or turning inward of the edge of the eyelid) or ectropion (a turning out of the eyelid) are serious faults.

Yellow eyes are very unattractive in Labradors as they give the dog a harsh expression. Very yellow eyes are called "bird of prey" eyes. Remember that the bright sun is unforgiving when it comes to eyes. A dog with bird of prey eyes might be rated as having only light eyes when judged indoors under artificial light. Eye color is only a cosmetic fault; it does not affect working ability.

The eye color should be darker in a black than in a yellow Labrador. Hazel to brown eye color is preferred in the chocolate. In general, the eye color should blend with the coat. A light eye renders a sharp, untypical expression.

Teeth

The teeth must be well aligned in a scissors bite wherein the upper incisors rest just in front of the lower incisors and the upper and lower canines mesh together. Serious faults are missing teeth, misaligned teeth, and overshot (upper jaw extends over the lower jaw) or undershot (lower jaw extends past the upper jaw) bites. If the teeth meet dead level in front, it isn't a serious fault, but the teeth will wear down faster.

Ears

The ears should be neat, carried close to the head, and rather far back. The ear set should be fairly high. Large, prominent ears are incorrect as they give the wrong expression. Long, lean skulls with houndy ears are incorrect. From a practical point of view, too-long ears will get their tips injured when the dog is hunting in rough cover. Flying ears are unattractive and ruin the dog's expression.

Muzzle

The muzzle, which is built to lie on the water, should be wide and fairly square with well-padded lips giving a rounded appearance. The head must be broader overall than it is deep, and the muzzle neither too long nor too short. The head should be clean-cut and free from fleshy cheeks. A snipey muzzle is a serious fault, as is a muzzle that is too long or too short or lacks depth. The jaws need to be moderately long so that the Labrador can pick up large game,

Eng., Am. Ch. Ballyduff Seaman (Ch. Ballyduff Hollybranch of Keithray ex Cookridge Negra), bred and owned by Mrs. Bridget Docking. A well balanced dog with a classic Labrador head. *Vivian Sirratt*

Ch. Briary Maytyme at Balamar (Ch. Davoeg Silky Beau ex Ch. Balamar Briary Blithe), linebred to Ch. Lockerbie Brian Boru and a granddaughter of Int. Ch. Spenrock's Banner, WC, owned by Sue E. May. She was Winners Bitch at two Labrador specialties enroute to her championship, owner-handled.

such as a Canada goose or a good-sized pheasant. A too-broad head with a short muzzle is faulty.

The foreface should be broad and level to the nose end, with no signs of a Roman (convex) nose, ending in good, wide nostrils. The nostrils should be wide with the lips curving away very slightly into the line of the underjaw. The depth from the stop to the underjaw should be a little bit deeper than the depth from the foreface at the nostril to the edge of the lip.

NECK, TOPLINE, AND BODY

Neck

The neck should be of proper length to allow the dog to retrieve game easily. It should be muscular and free from throatiness (an abundance of loose flesh under the chin, which spoils the clean outline of the dog). The neck should rise strongly from the shoulders with a moderate arch.

A "swan" neck is correct, but a "ewe" neck, which is found with straight shoulders, is wrong. The Labrador's head must flex at the poll and it needs enough reach of neck to be able to pick up game efficiently. The neck must be long enough to be in proportion with the body and legs.

The length and attachment of head to neck and neck to shoulders is a most important consideration. Short, thick necks are a fault, probably caused by breeding for short backs and tails, the vertebrae tending to become shorter along the whole spine.

Topline

The back is strong with a level topline from just below the withers to the croup. The loin should show evidence of flexibility for athletic endeavor.

The highest point of a dog's back is at the top of the withers (created by the tops of the shoulder blades). There is a gradual slope down to the level

Ch. Ahilo's Igloo Iggy, UD during Sporting Group judging at Fairbanks, Alaska; handled by owner Elaine Brock.

Ch. Delcrown La Contessa (Ch. Sailin's Proud Demension ex Braemar Miss Berryessa), owned by Jane O'Grady. *Vicky Cook* part of the back and the hindquarters should not be too high. There will be a slight slope to where the tail is attached. A low tail set is incorrect.

If a dog is fat rather than in hard, well-muscled working condition, there will be an unattractive rolling motion to the topline when the dog is viewed at the trot. Excess fat not only destroys the outline of the dog, it prevents the dog from moving properly and efficiently.

Body

The shoulders should be long and sloping. If they are straight, the hindquarter angulation is also affected. When a dog has straight shoulders (a very wide angle is formed where the scapula meets the humerus), its overall balance is upset because it invariably has a short neck and looks long through the ribs because the elbows are not set back far enough under the body.

A straight (too upright) short upper arm makes the dog move with short, mincing steps. The animal lacks the ability to extend his leg as far forward in a stride as is necessary for a sound, efficient trot. The incorrect pressures on the shoulder joint can cause lameness.

With correct shoulder layback, a plumb-line dropped from the top of the shoulder blade at the withers should fall just behind the dog's elbow. Often the mistake is made of thinking the shoulder is correct with the scapula well laid back but the humerus upright.

The length from the occiput (back of the head) to the withers will be longer in a dog with correct shoulders, whereas with incorrect, straight shoulders, the length from the top of the throat to the point of the shoulder will be longer. A poor shoulder can also be recognized by a foreleg that is set too far forward.

Because a Labrador is built for swimming, its shoulders must be slightly narrower than its hindquarters. Viewed from the top, the body should not be narrow behind the ribcage over the loin area. The shoulders must not be overdeveloped or laden with fat. Too much fat, as opposed to good muscling, causes a loaded front and unbalances the dog. If the Labrador's shoulders are too wide and overdeveloped as compared to its hindquarters, swimming will not be as efficient as when the dog has heavily muscled hindquarters and clean shoulders.

A typical Labrador is thick and strong. A dog with a good spring of ribs will have the lowest part of its underline from behind the elbows to the bottom of its chest. The underline will slope upwards toward the upper third of the hindquarters. A good spring of rib means that the ribs curve out from the backbone until they almost meet the breastbone underneath the body, tapering back from that point. Tied-in elbows or out at the elbows are both serious faults. "Spring" means that the ribs are not the same width all the way down the body. When ribs lack curvature, the dog is slab-sided and the ribcage will be narrow, which is faulty conformation.

Ch. Shookstown Solo Smasher, TD (Ch. Sandylands Midnight Cowboy ex Ch. Shookstown Gimlet), bred and owned by George Bragaw. Note excellent length of shoulder blade.

Ch. Windanna's National Dream (Am., Can. Ch. Rainel's Dynasty ex Ch. Windanna's Molly Melody), owned by Charles and Judith Hunt, winners of the Canadian Kennel Club Top Labrador Retriever Breeder Award in 1991. *Mikron*

Highlands California Cooler (Ch. Highlands Honey Dipper ex Hawkett's Holly Go Litely), owned by Lillian and George Knobloch. *K. Booth*

HINDQUARTERS

The hindquarters are broad, strong, and muscular, with well-turned stifles that are well let down to the hocks. The second thigh must be well developed with strong hams. Viewed from the rear, the quarters are wide and rounded with good muscling. Viewed from the side, the hindquarters must not look skimpier than the forequarters.

Straight stifles diminish the strength and soundness of a working dog. Incorrect hindquarters are a major fault, as this is the part of the body which gives the dog thrusting power on land or in water. A well-angulated rear plays a large part in giving the dog a proper outline when standing because it contributes to balance and correct shape.

Lack of sufficient angulation creates pounding stress on the joints, which leads to lameness and associated joint problems. A double-jointed hock is a serious structural defect in which the hock bends forward forming a nearly straight line from the stifle joint through the lower thigh and hock.

LEGS AND FEET

Small feet and thin legs are not correct in a breed where swimming ability is an essential quality. The legs should be of medium length with good bone, giving the dog a well-balanced appearance. Viewed from the front, the legs should be straight with strong carpal joints. The dog must not stand pigeon-toed, nor should the front feet turn out.

The pasterns should be strong, and instead of tapering into a thin wrist they should carry the bone straight to the feet. The pasterns are rather short and must not be upright, a cause for knuckling over. The feet should be compact, round, and have well-arched toes and pads. Flat, open, hare-shaped, or splayed feet are faults. Toenails must be trimmed to correct length to maintain good, tight feet.

Dewclaw removal for neatness and prevention of accidental tearing is advisable when puppies are three days old. While removing dewclaws from the front legs is optional, they should, if present, always be removed from the hind legs.

TAIL

The tail is the most distinctive feature of the breed, being very thick at the base and tapering toward the tip. It must be well clothed all around with the Labrador's short, thick, dense hair, thus giving it that rounded appearance known as an "otter tail." As for length, the tail should not fall below the hocks.

Tail set is important. A too-low tail set results in a sloping croup. There should be no feathering on the tail with hairs hanging straight down rather than curving around the tail. Tails that lack thickness at the base are undesirable, while a thin tail is a serious fault. Proper tail set and thickness are to be emphasized.

Am., Can. Ch. Campbellcroft's Angus CD, WC, and Campbellcroft's Anticipation, at seven and a half years old (Ch. Lockerbie Brian Boru WC ex Ch. Campbellcroft's Pede CD, WC), owned by Donald and Virginia Campbell. *Fox & Cook*

Windanna's Inachos (nine years old) with his daughters Windanna's Fairlady Goldberry (left) and Ch. Windanna's Pippin O Bucklebury CD, WC, owned by Charles and Judy Hunt, winning the Stud Dog class at the Labrador Specialty with the Westwind Sporting Dog Club in Canada. *Mikron*

The tail should be carried parallel to the ground at the trot. When excited it may be carried higher, but it must not curl over the back. The tail completes the balance of the Labrador by giving a flowing line from the top of the head to the tip of the tail.

COAT

The coat is another distinctive feature. It should be short, very dense, and should give a fairly harsh feeling to the hand. With a good undercoat, there may be some wave along the top of the back, which is not a problem.

The Labrador also has a weather-resisting undercoat that sheds water and protects a dog working in icy waters. The undercoat is soft and fluffy and waterproofs the dog, while the harsh topcoat repels water and keeps the undercoat from getting soaked. The undercoat is not visible at a glance, but can be seen when the topcoat is turned back. A good undercoat not only waterproofs the coat, but it also fills in all the angles and hollows, thus giving the dog the nice, rounded appearance typical of a true Labrador. A paper-thin, glossy coat is not correct. A coat that is too long, without undercoat, will not be weather-impervious as it will admit wetness. If a dog with such a coat is working in below or near freezing temperatures, it will have no protection and get very chilled.

I have seen my Labradors retrieve in water when the air temperature was below freezing. They would emerge with Canada geese in their mouths and while trotting toward me, one could see the wet part of the outer coat freeze, making them look frosty. The dense undercoat keeps a dog warm and comfortable.

Labradors do shed their undercoats once or twice a year. A female can be expected to shed after a litter or heat period. If shedding begins, a warm bath will help speed up removal of the dead hair. Shedding may occur over a period of several weeks. Undercoats will grow back quickly once they start to return.

Even when a dog is out of coat (a condition where the dog has shed most of its undercoat), some undercoat can be detected along the sides of the ribcage. This condition is not to be confused with a single coat. Any Labrador shown "out-of-coat" is at a disadvantage.

Proper coat is one of the Labrador's key points. The dog should be brushed and clean for a show, but trimming and scissoring on the underline and hind legs to create a "clean look" are not necessary, and in many cases make a dog look worse by narrowing the hindquarters. Trimming the whiskers is optional, as is trimming the few hairs that sometimes form a twist at the end of the tail. The Labrador is a working dog so the best presentation is the natural coat.

When I first exhibited Labradors in the 1960s, professional handlers made a great ceremony of trimming their charges. Judges were accustomed to looking at many out-of-coat Labradors. When they saw a proper coat, they didn't recognize it and penalized the dog for being fat or stuffy. This encouraged combing out the undercoat and scissoring to make a "clean" dog to win with. Eventually it became the practice to invite British breeders to judge Labrador Specialties. They preferred no trimming and dogs shown with full whiskers, and many American judges developed the same preference.

COLOR

Labradors can be black, chocolate, or yellow. A small white spot on the chest is permissible. The yellows range from pale cream to a deep fox red with

Ch. Hennings Mill Hase 'N To Kai Den with a normal faded nose; note the dark eye rims and muzzle. Owned by Jeannine Biddle.

Ch. Highlands Plain 'N Fanci (Highlands Regimental Brass by Eng., Am. Ch. Lawnwoods Hot Chocolate ex Grovetons Highland Holly). Owned by Lillian and George Knobloch.

variations in the shading of the coat on the ears, the underparts, and beneath the tail.

Chocolates range from light sedge to dark liver or chocolate, the darker shades being more attractive. Nose and eye rim pigmentation should be dark brown or liver-colored. Chocolate coats will sunburn, which turns them a lighter shade. Dogs being shown should be kept out of direct sunlight for prolonged periods.

A Labrador's nose should be black or dark brown. In both yellows and chocolates, fading to pink in the winter is not serious, but a "Dudley" nose, which is pink without pigmentation, should be penalized. Cold weather usually causes the black nose on a yellow Labrador to fade. Dogs that spend the winter in warmer climates do not lose the black pigmentation. Nose and eye rim pigmentation for show dogs should be black in blacks and yellows and brown in chocolates.

MOVEMENT

Movement should be free and effortless. A good Labrador should have a springy gait and move with drive and power. A shortened stride or high, hackney action is a fault.

As a good Labrador moves toward you, there should be no signs of elbows turning out. Instead, they should be neatly held close to the body with legs not too close together. The dog should move straight, without weaving or sidewinding (hindquarters not following the track of the forequarters). Viewed from the rear the hind legs should move as nearly parallel as possible, with hocks well flexed. At a brisk gait, the dog may single-track, but the hind legs should not cross in front of each other.

Viewed from the side, the shoulders should move freely and the foreleg must have the proper reach and extension. The hind legs must be well engaged under the body to provide thrust. If the dog is too short-coupled, the hind leg will not be able to reach far enough forward because it would hit the front leg that is coming back. Viewed from the side, the topline should remain firm. Rolling flesh on the topline is a fault.

If the dog is too straight in the hind leg, the whole leg will swing from the hip like a pendulum. There will be no spring to the stride and no flexion in the joints, thus exposing the dog to unsoundness.

Poor movement may be caused by a lack of condition and muscle tone, but it is usually the result of a structural defect, such as a straight shoulder with blades set too far apart, thus causing a rolling action at the trot.

Many Labradors enjoy pacing, a lateral gait with the two legs on one side moving together at the same time, followed by the two on the other side moving forward together. Exhibitors should not allow this in the show ring. The handler should slow down at once, give a gentle tug on the collar, which signals the dog to do something else, and then move forward at a trot. A trot is a diagonal gait with left fore and right hind moving forward while the weight is on the opposite pair of legs, followed by the right foreleg and left hindleg.

The speed at which the Labrador moves should be moderate. A Labrador is built for strength and endurance rather than speed. This does not mean that the Labrador can't step out smartly when required. Two of my Labradors, Ch. Spenrock Cardigan Bay and English and American Ch. Lawnwoods Hot Chocolate, could move with the best sporting dogs in Group competition. They were very strong movers, had great substance, and performed equally well in the field and in waterfowl retrieving.

In most show rings there is not enough space to move at the extended trot. However, specialties do use large rings that give the dog a chance to extend over a greater distance. Rapid movement should not be used to disguise poor gait. There have been instances where handlers with unsound dogs have moved them fast at all times, hoping that the judge could not detect the lameness.

STANCE

A good show Labrador stands with presence, gaits with power, and transmits his zeal to please. He should always move happily and always on a loose lead. I well remember that when I showed some Labradors at Crufts for Mrs. Docking, she told me to hold the lead down by the dog's shoulder with my arm stretched out and let the dog move along at a moderate pace on his own.

With head, tail, and eyes alert, the Labrador will enjoy showing himself off and will set himself up properly. A Labrador should not be stretched out or otherwise artificially posed. His tail does not have to be held up by his handler.

The Labrador in the show ring should be a standout for type, outline, and elegance. The shape of the head and body are important, while the coat and tail are two distinctive characteristics of the breed which are interrelated. To look like a Labrador rather than some other breed, the dog must have a close coat which is water-impervious, a tail like an otter, and a head with sufficient stop to preclude a Flat-coat profile.

A female should have a feminine head with a kind, sweet expression. A male will have a more rugged head, but nonetheless will also have an intelligent, kind expression.

FAULTS

Faults to be penalized are extremes in size and weight, snipiness of head, overshot or undershot jaws, too light or yellow an eye, narrowness between the eyes, lack of stop, straight shoulders, a bad dip in the topline, too long or narrow in the loin, straight stifles, narrow hindquarters, no development of the second thigh, straight upright pasterns, throaty neck, fat-loaded shoulders, chest not well let down, too much tuck-up, slab-sided, legs too long or too short, tail set too low, lack of bone, weak splayed feet, long thin tail, too much feathering on the tail, a tail that is not thick at the base, curled tail carriage, cow-hocked, sickle-hocked, no undercoat or a single coat, misaligned teeth, and sloping croup. Length of neck and legs must be in proportion to the body. Short, stuffy necks are a fault.

Obviously some faults are more serious than others. Those which interfere with soundness and type most are the worst.

DEFINING TYPE

Knowing the mixed background of the Labrador, conscientious modern breeders must avoid the characteristics of other breeds which are atypical of Labradors, such as Flat-coat heads or the slightly higher hindquarters found in Chesapeake Bay Retrievers. Feathered or thin, Pointer-type tails must also be avoided. The correct Labrador head is essential to breeding true type.

In the early 1980s, Mrs. Marjorie Cairns, of the Blaircourt Kennels in Scotland, judged a regional Specialty at the Labrador Club of the Potomac in Leesburg, Virginia. In her comments after the judging she said,

> It was a great pleasure to go over your animals. The intersex class was a joy although one feels sad to discard some lovely dogs. I had been led to believe that American Labradors were big and leggy. Happily this is not the case. The blacks, overall, seemed of better type and quality than the yellows. So to be critical, movement fore and aft could be improved, and some heads from skull to nose were too narrow. There were several hard expressions. Temperament and mouths were good. Some thin, houndy tails were in evidence. With careful thought most of these faults can be eliminated. I am sure with continued enthusiasm, the breed can only improve. Sincere thanks to everyone for making my visit a most memorable one.

Mrs. Cairns' Best in Specialty at that show was Ch. Bravos Black Magic of Wonwilo. She commented,

> A black in excellent bloom and condition, he is not overdone in any department, having a kind eye, pleasing expression, compact body standing on well-boned legs, and tight, well-padded feet, good muscle and angulation, and a nicely-set otter tail which he used to advantage. He looked the part, and in my opinion, deserved to win Best in Show.

chapter 5

Genetics for the Labrador

UNDERSTANDING GENETICS GLOSSARY

The science of genetics is intriguing, absorbing, and a challenge to all who would apply it to producing fine dogs. As with other scientific disciplines, genetics has its own language and a knowledge of this language is basic to an understanding of how inheritance works. The following glossary is provided to give you the important words and their definitions so you may better comprehend the text which follows and better use the natural laws it describes.

Acetabulum. The cup-shaped socket of the hip bone into which the thigh bone fits.

Agouti Alleles. Form hierarchy of five different genes that determine the color of hair pigment granules.

Allele. Alternative forms of the same gene that can occupy any location on a chromosome. The same developmental process is influenced, but in a different way. (Shortened term for allelomorph). The pair usually control contrasted characters.

Alleles, Multiple. A series of genes responsible for gradations of a certain character, occupying the same position (or locus) on a chromosome. Any one individual can carry only two members of such a series.

Anconeal. Pertaining to the elbow.

Autosomal. Refers to genes on the ordinary chromosomes. The gene is not sex-linked; it occurs equally in both sexes.

Ch. Great Scot of Ayr, a lovely head study. Owned by Nancy Martin.

Autosomal Dominant Inheritance. Affected dog transmits to male or female, who then transmit to one-half their progeny.

Autosomal Recessive. Faults in either sex (equally) are masked by dominant genes.

Back-cross. Mating of a hybrid back to one of its parents.

Catalytic. A counteracting agent employed to arrest pathogenic processes in an organism. A catalyst is a substance which either speeds up or slows down a chemical reaction, but which itself undergoes no permanent chemical change thereby.

Cell. Unit of living tissue.

Character. Observable or demonstrable property of an individual due to genetic similarities or differences.

Chromosomes. Gene-carrying bodies that inhabit a cell's nucleus. They are always paired; dogs have 39 pairs of chromosomes.

Congenital defects. Abnormalities of body structure or function present at birth.

Dihybrid. A cross between two individuals differing in respect to two pairs of alleles.

DNA (Deoxyribonucleic acid). The nucleic acids in a cell responsible for transmitting inheritable characteristics. DNA contains chromosomes and genes made up of complex chains of molecules called nucleotides.

Dominant. One pair of alleles whose characteristics are expressed to the exclusion of the effects of the other allele. One pair of genes has the power to mask the effect of the other member of the pair.

Enzyme. Any organic substance produced in an animal cell that causes changes in other substances by catalytic action.

Epistatic. Genes masking other genes. A dominant/recessive interaction between loci. The gene obscures others which are not the second member of the pair. A kind of non-allelic dominance.

Expression. Degree of appearance of a variable character. The expression of an anomaly is often referred to as varying from mild to severe.

Femur. The thighbone.

Gamete. A reproductive cell that can unite with a similar one to form the cell that develops into a new individual.

Gene Series. In the genetic hierarchy, some genes will dominate others. Superscripts are used by geneticists to identify each gene when this occurs in a series.

Genes. Units of hereditary information situated in linear fashion along the chromosomes.

Genotype. The genetic or hereditary makeup of the animal.

Germ Cell. A fertile cell from which a new organism may be developed. (Opposed to somatic cell.)

Hemophilia A. A severe bleeding disorder due to a deficiency of clotting factor VIII.

Heterozygous. Two different alleles for the same characteristic. Usually the dominant gene will show while the recessive one won't. Also carrying two different genes of a series of multiple alleles. A normal dog carrying a gene for a recessive anomaly. A given factor is inherited from one parent, and its opposite (or allelomorph) from the other.

Homologous. Of the same nature or of common descent.

Homozygous. Two genes in a pair that are the same. Inheriting a given factor from both parents.

Humerus. The bone of the forelimb extending from the shoulder to the elbow.

Hybrid. Heterozygous.

Hypostasis. Converse of epistasis. A hypostatic gene is one masked by the action of another which is not its allele, a kind of non-allelic recessive.

Incomplete Dominance. A condition in which both recessive and dominant members of a pair of genes (alleles) influence physical traits. This animal will have a characteristic that is intermediate between that expected from either of the two alleles.

Incomplete Penetrance. A genetic phenomenon in which a dominant gene doesn't always express itself in the physical characteristic (phenotype) of an animal. In some situations the phenotype may demonstrate the trait in a diluted form.

Impenetrance. The opposite of penetrance. The non-expression of an anomaly in a group of animals. This concept is important because such animals are bred from in the belief that they are normal.

Kindred. A group of closely related dogs within a breed.

Locus. Where the genes are located on a chromosome; usually stated in terms of its distance from other genes in the chromosome.

Metabolic. A change in form, structure, or function.

Mutation. Change in a gene or chromosome bringing about a heritable variation or alteration. A sudden variation in some inheritable characteristic, as distinguished from a variation resulting from generations of gradual change. A mutant is an individual resulting from such a change.

Pathogenic. Disease-producing.

Penetrance. A character produced by numerous genes acting in unison.

Phenotype. What the dog actually looks like. Visible characters indicate the genetic natures in contrast to genotype, which may not be evident without a breeding test. Phenotype is not an indicator of genotype.

Polygene. A combination of genes that has a specific effect such as modifying the intensity of color.

Polygenic. The combined action of an undetermined number of genes; for example, when a trait is influenced by more than one pair of genes (such as hip dysplasia).

Recessive. A gene whose effects are undeveloped or buried when associated with a dominant gene. The opposite of dominant. The phenotype of the individual will be that of the dominant gene. A recessive gene will only express itself when it is homozygous (paired with another recessive allele at the same locus.)

Rufous. Reddish or brownish-red color; rust-colored.

Sex-limited. A character which finds expression only in one sex.

Sex-linked. Genes on the sex chromosomes.

Sibs (siblings). Full brothers and sisters, not necessarily from the same litter.

Somatic Cell. Any of the cells which become differentiated into the tissues of the body, as opposed to the germ cell. Soma means the entire body of the animal with the exception of the germ cells.

Ulna. A bone in the dog's forelimb which articulates with the humerus and the head of the radius above and with the radius below.

X-Linked Disorder. Transmitted only by the dam to male progeny. Half of the males will be affected, half the females will be carriers. Does not apply to progressive retinal atrophy.

CONGENITAL DEFECTS

More than 400 hereditary diseases have been reported in dogs, some of which are specific to Labrador Retrievers. Genetic diseases manifest themselves in chromosomal defects or aberrations. Autosomal recessive traits are inherited when two apparently healthy parents (clinically normal) that each carry a normal and mutant gene (carrier gene) produce diseased puppies of either sex that have two mutant genes. All animals in the same litter are not affected to the same degree.

Each inherited disorder exhibits typical clinical signs early in the life of the animal. Usually the disease is chronic and progressive, although intermittent and late-onset presentations appear with some defects. The defect is present while the dog is very young, but the clinical signs may not appear until later in the dog's life. Other diseases may cause similar clinical signs, so routine and special laboratory tests are generally needed to confirm a clinical

RECESSIVE GENE INHERITANCE PATTERN

There are only six possible combinations of NORMAL, AFFECTED and CARRIER MATINGS. Pedigree analysis is difficult at best.

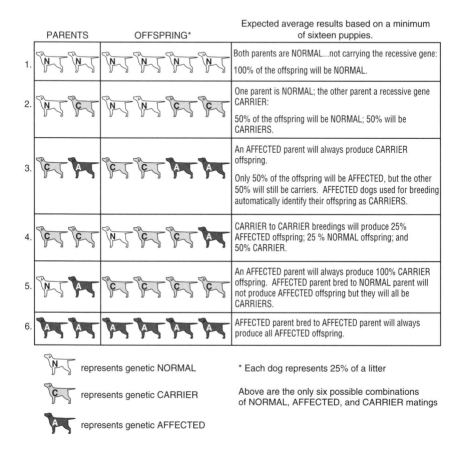

PARENTS	OFFSPRING*	Expected average results based on a minimum of sixteen puppies.
1. N N	N N N N	Both parents are NORMAL...not carrying the recessive gene: 100% of the offspring will be NORMAL.
2. N C	N N C C	One parent is NORMAL; the other parent a recessive gene CARRIER: 50% of the offspring will be NORMAL; 50% will be CARRIERS.
3. C A	C C A A	An AFFECTED parent will always produce CARRIER offspring. Only 50% of the offspring will be AFFECTED, but the other 50% will still be carriers. AFFECTED dogs used for breeding automatically identify their offspring as CARRIERS.
4. C C	N C C A	CARRIER to CARRIER breedings will produce 25% AFFECTED offspring; 25 % NORMAL offspring; and 50% CARRIER.
5. N A	C C C C	An AFFECTED parent will always produce 100% CARRIER offspring. AFFECTED parent bred to NORMAL parent will not produce AFFECTED offspring but they will all be CARRIERS.
6. A A	A A A A	AFFECTED parent bred to AFFECTED parent will always produce all AFFECTED offspring.

N represents genetic NORMAL

C represents genetic CARRIER

A represents genetic AFFECTED

* Each dog represents 25% of a litter

Above are the only six possible combinations of NORMAL, AFFECTED, and CARRIER matings

diagnosis. Veterinarians need better diagnostic tools to identify defects at an early age, rather than wait for some obvious symptoms to appear.

Fortunately, while laboratory tests to screen for healthy carriers are available only for a few inherited diseases, studies are underway to gain more knowledge in this important area. The Section of Medical Genetics at the School of Veterinary Medicine, University of Pennsylvania, has developed the first molecular screening test for a common inherited disease in companion animals. This test is for phosphofructokinase (PFK) in English Springer Spaniels, which is an enzyme deficiency in dogs with diseased red blood cells, preventing normal cellular function.

Another important area of research conducted by the Section of Medical Genetics at the University of Pennsylvania Veterinary School is the use of molecular genetic techniques to identify the carriers of recessively inherited diseases. These techniques use DNA isolated from blood samples to identify which animals in a breed are the clinically normal carriers of the gene mutation that causes the disease. When these techniques are perfected, it will be possible to eliminate a genetic disease from a whole breed population.

Research in veterinary medicine has made possible a significant reduction in environmentally caused diseases. Now the emphasis in research has shifted to genetic diseases. Dr. Donald Patterson, founder and chief of the Section of Medical Genetics (the first in a school of veterinary medicine) explained that "it is genetic medicine's ultimate hope to understand where every gene is on the chromosomes in every animal species and be able to identify those that cause disease." This is a lofty aspiration considering that there are between 50,000 and 100,000 genes in every mammalian organism, but it is not beyond the scope of modern science, which is aided by tremendous computer capability. The Section of Medical Genetics is creating a computerized genetic information system (funded by AKC) for a reference for practicing veterinarians. The Canine Genetic Disease Information System is a database and software program that will serve as a valuable tool for practitioners diagnosing genetic diseases and counseling breeders.

The work at Cornell University, New York State College of Veterinary Medicine, at the James A. Baker Institute for Animal Health, under the direction of Dr. Gustavo Aguirre, is specifically devoted to several breeds including Labrador Retrievers. (Funding is through the Morris Animal Foundation). This project is a molecular genetic study of canine progressive rod-cone degeneration (pred) in an attempt to eradicate progressive retinal atrophy (PRA) by identifying affected, normal, and carrier animals before they reach breeding age.

The Labrador Retriever Club has a Genetic Research Committee, under the direction of Dr. Frances Smith-Wilton, that is gathering information on conditions that occur in Labrador Retrievers. These conditions may or may not be hereditary and include PRA, hip dysplasia, elbow dysplasia, type II myopathy, retinal dysplasia with associated skeletal dysplasia (shortening) of the forelegs, malignant hyperthermia, hypothyroidism, and seizure disorders.

Purdue University has a veterinary medical database containing data on the results of eye examinations on Labrador Retrievers. These statistics may be of interest to some students of genetics.

In 1990 the Wind-Morgan Program for evaluating Labrador Retrievers for heritable joint diseases was established in association with the School of Veterinary Medicine, University of California at Davis/Department of Radiological Sciences, and administered by the Institute for Genetic Disease Control in Animals (GDC). The aim of this program is to provide a mechanism for orthopedic improvement in the Labrador Retriever. Data are being collected for the genetic analysis of these heritable disorders. As data accumulate, genetic counseling will be available through the GDC.[1]

Dog breeders should strive to have a program to control genetic defects. These defects can occur affecting a single anatomical structure or function, or as a syndrome combining more than one defect. The most frequently affected areas in Labradors are the eyes, bones, muscles, and central nervous system.

Some congenital diseases are inherited while others are caused by environmental agents, geographic locations, age of parents, and nutrition. Genetic diseases tend to run in families; however, it is difficult for the average breeder to collect enough accurate breeding data to determine the mode of inheritance. It is also difficult for veterinarians doing research because dogs' chromosomes are tough to look at and hard to sort out.

Furthermore, when these anomalies are discovered, one must keep things in proportion. The breed itself may not be riddled with the problem, while it can loom large in certain bloodlines. A widely-used and much-admired sire, for example, may subsequently be found to be a carrier of an anomaly. This fact was not known when the animal was first used for breeding; only after his offspring have multiplied does the problem become apparent. Inbreeding or linebreeding will ultimately bring into being multiple occurrences of the same anomaly. Possibly this abnormality had been hidden for several generations. It will now take many years of effort either to eliminate this anomaly or reduce it to a level where it is not a problem.

When planning matings, be aware that the characteristics of the animals are not transmitted through the blood. The two dogs mated do not give one half of their characteristics to their puppies. It is the reproductive gene cells that are the blueprint for what the dog will be. The building material is expressed in the chromosomes. One half of the genes from the male will be mixed with one half of the genes from the female, but it might not be the same half for each puppy in the same litter.

There is no way of telling which genes will be transmitted from the parents. It could be the good ones, or the bad ones. The parents could be passing on genes which they inherited from their parents, grandparents, or animals much further back in the pedigree.

A breeder should not rely too much on a particular stud dog until the dog is old enough to have several generations of offspring. Dogs theoretically make a larger contribution to the breed because of the number of offspring they can produce compared with a female. On the other hand, female lines can exert a tremendous influence on a breed, especially when they are mated to suitable dogs.

---

[1]*See Chapter 22 for statement by Dr. Autumn Davidson giving details about the Wind-Morgan program.*

Whenever extensive use of a carrier male coincides with his rising popularity in a breed, serious ethical and practical dog breeding problems can result. When owners discover a problem, they should be honest about it, notify those who are involved, and remove their dog from the breeding arena.

For many years dog breeders have lacked an early means of identifying anomalies, or means of identification may be available but ignored. For many years PRA could not be diagnosed until dogs reached four years of age or older. Not all people who breed Labradors get their dogs' hips and shoulders X-rayed prior to the mating. More than likely, out of the total population of Labradors (now the number one breed in the United States according to AKC registrations), only a small percentage receive tests for genetic defects.

DNA, which works like a data-processing computer, is becoming a tool to assist breeders because it can be used to positively identify parents. The integrity of stud books is no better than the honesty of the people submitting the paperwork. DNA is a fundamental universal molecule of inheritance that exists in everything; it is very stable and readily analyzed. Only a small number of hereditary diseases have been characterized at the molecular level. This genetic information is not only needed to better understand the mechanism of the disease process, but is essential for mutation-specific screening tests. A screening test to identify a suspected problem is developed by taking a couple of drops of the dog's blood from which the genetic code (DNA) is extracted and tested by a polymerase chain reaction, a modern laboratory technique. Dogs can be tested at any age, even newborns, thus allowing early detection.

As research progresses, gene splicing techniques will be applied to transfer genes from one organism to another. There are two basic forms of gene replacement therapy: germ line and somatic cell. The difference between the two is that in somatic cell therapy, the replacement gene is inserted in the somatic cell rather than the germ line, so the subject's offspring are not affected. There will come a time, in humans as well as animals, when disease-producing genes can be removed and replaced with normal genes. The research being done at the veterinary schools helps humans as well as animals.

Recombinant gene technology is being used by veterinary geneticists to locate defective genes and remove the breeding stock carrying them from the breeding pool. Many exciting things will happen in the future thanks to the new technology.

Markers on chromosomes will be identified, permitting these markers to detect defective, recessive genes in dogs with normal phenotypes. With the cataloguing of all defective genes, breeders will be able to have breeding stock analyzed to identify carriers. Several institutions are working to perfect the science of breeding healthy dogs.[2]

---

[2]*Michigan State University & the Univ. of Michigan joint project sponsored by The Morris Animal Foundation, AKC, and the Orthopedic Foundation for Animals (OFA).*

Ch. Breton Gate Cairngorm, CD, winning BOS and Best Brood Bitch at Golden Gate Labrador Specialty, 1988, with Campbellcroft Happiness and Campbellcroft Highlander at one year old; owned by Virginia and Donald Campbell. *Fox & Cook*

DIAGNOSIS OF GENETIC DISEASES

It is easier for a veterinarian to diagnose a genetic disease if the breeder has kept careful records of as many of the dogs he/she has bred as possible. Breeders must be honest and observant while keeping precise records. A veterinarian can only make inferences from pedigree analysis. Pedigree analysis alone is not enough because as you look at pedigrees with lots of common ancestors, the further back you go, the more you find the dogs are closely related. Growth records are very useful because genetic diseases are usually found in the bottom third of the growth profile.

Better diagnostic methods are needed. There can be a wide spectrum of disorders within a disease. The clinical signs of disease with genetic deficiency are similar in all species, including humans. In polygenic diseases, however, it is difficult to narrow the problem down to one gene.

For many years, breeders had no knowledge of certain problems because diagnostic equipment had not been invented, and even after it was available, not all veterinarians had training in its proper use.

To avoid misdiagnosis, veterinarians must look at the entire profile of the animal to make sure they aren't missing other diseases. For example, according to Peter F. Jezyk, VMD, PhD,

> Hyperthyroidism is the most over-diagnosed disease in dogs. Many of the manifestations are common to other defects. You must rule out other genetic and endocrine disorders. The dog probably has a genetic predisposition for autoimmune disease rather than a defect for hyperthyroidism. You have to rule everything out.

Hip dysplasia and osteochondrosis existed in dogs long before the advent of the x-ray machine to confirm the condition. I can remember trips to

Ch. Sandylands Spungold (center, handled by Stephen Shaw), winning Best Brood Bitch at a LRC Specialty under Percy Roberts with her get by Ch. Lockerbie Sandylands Tarquin: Ch. Lewisfield Spenrock Ballot WC and Int. Ch. Spenrock's Banner WC, owner-handled by Janet Churchill (left) and Ch. Great Scot of Ayr, owner-handled by Nancy Martin (right). *Shafer*

England in the 1970s when breeders there told me that the dogs "had growing pains" when I asked them about shoulder and hip lameness. The first X-rays that I had made in England of dogs that I imported did not position the dogs according to OFA standards. Now there is discussion among some veterinary radiologists about using a more relaxed position of the legs as the most accurate means of diagnosing hip dysplasia.

Metabolic diseases should be tested for when the veterinarian observes clinical manifestations connected with them, most of which are non-specific. Clinical manifestations of inborn errors of metabolism in dogs include growth retardation, facial dysmorphism, organomegaly, or skeletal malformations. There are limits to what veterinarians can do with enzyme analysis.

Genetic probes are the key to diagnosing carriers, as one can't always be certain with an enzyme test. When you identify the carriers you can effectively eliminate the disease from your breed. If we look only at phenotype, the defect will be around forever.

In the future it will be possible to identify defective, recessive genes in dogs that appear to be normal and replace them with normal genes from another bloodline. Breeding techniques will change and dog breeding will become more of a science than an art.

SELECTIVE BREEDING

Selective breeding is necessary to maintain consistency and uniformity of type in a breed. Only the best dogs in a litter should be used for breeding. There will be times when none of the dogs in a litter are suitable. When selecting a mate for a dog, you must consider the qualities you are trying to preserve and those faults you need to correct. It may take several generations to accomplish your goals.

Most defective dogs are not used for breeding. Although two defective parents mated together produce only defective dogs, most defective dogs are produced by normal-appearing parents. Each normal parent that produces a defective dog transmits one of the two abnormal genes needed to produce a defective offspring. Recessive defects can be carried generation after generation by normal-looking animals before being expressed, and then suddenly certain combinations of genes will allow the defect to show up. Eliminating defective dogs from breeding will help to keep recessive defects at a low incidence. However, it is extremely difficult to breed out recessives.

Very few faults are dominant but these are easily eliminated. Genes work differently in different breeds. Labrador genetics shows the influence of some of the other breeds that were mixed with them many years ago. Mutations and incomplete dominants also complicate the picture.

Recessive faults in the Labrador include sickle hocks, undershot jaw, dropped premolars, black and tan color, short upper arms, long wavy coat, splayed feet, and long ears.

YOUR BREEDING PROGRAM

Choosing a foundation bitch from the best stock available is fundamental to a breeding program. If you begin your breeding program with a mediocre pet you are likely to end up with similar puppies. You must have a set goal in mind and know what constitutes proper type. Start by improving the major faults first. Performance also enters the picture with a working dog such as the Labrador. Investigate the working ability of the parents and grandparents if you will be breeding dogs for hunting purposes. Those working with guide dogs will want to use stock selected as suitable for the role of working, in a dignified and intelligent manner, with a blind person.

Breeding for perfection all at once is not possible. The object in breeding dogs is for each generation to be superior to the preceding one and to preserve breed type. Good dog breeders study the breed and learn what to aim for. The top breeders have usually been in the breed for 10 years or more and have consistently produced good type and soundness. They know the genetic faults carried by certain bloodlines and use all analytic tools available to avoid problems. They must also be free from "kennel blindness" or the inability to recognize faults in the dogs they own and love.

Prepotency in breeding stock is the ability of the animal to stamp its offspring with good characteristics. These dogs usually come from lines of prepotent dogs and bitches, but this does not mean that they will not transmit unwanted recessives. The prepotent dog will have many characteristics transmitted by dominant genes. The recessives may be apparent in the offspring only when carried by both parents. This is why it is important to research the pedigrees of dogs considered for breeding.

A male dog will have a more far-reaching effect because he is able to sire many more puppies than a single bitch can produce in her lifetime. The produce of a potential sire for your litter should be studied carefully. In evaluating any particular litter, however, remember that the bitch has as much influence as the dog. The bitch has the greatest impact on the puppies because she will teach them and raise them according to her temperament. Disorders on the bitch's x-chromosomes will be transmitted by x-linked recessive inheritance. For example, hemophilia A has been detected in Labrador Retrievers. A blood test is available to detect this disease.

In selective breeding, linebreeding, inbreeding, or an outcross will be used. Experienced breeders will use whichever method best suits their needs. However, until you have a great deal of experience breeding Labradors, do not inbreed and be careful of outcrossing.

Outcrossing gives the widest variation in type. Generally speaking, there are no common ancestors for at least five generations in an outcross. Outcrossing is usually used to eliminate a particular fault. At the same time undesirable recessives may be introduced into your breeding program, and this can't always be determined for several more generations.

Inbreeding is the mating of closely related animals such as father-daughter, brother-sister, or mother-son. Rigid selection must be exercised and this form of breeding should be avoided by all except the most experienced breeders. It is a way to establish type, but at the same time defective individuals are more likely to turn up. These should never be used for breeding.

Inbreeding will increase the percentage of gene pairs that are alike and make the animal more homozygous. Inbred animals breed "truer" or are more prepotent. The puppies not only look like their parents, but as adults they should perform and look alike. The progeny of inbred animals tend to be more alike because they have received the same genes from their parents when compared with non-inbred animals.

Inbreeding will bring harmful genes into the open, so once these are recognized, the animals should not be used for breeding again. Critical selection is necessary or there will be disastrous results. Another caveat is the loss of performance because as the level of inbreeding increases, the performance (in the field or working, as well as producing progeny) decreases. Therefore only the most experienced breeders should use inbreeding, and then sparingly. Even though inbred animals are more prepotent, it may not be worth the risk of increased incidence of defects and decreased performance.

Linebreeding done properly will work back toward the norm. This makes it possible for a bitch on the small side to produce normal-size offspring when bred to the proper stud dog. Breeders need a thorough knowledge of pedigrees to make prudent selections of stud dogs.

Linebreeding is used in a long-range breeding program and usually concentrates on common ancestors that are many generations back in a pedigree. There are dogs and bitches whose qualities are excellent and historically the most influential in the breed. Linebreeding to them helps to maintain their good points in later generations. Linebreeding tends to separate a breed into distinct families closely related to superior ancestors. The use of linebreeding should be limited to the knowledgeable breeder using superior animals.

Linebreeding and inbreeding used incorrectly can perpetuate serious problems if breeders inadvertently use stock that carries defective genes. In the past, some of these defects couldn't be identified until the dogs were two to four years or older. This means that breeders might decide to have a litter using two-year-old parents, not knowing that these normal-appearing dogs would later exhibit defects.

Superior results may be obtained by "nicks," where daughters by a particular sire are mated to a stud from another bloodline. This is a mating system which can change phenotypic or genotypic frequencies by creating specific gene combinations that work. However, "nicks" will not necessarily lead to genetic progress, which by definition would increase positive or favorable genes in the Labrador population.

Phenotypic selection refers to selection based on the dog's performance and is more prevalent in breeding field trial dogs where speed, trainability, and other characteristics for winning field trials are of more importance than conformation. Here, dogs with outstanding performance records are selected as breeding stock.

Selection for performance is valuable with medium to highly heritable traits. It does not work as well when based on lowly heritable traits where environmental influences must also be taken into consideration. Examples of highly heritable traits are marking ability, soft mouth, and willingness to re-enter water.

Congenital defects may also be inherited in a polygenetic manner with many genes involved. Hip dysplasia (HD) or subluxation, for example, is one problem that is believed to be heritable, as is osteochondrosis or shoulder lameness. The Orthopedic Foundation of America (OFA) used to give Labradors passing grades at one year of age. These dogs might then be used for breeding, only to discover later that they did have HD. To avoid this problem OFA changed the age for receiving OFA certification (with a grade and number) to two years of age.

However, usually the preliminary changes in the joint are evident on X-rays by five to ten months, so it is wise for breeders to get preliminary radiographs made.

Hereditary eye diseases, discussed in another chapter, are also identified at earlier ages now because of modern testing.

Congenital defects or disease susceptibility in Labradors include bilateral cataracts, retinal dysplasia, central progressive retinal atrophy (CPRA), progressive retinal atrophy (PRA), cystinuria, hemophilia A, craniomandibular osteopathy, and carpal subluxation.

Cystinuria is a congenital defect in the canine urinary system. It is a sex-linked recessive causing excess cystine in the urine, predisposing the dog to calculi. Another sex-linked recessive is cryptorchidism, which is unilateral (resulting in sterility) or bilateral non-descent of the testicles. Hemophilia A is a sex-linked recessive causing prolonged bleeding.

Craniomandibular osteopathy, or lion jaw, has been reported in Labradors. This is an irregular osseous proliferation of mandible and tympanic bulla which causes fever and discomfort in eating. It begins around four to seven months for a few months and then may stop or regress. It may be caused by malnutrition rather than heredity.

In bilateral carpal subluxation, the gene is allelic to the gene for hemophilia A. Subluxation of the carpus in dogs is an x-chromosomal defect closely linked with the locus for hemophilia A. Partial carpal dislocation has been attributed to a sex-linked recessive gene.

Elbow dysplasia, or nonunited anconeal process, probably has the same mode of inheritance as hip dysplasia. It is the failure or nonunion of the anconeal process to the ulna, resulting in osteoarthritis. Clinical signs range from mild to severe unilateral or bilateral front leg lameness. It most commonly affects dogs from five to nine months of age.

Hip dysplasia, caused by a polygenic mode of inheritance, is the most common canine defect. It is manifested in deformed coxofemoral joint(s) with clinical signs ranging from no signs at all to severe hip lameness. Radiographs (x-rays) of the hips may show a shallow acetabulum, a flattened femoral head, subluxation, and/or secondary degenerative joint disease.

The severity of hip dysplasia varies considerably and it has been shown that selective breeding can reduce both the incidence and severity. OFA provides guidelines for selective breeding to eliminate hip dysplasia.

A recessive gene has been found to be responsible for "overshot" jaws in some breeds. This is a case where the lower jaw is unusually short. An "undershot" jaw is the opposite problem. Dogs with overshot or undershot jaws will not have the proper "bite" or scissors meeting of the teeth. They should not be used for breeding or showing.

Cleft palate is apparently due to heredity in some cases. The situation is unclear, as it may arise as part of a syndrome not having cleft palate as the prime anomaly.

Epilepsy has been suspected to be inherited, but it may also be caused by environmental factors, disease, parasite infection, and injury to the nervous system. The epilepsy data bank of the Institute of Genetic Disease Control (GDC) should help breeders to understand the inheritance pattern of epilepsy.

Idiopathic epilepsy in Labradors represents a collection of different hereditary seizure disorders, each with a different genetic cause. The pattern of the seizures and mode of inheritance is usually consistent within a kindred, but idiopathic epilepsy can be inherited differently even in kindreds. Most forms of epilepsy are polygenetically controlled in a kindred; thus close relatives of epileptic dogs are most apt to carry a subclinical threshold of these genes.

Labrador Colors

Labradors may be one of three solid colors: black, yellow, or chocolate (also called liver). According to the AKC Standard, a white spot on the chest is permissible. In spite of the fact that the original, true color of the yellow Labrador was a dark golden, the term "golden" Labrador is incorrect. In 1925, to avoid confusion with the Golden Retriever, the English Kennel Club assigned the word "golden" to the Golden Retriever. Yellow is used for the Labrador Retriever and describes many shades from a deep fox red to a pale cream.

The mode of inheritance is basically simple. Genes function in pairs with one inherited from the dam and one from the sire. There are two kinds, dominant and recessive. To complicate matters, there are also mutations or alterations. A dominant gene can influence a characteristic by itself, whereas a recessive gene must be coupled with another recessive gene to express its characteristic. When dominant genes are paired, or a dominant and a recessive, they can produce the same visible characteristic. However, a recessive must be paired with a similar recessive gene to produce a visible manifestation of the recessive characteristic. This means that many generations may pass by before two unsuspected recessives appear visually, either as a color or some other manifestation.

Ten pairs of genes govern coat color in the Labrador. The genetics can be very complex, but basically the various combinations of genes produce the three colors, black, yellow, and chocolate. For many years in England, yellow was the most popular color. As time went on the original dark golden color became diluted as the pale cream and biscuit colors were fancied. Chocolates were not around in great numbers, partly because when they did appear, the breeders disposed of them as undesirable. The color was much maligned for "fashionable" reasons. Chocolates can be of excellent type and

Mother and daughter triple champions: Ch., FT Ch., OT Ch. Whistlewings Kitty McGee, WCX at five years of age (by Am. Can. Ch. Monarch's Black Arrogance WC, CD) at left; her dam at right, Ch., FT Ch., OT Ch. Kenosee Jim Dandy, WCX (FT Ch., AFT Ch. Pelican Lake Andy ex Kenesee Jo) at ten years of age.

also great workers in the field. The color is now sought after by many admirers. The chocolate coats are subject to sunburn, so appropriate precautions are indicated if you own a chocolate.

BLACK LABRADORS

Blacks are either dominant for black, in which case they produce only black when mated with any of the three colors, or there may be blacks that can produce all three colors (even in one litter). The black coat color is determined by a dominant B allele at the B locus on the chromosome. The black coat color allele is dominant to the recessive chocolate allele.

Pure dominant black Labradors will produce only black with no yellow genes. If the black is impure, then the dog carries a yellow or chocolate gene; if mated to another black, then the offspring will all be black, but half will carry the genetic makeup for pure black, while the others will carry the yellow or chocolate gene. It is possible for two blacks (when one is not a pure dominant) to produce a chocolate with a chocolate nose, a yellow with a black nose, or a yellow with a chocolate nose (the latter would be least probable).

Remember that you can't tell just by looking at an animal if it is a pure dominant for black or not. This can only be established by observing offspring. You may know about several generations of the dog's pedigree, but it is unlikely that you will have knowledge of all the dogs in the pedigree going back to its original ancestors. The colors that result from breeding two black Labradors are always a matter of probability, because even though they may have produced only black puppies in several litters, one can't assume that both are BB, but certainly one of them is.

One of the most famous English imports to America, Grace Lambert's famous English, American, and Canadian Ch. Sam of Blaircourt, a lovely black dog long used as a model for the breed Standard, did not carry any genes for yellow. If a yellow bitch was bred to him, she would produce only black puppies. However, these puppies would now carry a yellow gene (from their dam), so even though black, they could produce yellow offspring. The only way to have no black puppies is to breed yellow to yellow.

YELLOW LABRADORS

Yellows are recessive to blacks. The yellow coat color is determined by

a simple Mendelian allele at a single E which is separate from the B locus. The yellow coat color allele is recessive to a dominant allele that allows full expression of the B locus alleles. When the yellow allele is homozygous, it is epistatic to the B locus alleles. In Labradors, the coat color produced by the e/e genotype varies from creamy-white to copper red through gene interaction with the e/e genotype and other modifying genes.[1]

The yellows can produce all three colors, but yellow mated to yellow will produce only yellow. Two yellows cannot produce black puppies, even though they both came from black parents. However, two blacks can produce yellows if they both carry the yellow gene.

A yellow Labrador should have dark pigment expressed in black eye rims and a black nose. There are yellows that carry alleles which prevent the expression of dark pigment, which results in a yellow with liver nose, liver eye rims, and light eyes. Yellow should not be bred to chocolate because usually the offspring will lack dark pigment and have light eyes.

Yellow dogs can exhibit an absence of pigment when they carry the two recessive chocolate alleles. This happens only when both parents carry chocolate. Both parents may have been black, yellow, or chocolate. Because of probabilities, chocolates are not usually bred to yellows, but this is not enough to prevent the lack of pigment, and indeed, it is possible for some chocolate-to-yellow matings to have correct pigment. This is best accomplished if the yellow used in the breeding does not carry chocolate. That way the resulting yellows, if the chocolate parent carries yellow, will have black pigment and the remaining puppies will be black. The next generation of puppies would all carry chocolate so the color could be continued thereafter from that mating.

Normal black pigment on the yellow Labrador's nose will turn pinkish in cold winter weather but will return in the summer. This is not the same as a "Dudley" nose, which is described as pink without pigmentation. A "Dudley" nose would be penalized in the show ring, while a "winter nose"

---

[1]Templeton, Stewart, and Fletcher. "Coat Color Genetics in the Labrador Retriever," The Journal of Heredity, 68:134–136, 1977.

A chocolate and yellow litter, sired by Ch. Kai Den Jet, CD, WC, owned by Jeannine Biddle. Note that yellow pups to the right have the double chocolate gene while the yellow puppies to the left have dark pigment. *Mike Johnson*

Ch. Ahilo's Igloo Iggy, UD, a lovely yellow BIS dog, with darker shading on his ears, muzzle, back, and tail. Owned by Elaine Brock.

is not a fault. The liver nose color in a yellow resulting from a chocolate gene is not the same as a winter nose. The yellow with correct pigment will exhibit dark eye rims even with a winter nose. This yellow results when either one or both parents can produce yellow or chocolate colors. Labradors that spend the winter in warm climates will maintain black noses.

CHOCOLATE (LIVER) LABRADORS

Chocolates inherit their color from a time when other retriever breeds were interbred with Labradors. Chocolate is an alternative form of the black coat color. All chocolates carry recessive alleles that inhibit black pigment anywhere on the body, thus making it unlikely that one can breed chocolates with dark points. These same alleles give some yellows brown, rather than the desirable black, pigment.

Chocolate-to-chocolate breeding can produce yellow or chocolate puppies. If a chocolate that does not carry a yellow gene is bred to a yellow that carries the gene for a brown nose and brown eye rims, the resulting puppies will be normal-appearing chocolates. However, if the chocolate carries the yellow gene, the probability is that half the offspring will be yellow with chocolate pigmentation on the nose and eye rims and half will be normal-appearing chocolates. If you breed a chocolate to a yellow that is homozygous for dark pigmentation, the puppies will be yellow with normal pigmentation.

However, if the chocolate is bred to a yellow that is heterozygous for dark pigment, then the puppies will be yellow but half of them will be carriers of incorrect pigmentation while they themselves look normal with black pigmentation. The other half of the litter will have liver pigmentation. This means that breeding a yellow Labrador to a chocolate Labrador is unwise and should not be done. If either parent has the ability to produce chocolate, it is extremely likely that yellow puppies with liver pigmentation will result. It is possible that neither parent can produce anything other than its own color but they still are heterozygous for the yellow and chocolate genes that, in future generations, will cause pigmentation problems.

Chocolate-to-chocolate matings are relatively safe in that they produce the chocolate color. However, to improve conformation and darken the coat and eye, breeding to a black of correct type, which carries chocolate genes, is the way to go. Too many generations of strictly chocolate matings can dilute the rich chocolate color. If a chocolate has the homozygous recessive genes, the pigment will be spread sparsely throughout the hair, diluting the color.

Famous Chocolates

In 1892 two liver-colored puppies were born at the Buccleuch Kennel at Dalkeith, Scotland. Even earlier, when shows began, red or liver-colored retrievers were exhibited. Many early field trial winners in England were liver-colored retrievers. The first field trial winner, in 1900, was a wavy-coated liver bitch.

In the 1930s in England Lady Ward (Chiltonfoliat Labradors) established a chocolate strain. At that time the larger kennels had their favorite colors, and usually concentrated on them and eliminated others. In 1929 Mrs. Marshall Field imported one of Lady Ward's chocolates, Diver of Chiltonfoliat (by Hayler's Joker ex Hayler's Fantasy), to the United States. Mrs. Field maintained two kennels, a yellow kennel and a black kennel, so she kenneled Diver with the yellows.

The first chocolate bench champion in the United States in the late 1950s was Ch. Invails Pogey Bait, owned by Mrs. Rita Haggerty. Ch. Kimbrow's

General Ike (Gault's Black General ex Far Away Bonnie), a Canadian-bred owned by Mrs. Reginald M. Lewis, became the first chocolate field champion. Ike was a good-looking dog and could have been a dual champion. Not many breeders used him because his color was unfashionable at that time.

Breeding chocolates was genetically difficult until more recent times, when Ch. Sandylands Tweed of Blaircourt, Ch. Sandylands Mark, and Ch. Follytower Black Stormer, top black English stud dogs that carried chocolate, were used extensively.

The first liver champion in England was Ch. Cookridge Tango (by Ch. Sandylands Tweed of Blaircourt ex Cookridge Gay Princess), a lovely bitch of excellent quality. Tango was the first liver to be awarded a Challenge Certificate under noted author and judge Mary Roslin-Williams. Tango was bred and owned by Mrs. M. Y. Pauling, whose Cookridge kennel did much for Swedish Labradors, especially those of Mrs. Brit-Marie Brulin's Puh prefix.

The second chocolate champion in England was also a bitch, Mrs. Margot Woolley's Ch. Follytower Merry Go Round at Brentville, sired by Ch. Follytower Merrybrook Black Stormer. Stormer also sired the first English male chocolate champion, owned by the author, English and American Ch. Lawnwoods Hot Chocolate. Campaigned at some shows in England and Ireland, Chock set quite a record before coming to the United States, where he enjoyed a great show career and spent many happy days hunting waterfowl with his owner.

Chock's breeder, Marjorie Satterthwaite, had sold him as a puppy to a policeman. Chock was a handful for his new family, so when he was about a year old, he went back to Mrs. Satterthwaite, who at the time was searching for a young black male for the author. Having no objection to what was then not a popular color, she bought the dog. Chock had a mind of his own and was very much an alpha dog. Special arrangements were made for him to travel in the cabin of a cargo plane. He had never been in a crate before, so Chock flew over loose in the forward cabin, and upon arriving at Kennedy International Airport in New York, the captain led him off the plane. Chock had to clear customs. The customs agent looked and made a comment about an old brown dog, while "Chock's" owner nodded in agreement (keeping in mind that this was the first chocolate champion male Labrador now arriving in the "Colonies"), and that was it. I was on hand with my small plane with a crate on the back seat. Chock got in (not knowing what it was) and then tried to take the crate apart to get out as we flew away. He was so provoked about the situation that for the next six months the only way to crate him was to back him in.

Chock always liked flying and eventually was so well behaved in the plane that he didn't need a crate. He would lie on the back seat, sleeping, except for looking out the window during takeoff and when it was time to land. His favorite trip was from Maryland to Connecticut one day to breed a bitch

Windshire Princess of Bree, a daughter of Eng., Am. Ch. Lawnwoods Hot Chocolate, owned by Lillian and George Knobloch.

Am., Can. Ch. Highlands Chivas Regal (Ch. Highlands Bronze Chieftain ex Windshire Princess of Bree), winning the Veterans Class at the LRC National Specialty in 1993, owned by Lillian and George Knobloch.
S. Booth

owned by Lorraine Robbenhaar. This was not the usual procedure, but the mating was accomplished in short order behind the hangar at the airport in Connecticut, and then Chock was flown home, sitting like a king on his back seat. Ch. Clemmsen of Killingworth, a Best of Breed winner at the Westminster show, resulted from this expedition.

Chock had been field trained in England so he could be a full English champion. He always wanted to do things his way, but eventually was willing to learn. He was extremely enthusiastic and was an excellent gun dog. I never ran him in field trials, but no doubt he would have performed with gusto.

Chock was very strong in the show ring and attempted to run the situation to his liking. He saw no need for the assistance of a handler and it was easier to let him do it himself, as he seldom put his feet down wrong. Once in a Sporting Group in Kentucky, handled by his owner, the ring was large, the pace when all dogs went around was fast, and it looked like his owner had a death grip on his lead. The judge said, "Now move on a loose lead," which he may have thought would eliminate the handsome Labrador. Not so. I dropped the lead, the dog cooperated, trotting perfectly on a loose lead. He was awarded a Group second that day!

Soon after I acquired Chock I judged a Labrador Specialty show in California. It seemed that every chocolate west of the Mississippi was there, as exhibitors thought they could win with my "favorite color." They were all of poor type and many had light or yellow eyes. Color has nothing to do with excellent breed type, just as sex has nothing to do with color selection. While a judge may have a personal color preference, certainly a poor specimen of the breed in a favorite color won't be put up over an excellent type of another color.

Edna Pillow—Cacao Labradors

Edna Pillow has been raising chocolates for over 34 years in New Hampshire. Her lines go back to Ch. Indian Valley Raed Wulf, an English import bred by Marjorie Cairns, and one of the first chocolate champions in the United States. In more recent years she has used dogs from Puhs (Sweden) and Follytower (England).

When Mrs. Pillow first started breeding and exhibiting chocolates, most people thought they were Chesapeakes! The first judge she showed a chocolate under said, "The Chesapeakes aren't being judged in this ring." Other people at ringside said, it looks like a Lab, but what is it? In spite of these remarks, Mrs. Pillow stuck to her guns, saying, "I will have some champion chocolates before the sod is over my grave, and I have succeeded after a long tough fight."

Her first Labrador, Ace from Trollgaard Kennels in New Hampshire, was black, but his dam was chocolate. Immediately Mrs. Pillow fell in love "with the luscious brown color." Three years passed before she was able to get a chocolate puppy from Jo deBesche, which she named Deuce.

As time went on she desired a chocolate bitch puppy. Mrs. Pillow contacted Dorothy Howe (Rupert Kennels) and Mrs. Howe wrote the breed column in *Popular Dogs*, where the letter was published. From this came a chocolate bitch puppy from Could Be Kennels in Missouri, named Could Be's Flaming Rock. "We called her Firey; she had a good pedigree and a delightful temperament and was as sound as a dollar, and to me that is what it is all about," recalls Mrs. Pillow. Firey had Ch. Indian Valley Rob Roy behind her, a brother to Ch. Indian Valley Raed Wulf. Mrs. Jean Willey imported these dogs directly from Mrs. Cairns in Scotland.

Mrs. Pillow's first chocolate bitch was bred to a black who carried the chocolate gene. She produced one black and six chocolates. At that time the gene pool for good chocolate stud dogs was very lacking. "I guess I was lucky to have bred to a black," recalled Mrs. Pillow. "I got dark eyes, dark coat color, proper coats, substance, and bone. I kept two puppies from that breeding and that was my foundation start."

Ch. Puhs Miss Swiss Miss (Swedish, Finnish Ch. Kamrats Buse ex Swedish Show Ch. Puhs Tongue-Twister). Owned by Edna Pillow.

In addition to breeding to American chocolates, Mrs. Pillow bought a lovely chocolate bitch, Ch. Puhs Miss Swiss Miss (called Flicka), from Frau Britt-Marie Brulin in Sweden, thanks to arrangements made by Helen Warwick. "I finished her championship quickly and to many she was one of the nicest chocolate bitches shown." She lived to be 15 years old.

Mrs. Pillow's next acquisition was Follytower Augustus from Mrs. Margot Woolley in England. "He never quite finished, but did sire eight chocolate champions and was the sire of my Anderscroft Brown Sugar who to me was a very valuable brood bitch," recalled Mrs. Pillow. Mrs. Pillow said that bringing in new bloodlines to combine with her old original lines really paid off.

Breeding chocolates has been a great challenge to me and I enjoy seeing some nice chocolates in the show ring and over the years there has been a great improvement. I have recently introduced the newest bloodline to my kennel through Glosmere Chocolate Soldier, an English import and a Ch. Comedy Star grandson.

I have always been most selective in the use of my stud dogs to other people's dogs, and in so doing, have had good results. I will not breed chocolate to yellow or to dogs carrying yellow. I feel that this is where the problem (with eye color and pigment) lies, combining the two colors. Once light eyes crop up in a line, it is almost impossible to breed out.

The days are gone when chocolates are rare! Yes, there are some nice ones out there but the overall quality still has a way to go. When chocolates started to become popular, many people jumped on the bandwagon with no thought of what was behind the dogs on paper. They bred for COLOR and in my opinion, that is why so many poor chocolates came about. It did a job on the chocolates' reputation and only careful breeding can correct this error that was made long ago.

Over the years for the most part, I have bred chocolate to chocolate and now and then going out to black and then coming in again to my chocolates. As I am called "Mrs. Chocolate," The Chocolate Lady," and "The

Ch. Cacao's Chief Mini-Willey (Cacao's Tully Wulf ex Anderscroft Brown Sugar), bred and owned by Edna Pillow. He is her best producing dog and the sire of several champions. *Gilbert*

Ch. Cacao's Mr. Personality (Ch. Cacao's Chief Willey ex Cacao's Christmas Carol). Bred and owned by Edna Pillow. *Tatham*

Chocolate Pioneer," I have no regrets for hanging in there when, at times, you felt as welcome as a skunk at a lawn party. I have met some wonderful people and have made some great friends.

BREEDING FOR COLOR

Labrador owners with a breeding program need to study more than the pet owner who is merely interested in color inheritance. In a breeding program, color is one consideration, along with breed type, conformation, and performance. According to Debby Kay, who has done extensive research on color genetics, "The overall quality of the dog is controlled by so many genes you cannot expect to accomplish your goals of color richness and clarity along with type with any quality in just one or two generations."

Yellow coat color in Labradors can range from a solid fox red to a very pale shade with extreme shaded cameo or chinchilla yellow or a pale cream. "Chinchilla" is a term used to describe the amount of shading, from a dark

A yellow with splash marks at four months of age. These persisted all her life, only on one leg and base of tail on back. *Photo from Debby Kay collection.*

to a lighter hue, on the hair shaft. Chinchilla shading appears in all three recognized Labrador colors. The gene is carried by the black but rarely seen except for dogs occasionally reported as silver or ghost Labradors.

"Cameo" refers to the dilute or cream shade and the presence of shading. The yellow gene in Labradors has many versions, some dilute with shadings and some solid. Many yellow Labradors have white markings which blend in with the overall coat color. Some are shaded to the extreme chinchilla so that they are almost white.

A uniform yellow coat will have the same coat shade on the ears and throat, whereas the non-uniform coat will have an overall body color of cream or beige with a predominantly darker color on the ears or edges of the ears, usually brown or cinnamon. Other areas such as the shoulder and back will be shaded with tones in between the cinnamon ear color and the cream or beige coat. Either the solid yellow coat or the yellow coat with shadings is acceptable for the yellow Labrador.

According to Debby Kay,

Some of the nicest-looking Labradors are the darker yellows with the chinchilla gene. The shading falls around the shoulders and underbelly to create a most striking illusion. A very pale yellow with the chinchilla gene, on the other hand, tends to look like a dirty white and often loses its expression.

Debby Kay has found the following in her research with Labradors:

As the shading factor is introduced, there is an additive effect on the intensity of the color. The intensity is reduced with successive generations. The degree varies with different lines. The shaded gene in a dog's pedigree can cause some strange things to happen even if the dog is chocolate or black. I have seen chocolates that have a yellow undercoat and blacks with a

A dark yellow dog, Ch. Gunslinger's Tawny Boy (Ch. Lewisfield Gunslinger ex Littlemore Rose of Trailee), bred by Anna Metz and owned by Col. Jerry Weiss, handled by Lisa Weiss Agresta in 1971 under Larry Downey. *Gilbert*

A fox-red Labrador (left), Lady Brittany VI at five years old (Mr. B. Thornapple ex Beulah Mae Spade) and Acme Creek's Lady Chelsey at four months of age (Ch. Triple L's Davey Crocket ex Ignots Beaver Creek Abby), owned by Joni Sterenberg.

silver cast. These usually do not persist, so most people do not pay attention to them.

I have come across genes that cause brindling, white spots, and black and tans. These factors are all simple recessives. Brindling is sometimes referred to as splashing or splashmarks, due to the fact that it appears as though the dog has been splashed with mud. On chocolate dogs this would be difficult to see unless there is a distinct difference in the shades of brown.

I have also seen the black and tan gene, which seems to occur almost twice as frequently as the brindling gene. In recent years, this gene has been cropping up with more regularity, which is not surprising since more intensive linebreeding is being done nowadays. This trait probably comes from crosses with setters in the early 1900s. Helen Warwick mentions the black and tan factor in her book (*The New Complete Labrador Retriever*) but offers no explanation as to its mode of inheritance. My own litters with the trait support the recessive mode of inheritance; in order to show up the dog has to carry both the recessive tan factor genes. This is why the gene is not seen on self-colored dogs. The intensity of these tan markings, particularly on the cheeks, may vary from very slight reddish hues to distinctive tan marks.

COLOR HUES AND SHADES

Polygenic inheritance works to produce all shades, depth of color, and clarity in Labradors. Blacks are usually a deep color but some are born with a brownish cast. Chocolates range from light cocoa to the deepest dark chocolate shade. Yellows can range from a deep fox red to dark mustard to a pale, ivory cream. The dark, rich colors are dominant, and as with all desirable dominants are the most difficult to keep. The mid-range tones are the most numerous while the lightest pale colors are the most recessive and easy to maintain by doubling up on recessives. The depth of color, from the dark red Labrador to the pale cream, is caused by rufous polygenes. The very pale yellows, usually called cream color, get their very pale coloration from the addition of the chinchilla gene.

The shading comes in hues of white, cream, tan, and golden brown on the main hair shaft root. This is not the undercoat hair. If you decide to breed for a specific color, you will have to select for color first in planning your matings. Debby Kay reminds us

> . . . that hue in the Labrador coat is not universally defined. What I call dark chocolate someone else may call sedge, and the same for fox red. If you are determined to breed a particular hue of a color then you will need to establish a color chart to compare and grade your breeding stock's colors against. This will allow for consistency. The keeping of records in a color breeding program is very important.
>
> Regarding color "problems" in Labradors, these are minor and should be kept in perspective. If your dog is well-built and from a solid foundation, do not scrap it from your breeding program because of color. Color is superficial and usually easy to deal with since most all the color genes except black are recessive. In two generations of strict color breeding the trait can be eliminated.
>
> The preferred method of breeding where two traits (solid color and a particular color hue) are involved is called convergent improvement.

Ch. Starpoint Blackthorn Blonde CD, an example of a yellow with chinchilla. Note color on ear, tips of toes, and tip of tail. This bitch was Best in Sweeps in 1986 at the Golden Gate LRC under Lorraine Robbenhar-Taylor and later that year won a class under Mrs. Margie Cairns (Blaircourt). Owned by Janice Byer.

Ch. Windanna's Pippin O Bucklebury CD, WC, was Best Puppy at 11 months of age in Edmonton, Alberta in 1993. She won a Group at 14 months of age. Note the shadings on head, ears, back, tip of tail, and hind legs. Owned by Charles and Judy Hunt. *Mikron*

Simply put, convergent improvement is when two separate lines, each pure for one of the traits, are developed, then crossed with each other and back-crossed to the parent line until the desired combination of traits is obtained. To get rid of or enhance a particular trait, you simply use the same method as dealing with any recessive trait. Identify your carriers and take steps from there to eliminate the unwanted trait. To control the hue of the color in chocolates or yellows takes an in-depth study of color genetics. Control over color in a breeding program is possible, but remember that color then is the primary selector. Conformation and temperament, in these instances, can suffer at the expense of color. Is it worth it? I don't think so, but then color is not my goal in my Labrador breeding program.

Other Markings

The genes that govern Labrador coat colors also combine to affect pigment, shadings, mismarkings, eye rim and nose color, and eyes. There were once Labradors in England that were black with white specks. They were of excellent type and thought to originate with some of the early water strains, but not being of a solid color, this strain was not perpetuated.

Mary Roslin-Williams, who started with Labradors in 1939 in England, told me about blacks flecked with white spots which were well liked at one time. These were known as "Hailstone" Labradors, thought to have originated with an old strain of waterdogs on the Solway. The outstanding British breeder, Lorna, Countess Howe, approved of this color, but it never became a recognized color.

White Spots

The AKC Standard permits a white spot on the chest. However, white marks may also appear on the feet, chest, and underbelly, some of which may be rather large. This marking has appeared in Labradors from the beginning of the breed and is probably one of the most common recessives. Being a recessive, the trait for white can skip many generations before showing up. Due to an additive effect, the more dogs in the pedigree carrying the gene, the greater the amount of white that may appear. However, the trait can be eliminated by breeding "clean," i.e. non-carrier dogs, to other non-carrier dogs.

A piebald white spotting can occur. It is rather wild and manifests itself with jagged white areas on the neck and body, one or more feet and pasterns, and also the underbelly. This of course is very undesirable and is a throwback to some other breed that was crossed with the Labrador at some time. Probably some variation of the piebald spotting allele is responsible for dogs having large white spots on their coats.

There are many yellows with white spots, but most of these go unnoticed since they blend in with the shading of the undercoat.

White Labradors

Helen Warwick's book on Labradors mentions a report from a 1933 issue of *The Gamekeeper* referring to a strain of "white Labradors" that were raised by Mr. Austin MacKenzie at Carradale, Argyllshire, in Scotland. These dogs were traced back to the Duke of Buccleuch's imported (from Newfoundland) strain of blacks. One white bitch from this kennel was later mated to Lord Lonsdale's Blanco, a bluish-white dog by Captain Radclyffe's Ben of Hyde. Eight white puppies were born "and the color was apparently fixed."

These animals were probably very pale cream rather than white. A pure white dog would be called an "albino," which indicates a lack of any pigment; also, albinos have pink eyes. None of the early writings about Labradors mention white dogs with pink eyes.

White Hair Condition

Puppies may have white hairs from two to five months of age. The hairs will appear singly on the feet and legs, and then on other parts of the body. The amount will vary, even among littermates. When there is a gray undercoat the puppy will have a salt-and-pepper appearance. The guard hairs turn white,

Chucklebrook Tabuka was temporarily gray from three to eight months before turning solid black. Photo courtesy of Diane Pilbin. *Gilbert*

not the undercoat. By the time the puppy is about a year old and has shed its puppy coat, its color will be normal and the white hairs will not reappear.

The problem seems to be widespread in unrelated lines and exact causes have never been determined. There may be environmental causes where a particular dog has an allergic response which causes a temporary loss of pigment in its coat. Pollen, vaccinations, diet changes, or pollutants in the air are all possible determinants. Canine allergies are very complex.

To make sure that a puppy will turn black at maturity, the breeder must be able to recognize the difference between this temporary condition and true white mismarkings in which white patches are present on otherwise black puppies at birth.

Black and Tan or Splashed Markings

Splashed markings usually occur on the underpart of the flanks and on the inside of the lower part of the legs when a puppy is about four months old. The brindling may also appear on the tail. This is a throwback to some unknown ancestor. Such coloration is not allowed in show dogs.

Black and tan markings, also a throwback, are more serious faults. These markings on the legs, cheeks, and chest, under the tail, and spots over the eyes may be an obvious brown or golden color, or on a dark dog, they may be barely visible. It is especially difficult to see the tan markings on a chocolate dog because of the similarity of the colors. However, one can sometimes detect a circle of light hairs in the anal region.

Labradors carrying the tan allele should not be used for breeding. The offspring of two Labradors heterozygous for the tan allele will continue to carry the allele. It could be many generations before it is expressed visually.

Labrador breeders must remember that the modern Labrador (as with other retriever breeds) is a combination of many other breeds, some now extinct. There were various types of spaniels, setters, pointers, and Newfound-land types (notably the St. John's or Lesser Newfoundland). Furthermore, breeding records were not kept. Other breeds were also used as crosses, notably the Foxhound and possibly the Rottweiler.

The English Kennel Club first accepted the Labrador as a foreign breed in 1902, and then in 1905 as a retriever variety. Until at least 1919 the retriever breeds were interbred; interbred retrievers were registered as such. The commonest crosses were Flat-coats and Labradors. It is most likely that the Gordon Setter influenced the black and tan markings.

The Labrador Standard calls for a solid color; therefore it is never wise to breed from mismarked animals. Mismarked progeny should be sold or given away without papers.

Colors in Undercoats

A true-bred black will have a thick undercoat which may vary in shade from black to a mousy color. Chocolates usually have excellent undercoats, in most cases the same color as the coat or just a little lighter. Mary Roslin-Williams told me this probably comes from their Chesapeake ancestors. The author agrees, as the Labradors and Chesapeakes trace their ancestry back to the dogs in Newfoundland. Undercoats in yellows vary from the same color to a much lighter shade.

Single-coated Labradors are incorrect even though they may have shiny, sleek coats. The undercoat is essential to waterproof and protect the Labrador when it swims in icy, cold water.

COLOR GENE CHART FOR LABRADOR RETRIEVERS

[A capital letter represents a dominant allele while a small letter represents a recessive allele. An additional symbol tells of the particular type of allele present at that locus.]

A Locus   A - This indicates a solid-colored dog.

a - Tan points, normally seen on the cheeks, above eyes, front of the legs, and under the tail.

B Locus   B - The dominant member of the group, makes a dog black.

b - The recessive member of the group, makes a dog chocolate.

C Locus   C - Full pigmentation of the hair color.

c - Causes complete albinism and does not exist in the Labrador breed. There are rare white Labradors but it is due to a different gene.

c - Chinchilla, hypostatic to C. Epistasis is the situation whereby a gene at one locus can influence the expression of a gene at another locus. When geneticists term a gene epistatic (above) to another gene, it will mask the effect of the gene it is above. When the term hypostatic (below or under) is applied, that gene is marked.

Therefore a dog coded CC will have the deepest color, and the dog coded Cc a more reduced color.

D Locus   Intense pigmentation, richness of color.

Labradors do not have d, which indicates "blue" puppies.

E Locus   Alleles at the E locus give interrelationships and variable expressions which may be confusing.

E - Extension of dark pigment.

e - The red/yellow pigmentation.

e - Produces brindling, is epistatic to e in most breeds, but in some dogs is hypostatic to e.

S Locus   S - Self-colored. Labradors are one color, not merle or some other combination of colors. Nonetheless, there have been Labradors of more than one color (black and yellow) and a case of a mosaic Labrador has been recorded; this is very rare.

s - Controls the distribution of white spots, pencil marks, etc., on the dog. It has an additive effect; the more a dog with this gene is bred to another with the same gene, the larger the areas of white will become in the progeny.

T Locus   This is responsible for ticking. It is possible that this gene is carried by some Labradors.

Finally there are the g and m loci. All Labradors carry the hypostatic g and m. The g controls graying and does not allow it to occur. Labrador puppies are not black and turn gray by one year. Thus we know that Labradors carry the g and not G. M produces merle and does not occur in Labradors; therefore all Labradors are m.

With the above information you can construct the color code for your dog. For example, you have a dog that produces a puppy with tan markings. His code would be: Aa EeBB. If you breed that dog to a dog that carries the same tan marking gene, the chances are greater that you will get a puppy with tan markings. Or you may have a litter in which all puppies are black or yellow except for one brown or pink-nosed yellow that has brown eye rims and pads. This puppy carries two chocolate genes, so it has to have that kind of pigment. This happens for the same reason that a yellow puppy with pink pigment (actually the lack of black pigment) will result from breeding two chocolates that carry yellow together, or a yellow that carries chocolate to a chocolate that carries yellow. These puppies are all eebb or "double" chocolate gene carriers.

POSSIBLE LABRADOR GENOTYPES:

B = dominant allele, black pigment

b = recessive allele, liver pigment

E = dominant allele for expression of dark pigment

e = recessive allele, restricts dark pigment (ee always gives yellow pigment)

COLOR PHENOTYPE	COLOR GENOTYPE	COMMENTS
Black	BBEE	Dominant black.
Black	BBEe	Black carrying yellow.
Black	BbEE	Black carrying chocolate.
Black	BbEe	Black carrying yellow and chocolate.
Yellow	BBee	Very dark pigment not expressed.
Yellow	Bbee	A yellow/chocolate; ee alleles mean dark pigment not expressed. Produces a yellow with brown nose, eye rims, and light eyes. Carries chocolate.

| Chocolate | bbEE | A chocolate which does not carry yellow (no e allele present). Could produce black or chocolate. |
| Chocolate | bbEe | Chocolate carrying yellow. Can produce all three colors. |

chapter 7

Your Labrador Breeding Program

Fanciers should have definite goals in mind before embarking on a breeding program. They must understand linebreeding and outcrossing and be thoroughly knowledgeable about genetic problems in Labradors. They must be able to commit the time and money that go into a successful breeding program. Their aim should be to improve their stock. Conscientious breeders must be concerned about the welfare of each puppy they breed.

Dedicated breeders realize that success may not come in any one litter. It may take years to reach a goal. There are many people in Labradors who have been breeding successfully for a long time. It is interesting to see what they have accomplished over the years by following a careful breeding program.

THE FOUNDATION BITCH

A foundation bitch is the heart and cornerstone of a breeding program. A great foundation bitch may not necessarily be a top winner but she will conform to the breed standard and have the proper temperament and working ability. A large kennel is unnecessary as excellent progeny can come from limited parental stock.

To identify a potential foundation bitch, a breeder needs knowledge of her genetic background so as to avoid a vast amount of wasted effort and false starts. A foundation bitch must be predictable and produce consistently the qualities she possesses in genotype and phenotype. She should be able to increase the desirable qualities in her progeny. The foundation bitch should be purely dominant herself so she can be purely dominant in her gametes.

103

Three very influential Labrador littermates by Ch. Lockerbie Goldentone Jensen ex Int. Ch. Spenrock's Banner WC, pictured at 11 years of age: left to right—Ch. Spenrock's Cognac (owned by Jerry and Lisa Weiss Agresta), Ch. Spenrock's Bohemia Champagne (owned by Diane Pilbin), and Ch. Spenrock's Cardigan Bay (owned by Janet Churchill). *Gilbert*

Ch. Lobuff Tequila Sunrise (Ch. Spenrock Heatheredge Mariner ex Ch. Spenrock's Cognac) winning a brood bitch class at the Miami Valley LRC, with littermates Ch. Lobuff's Missouri Breaks and Ch. Lobuff's Indiana Jones. Five finished from this litter sired by Ch. Northwood Sandman. Owner and breeder, Lisa Weiss Agresta. *Alverson*

Two parents with any factor as pure dominants in the gametes from both will produce in their immediate progeny pure dominants as pertain to that factor. This would be a way to produce an excellent foundation bitch. However, if the two parents have any factor or attributes as recessives in the gametes of both, they will produce in their immediate progeny only recessives as pertain to those factors. This could cause a regression in a breeding program if the recessive is undesirable.

If one of the two parents in a mating is pure dominant for a given trait, and the other is recessive for that trait, all the immediate progeny will be hybrid-dominant for that trait. In these cases a bitch produced from such a mating may be an excellent show specimen but a disappointing producer. Such a bitch has a nonhomozygous genetic framework. She usually lacks a linebred pedigree (no common ancestors in the first five or six generations), and most

Ch. Breton Gate Cairngorm, CD, JH, WC, (Am., Can. Ch. Campbellcroft's Angus, CD, WC ex Ch. Breton Gate Omega Boom), was Best Brood Bitch at Rose City LRC Specialty, 1991, with her puppies Shandy, who took WB, BOW, and BOB; and Happy, who took Second Open Black Dogs under Mrs. R.V. Hepworth (Poolstead). *Callea*

Donald and Virginia Campbell at home, 1989: front row: (l to r) Ch. Breton Gate Cairngorm, CD, JH, WC; Am., Can. Ch. Campbellcroft's Angus, CD, WC; Ch. Agber Daisy of Campbellcroft, CD, WC (at 15 years old). Back row: Ch. Campbellcroft's Top Drawer, CD, JH, WC; Ch. Campbellcroft's Pede, CD, WC; Campbellcroft's Piper, CDX, WC.

likely will not produce type consistently because of her hybrid dominance. Statistically, if such a bitch had many puppies, 25 percent of them would be recessive, 50 percent hybrid-dominant, and 25 percent pure dominant when bred to a hybrid-dominant stud.

Your foundation bitch must be evaluated, not for what she is, but for what she will produce. A breeder must aim for the purity of dominance. If a breeder allows various sets of genes to become hybrid-dominants because of a poor stud selection, a breeding program will suffer a setback in just one generation, because now the bitch's progeny will fail to produce the past excellence of the line.

A foundation bitch may even be somewhat inbred provided that the dogs in her pedigree, and the bitches in particular, have produced within their litters excellent pups with uniformity as to breed type and qualities. The foundation bitch should have great intelligence, be as near to the Standard as possible, and have strong hybrid vigor and nurturing qualities that she will

Ch. Chucklebrook Tuc O'Aspetuck at 11 months (Ch. Killingworth Thunderson ex Ch. Spenrock Bohemia Champagne), owned by Selene Weaver (left); and Ch. Chucklebrook Helen (Eng., Am. Ch. Ballyduff Seaman ex Ch. Spenrock's Bohemia Champagne), owned by Diane Pilbin.

Ch. Killingworth Thunderson (Ch. Torquay's Scorpio ex Killingworth's Snipe), owned by Lorraine Robbenhaar-Taylor, a dog behind many pedigrees.

Four generations of Labradors: l to r - Whistlewing's Que Sera CD (FT Ch., Am. FT Ch. Gahonk's Leave It To Jessie ex Whistlewings Kitty McGee); Can. Triple Champion Whistlewings Kitty McGee, WCX; Can. Triple Champion Kenosee Jim Dandy, WCX. The puppies are sired by FT Ch., Am. FT Ch. Walmarc's Postal Code. Pictured with Megan, Lori, and Garrett Curran.

A lovely bitch in whelp: Hampshire's Secret (Ch. Cacao's Chief Mini-Willey ex Ch. Puhs Sea Coral). Owned by Edna Pillow and Mel Pfeifle.

Ch. Highlands Ruffian, JAM (Ch. Beechcrofts Edgewood Tomarc ex Anderscroft Encore). Owned by Lillian and George Knobloch.

Ch. Coalcreek's Gimme A Break (Am., Can. Ch. Coalcreek's Briary Breakthru ex Ch. Scrimshaw My Sin). Number One Labrador in 1988, he sired many outstanding offspring, including the 1989 #1 bitch, Ch. Highlands Break of Dawn (Group winner); sire of breeding stock for Guiding Eyes for the Blind as well as therapy dogs, search and rescue dogs, and service dogs. *Alverson*

pass on to her daughters. Good fertility and ease of whelping are also important attributes. A good foundation bitch is the rock upon which successful kennels are built.

CHOOSING A STUD DOG

A good stud dog should be prepotent. He should have the ability to carry on excellence in his progeny and he should be able to produce better than himself. The stud dog should stamp his puppies with his own distinctive look. When selecting an appropriate stud dog for your bitch, study him genetically and phenotypically, looking for prepotency and dominance. Don't just choose stud dogs from pictures in magazines (some pictures may be retouched to give a better top line or correct some fault). Study a dog's progeny in the show ring or in the field and try to predict which sire would be most likely to complement and/or correct faults in your bitch. A strong bitch line is very important in a sire. You must also do a careful pedigree analysis of the dog, as well as checking hip, elbow, and eye clearances.

Most heavily used stud dogs will produce everything in their career. If a dog consistently produces the same problem, then you know there is trouble. Dogs, of course, have the opportunity to produce many more offspring in a lifetime than bitches. Bitches don't usually have enough puppies in their lifetime to produce the total spectrum of genetic problems that they are capable of producing under certain circumstances. The genetics are complicated but as you come to understand them you will learn that breeding is a constant process of selecting the best and culling the problems.

chapter 8

Hereditary Eye Diseases in Labradors

Hereditary blindness has been a problem in Labrador Retrievers for many years. Dr. Keith C. Barnett of the Animal Health Trust in England was one of the first to be aware of the problem and to try to work out a solution through examination of dogs' eyes. Dr. Lionel Rubin, at the University of Pennsylvania, was one of the first American veterinarians to examine dogs for hereditary blindness. Gustavo D. Aguirre, VMD, PhD, has conducted research for many years and is director of the James A. Baker Institute for Animal Health at Cornell University's College of Veterinary Medicine.

PROGRESSIVE RETINAL ATROPHY

Progressive retinal atrophy (PRA) was first recognized in Sweden in 1906 by Dr. Magnusson as a form of hereditary blindness which he called *retinitis pigmentosa*. The affected dogs were Gordon Setters sired by a dog from England, so actually the disease originated in England. By the 1930s the disease was called progressive retinal atrophy, but not much was heard about it until the 1950s, when veterinarians divided it into two forms, general and centralized.

Dr. Barnett and other ophthalmologists in England used the term PRA for many years in regard to the Labrador Retriever to refer only to centralized PRA. It was not until the late 1970s that they recognized that the generalized form of the disease occurred also in the Labrador.

PRA is an hereditary abnormality in which a degenerative disease of the retinal visual cells may result in blindness. The disease affects the functioning of the photoreceptor layers of the retina, the light-sensitive lining at the back of the eye, causing the dog to go slowly blind. "Atrophy" refers to the gradual thinning or wasting away of the tissue of the retina. Once the nerve endings atrophy, there is no means of recovery for the dog's eyesight.

In early studies of the mode of inheritance in England it was incorrectly believed that the cause was a simple dominant gene with high but incomplete penetrance. (This applied only to central PRA, a belief which also turned out to be incorrect). Eventually researchers found that the gene was a recessive trait so it could be passed on without regard to the mate also having the gene, with the result that a percentage of the offspring would be blind (eventually), while the others would not go blind, but could be carriers.

The major difficulty many years ago in England was that the veterinarians had only ophthalmoscopic examination for detecting the blindness. Dogs were examined at a year of age and every year thereafter until four years old. They were given an interim certificate if they passed the examination at one, two, and three years and a permanent certificate at the age of four.

Unfortunately many dogs were used for breeding prior to age four, not all dogs went blind at a certain age, and dogs clear of PRA at four often went blind a few years later. Unless it hit home, not all breeders used the tests. Also, at that time very few breeders or veterinarians understood the genetics of the disease. Certification was troublesome and expensive and it never was a guarantee that a dog would not transmit blindness. Carrier dogs could pass the ophthalmoscopic examination and receive a certificate and yet transmit blindness. There were also instances of misdiagnosis.

Complete eradication of the disease was very unlikely under the circumstances. As early researchers found that the disease skipped generations, they realized that a recessive gene was involved. Breeders were hampered by the fact that a dog which appeared normal could later go blind. Dogs could pass on the disease without ever going blind, and no test was available for detecting carriers, other than test matings, which by nature were impractical. Breeders would sell puppies which appeared normal, and the parents could both hold PRA certificates as being normal even though they might go blind at a later age, or were carriers.

Thus the problem has filtered down through Labrador bloodlines and at times wiped out a person's entire breeding program. In the United States information was not readily disseminated, so many breeders had no knowledge of PRA. The only way to eliminate PRA is to stop breeding from dogs that are carriers. To do this, those dogs need to be identified. PRA Data, Inc. has published three books (as of 1994) of pedigrees of affected Labradors.[1]

---

[1]*PRA Data, Inc., 15624 N.E. 164th Street, Woodinville, WA 98072 USA. The cost in the USA and Canada is $12.50 per volume (includes postage); in other countries, $17.50 (US dollars).*

PRA Data is a nonprofit organization dedicated to compiling voluntary data on Labrador Retrievers that have been clinically confirmed as having hereditary generalized (not centralized) PRA.

Because the blindness caused by PRA is completely painless, many Labrador owners are not aware of it until the problem has become quite advanced. Some of the symptoms are a loss of night vision, followed by a progressive loss of day vision and poor "marking" or the inability to see stationary objects. As the rods and cones in the eye atrophy, more light shines on the tapetum which in turn reflects it out. As the retina gets thinner, more light is allowed in and reflected. As fewer and fewer rods function, less reflected light is picked up and gradually the dog loses sight until eventually total blindness results. A dog will adapt to the increasing blindness and develop its other senses to compensate for the onset of poor vision. This may lead the owner to believe that the dog is normal. The coat color and eye color have no bearing on the disease. However, the dilated pupil in a dog with generalized PRA may appear as a darker eye.

Generalized PRA is passed on by a simple autosomal recessive gene, one of the three types of inheritance. Most inherited diseases are spread by inbreeding or linebreeding back to a limited number of different ancestors. If you look at the tenth to fifteenth (or perhaps further back) generations of a pedigree, you may find many of the same dogs in the various lines.

Diseases are genetically different in different breeds. Even though PRA appears to be identical in different breeds, different genes control the disease in each affected breed.

Carriers are phenotypically normal, but a carrier-to-carrier mating may produce some affected dogs. A carrier has a single recessive gene and an affected dog has a double recessive gene. A dog must inherit the defective gene for PRA from both parents in order to become clinically blind.

Affected mated to affected produces all affected. In a mating of affected to carrier, half the offspring will be affected and half carriers. Normal bred to affected produces all carriers. Carriers bred to normal never produce affected pups but they distribute the undesirable genetic trait to half their puppies. (The succeeding generation would have a 25 percent chance of having carriers.) Clinically normal bred to normal can produce affected, clinically normal but a carrier, and clinically and genetically normal.

The worst thing breeders can do is to breed carriers to each other, as the unwanted gene will be distributed to half the progeny and there is no way to know which half will get the affected gene. If a genetic disease is dominant, it can be removed in one generation. However, in the case of PRA, if one selects against affected dogs, it takes 10 generations to reduce the incidence of the disease to 25 percent—the lowest it can be.

This should indicate to Labrador breeders that removing affected dogs from breeding programs by itself is not enough. Breeders must disclose the identity of affected dogs and remove all affected and/or carriers, as well as the progeny of these animals and those likely to be carriers, from their breeding stock. Any dog which has a 50 percent chance of being a carrier must not be used for breeding. If a carrier dog is clinically normal, it is not considered safe to use its grandchildren for breeding. If a carrier is never bred to another carrier, it will never produce an affected dog. Unless a dog produces an affected dog, the only way to prove a dog is a carrier (until a DNA test is developed) is by test breeding.

Test breeding is a difficult task but it is the only method available at this time to identify carrier dogs. Fairly large litters are needed in test breeding to determine percentages, and then the results are not absolutely true, as statistical rather than absolute guarantees are the outcome.

A suspected carrier must be bred to an affected dog. To test the progeny, a minimum of six puppies is needed. Ten would be better, even if it were necessary to breed two litters to get that number. The test puppies must survive to the testing age in order to obtain a greater than 95 percent confidence level that the tested dog is not a PRA carrier, and then there is still a chance for error because 100 percent never happens. According to Dr. Aguirre, "A minimum of six puppies gives 96.5 percent confidence that the test-mated dog is not a carrier; as the numbers increase, the confidence increases to over 99 percent, but never 100 percent."

CENTRAL PROGRESSIVE RETINAL ATROPHY

Central Progressive Retinal Atrophy (CPRA) is a totally different eye condition from GPRA, with its own histopathological and ophthalmoscopic features. Central PRA is recognized by a pigmentary disturbance in the tapetum lucidum due to hypertrophy and migration of the pigment epithelium cells. Photoreceptor degeneration occurs secondary to the disease underlying the pigment epithelium. Progression is slow, and in fact, some dogs never lose vision.

In contrast to GPRA, affected dogs may have better vision in dull light than in bright sunlight. The peripheral vision will remain normal until late in the disease, enabling dogs to see moving objects, while at the same time causing them to collide with stationary objects in their path. Dogs with CPRA also have poor near vision.

The mode of inheritance in CPRA is different from GPRA. In CPRA it is autosomal [2] but dominant, probably with incomplete penetrance of the gene—which means that even though present, the gene may not express itself. The disease has had a limited geographical distribution confined to Europe, leading researchers to suspect environmental or nutritional causes rather than

---

[2]Autosomal *means that the gene is not sex-linked; it occurs equally in both sexes.*

inherited factors. Dr. Aguirre reports that "the evidence coming out of England, which is still unpublished, is that the disease is probably a nutritional one resulting from deficiency of antioxidants."

The majority of dogs with CPRA are affected by two to three years of age and the disease is usually found with an ophthalmoscope by four years of age. The eye examination will show brown pigment spots in the tapetal fundus. Affected dogs may exhibit a strange expression because they have enhanced peripheral vision as they compensate for loss of central vision.

DIAGNOSIS OF PRA

PRA lesions are very typical in Labradors. The lesions are probably present by nine months of age, even though they can't be detected at that age. There are at present three ways to examine a dog's eyes: the slit-lamp microscope, an ophthalmoscope, and an electroretinogram.

The slit-lamp microscope examines only the front of the eye. No one can diagnose PRA using a slit-lamp because it does not look into the retina. It is, however, critical for diagnosing diseases of the lens and cornea.

Two types of ophthalmoscopes are used to examine the retina: a direct or hand-held, and an indirect. The direct has limitations. The indirect is the most important ophthalmoscope as it allows an earlier diagnosis than could be determined with a direct scope. Examinations must be made by trained ophthalmologists. The age of diagnosis of PRA with an indirect ophthalmoscope is usually after four years of age.

The electroretinogram (ERG) measures the function of the retina and can show marked functional abnormalities indicative of progressive rod-cone degeneration by 18 months of age, which is before the disease can be recognized clinically. With an ERG Dr. Aguirre can detect PRA conclusively by 18 months of age. However, unless they have special training, other veterinarians may not be able to do this. Merely buying expensive equipment is not the answer; equipment is the least important part of an ERG. A veterinarian can get adequate used equipment, but she/he must know how to correctly stimulate the retina to obtain a valid diagnosis.

The basis of an ERG exam is stimulating the retina, which must be done properly or results will be misleading and inconclusive. The ERG must be done under anesthesia because the ERG response is 1000 times smaller than a blink and dogs that are awake will twitch, thus making an awake ERG useless. Good recording equipment is essential.

The ERG is performed by anesthetizing the dog and dilating its pupils. Using a moist solution, contact lenses are placed over the corneas of the eyes (the outer edges). The contact lenses then record A waves and B waves on an oscilloscope using complicated equipment. Electrodes are attached to the eye to measure the response of varied light stimuli of different color, intensity, and duration. The responses of millions of retinal cells are recorded.

The ERG is able to diagnose PRA while the retina still looks normal. Degenerative diseases progress very slowly, which makes it extremely difficult to detect them while the dog is quite young. Misdiagnosis of eye diseases exacerbates the problem for dog owners. Inflammation in the back of the eye can destroy the retina, but inflammatory retinal disease should not be misdiagnosed as PRA. Furthermore, rumors should not be spread about a dog's alleged condition, because the rumor may be based on a misdiagnosis.

According to Dr. Aguirre, 80 percent of Labradors show a typical rate of progress. There are variations in the age of onset. The clinical signs of the disease are indistinguishable from normal when the dogs are young. Usually there are early lesions by four years of age and blindness at seven years, but not all dogs follow the rules. Dr. Aguirre has divided PRA into two groups: one has clinical signs as early as six months up to two years with total blindness early; the other is a late onset clinically, with blindness not occurring until five to seven years of age.

Histology is another method of detecting PRA, but subtle errors can occur at all levels. A special laboratory processes the tissues when the dog is at least eight to ten months old. It takes a full-time technician to do histology and it is costly because standard methods of histology will not work. The tissue processing is very critical. Most laboratories are not set up to do this for Labrador Retrievers because of the difficulty involved. Because of the time and expense involved, research labs do not have time for histology.

DNA TO IDENTIFY CARRIERS

Studies are underway to identify gene markers for specific traits. DNA or genetic fingerprinting will be used to detect animals carrying the PRA gene. The Animal Health Trust in England has received funding from the Guide Dogs for the Blind Association (also of England) for research on the molecular biology of the canine genome (chromosomes). A canine DNA linkage map will be established by a number of markers distributed throughout the chromosomes. One goal is to discover the gene responsible for PRA (by comparing the DNA of affected and unaffected dogs) so that a screening test can be established which can be carried out on a blood sample to detect a PRA carrier. This technology can also be applied to other inherited diseases, such as cataracts.

This program is of vital interest to The Seeing Eye and other guide dog schools because affected Labradors (and other breeds) would not be placed in the training program, and carriers would be identified so that a scientifically sound breeding program could be undertaken.

The James A. Baker Institute at Cornell University (New York) headed up by Gustavo D. Aguirre, VMD, is working to define and characterize the various forms of PRA. Their project is called "Molecular Genetic Studies of Canine Progressive Rod-Cone Degeneration (PRCD)." The study is funded by Morris Animal Foundation with significant funding sponsorship from The Seeing Eye, Inc. Many dog clubs have also made contributions.

The investigators propose to clone the PRCD gene and develop a reliable blood-based DNA diagnostic test to identify dogs that are genetically normal, affected, or carriers for the PRCD mutant gene. Since the PRCD blindness can't be treated medically, it makes sense to eliminate it genetically. With such a test, owners could breed carriers to genetically normal dogs and keep the genetically normal progeny as future breeding stock. Abnormal puppies would be neutered. Valuable breeding lines would be preserved by this method while the mutant PRCD gene was being eliminated altogether.

Molecular genetics of canine ocular diseases will be used to score or identify the marker genes as a means of fingerprinting the alleles. After the defective genes have been identified, a screening program will be set up whereby affected and carrier animals are identified and normal dogs cleared. The Inherited Eye Disease Studies Unit (IEDSU) at Cornell University is performing research studies on the molecular genetics of inherited retinal degenerations to develop a method for testing DNA in blood samples to unequivocally identify affected, normal, and carrier dogs at an early age.

A recessively inherited genetic defect which can't be identified until after the animal has reached breeding age has presented breeders with a difficult problem. Progressive rod-cone degeneration, the most common form of progressive retinal atrophy (PRA), has been difficult to identify and, as a result of a mutant gene, it is widespread. Experts estimate that 24 percent of Labradors are carriers. Until the DNA test can be perfected and used, the only effective means to control PRCD is to test-breed dogs in order to identify carriers and eliminate affected dogs and heterozygotes from breeding. If this test breeding were feasible, a large segment of the Labrador population (from 24 percent to 50 percent) would be eliminated from breeding stock. Colorado State University is doing research on an amino acid test to identify carriers.

RETINAL DYSPLASIA

by Dr. Autumn Davidson

Retinal dysplasia (malformation of the retina during fetal development) is both congenital and inherited. Two forms of retinal dysplasia have been described. Generalized retinal dysplasia was reported in Sweden in 1970 as a recessive trait with complete penetration. Multifocal retinal dysplasia has been reported in the United States, and has incompletely dominant inheritance. Dominant traits, when inherited, are present and detectable in an individual. Unfortunately, a trait that has incomplete dominance is not always present in the same form in each affected individual. The eye lesions of retinal dysplasia thus vary from small, asymptomatic folds in the retina to retinal detachment with cataracts and corneal opacification associated with blindness. Ophthalmologic examination by an individual trained to recognize the lesions of retinal dysplasia, and how they can vary from subtle to severe, is essential.

Retinal dysplasia has been found to be associated with skeletal abnormalities causing chondrodysplasia (dwarfism). A genetic study producing 124 Labrador puppies found that this "ocular and skeletal dysplasia" syndrome is controlled by one gene, and thus inherited together. Dogs that are heterozygotes (inherited one affected gene from only one parent) have only ocular abnormalities. Dogs that are homozygotes (inherited a pair of affected genes, one from each parent) have both ocular and skeletal abnormalities. Skeletal abnormalities associated with this syndrome include retarded growth of the forelimbs resulting in shortened legs, elbow and pastern abnormalities, and excessively straight rear limbs.

What seems like a straightforward problem for breeders to identify and eliminate is further complicated by another fact: The adult parents of affected puppies can appear phenotypically normal in every respect, showing no visual problems and no abnormalities during a veterinary ophthalmologic examination (pre-breeding) for heritable eye conditions. This is because subtle lesions of retinal dysplasia, usually retinal folds, can become less distinct as a dog ages, and were only detectable when the dog was a puppy. This has been named the "go normal" phenomenon. Individuals whose lesions disappear are, unfortunately, not genotypically normal. Ophthalmologic examination of a Labrador Retriever starting at six to eight weeks of age is the only way to be certain that retinal dysplasia does not exist in an individual. Finding stud dogs and brood bitches who were examined as puppies is a rarity that needs to be corrected. Litter examinations at six to eight weeks should be part of a breeder's duty to the fancy before placing the pups.

A breeder using stock that has been certified clear of heritable eye diseases may have no indication of the presence of retinal dysplasia in a litter of pups unless the visual deficiencies are marked, or the puppies are individually examined by an ophthalmologist.

Genetics dictates that the only way to eliminate retinal dysplasia from the Labrador Retriever gene pool is to perform ophthalmologic examinations on every individual puppy in a litter and use only dogs from cleared litters for breeding. Furthermore, because of the variable penetrance of the trait, individuals related to dogs diagnosed dysplastic should not be used as breeding stock. Clearly, elimination of the disorder of retinal dysplasia will be costly and full of disappointment, but the potential for creating puppies with devastating problems makes such an effort very worthwhile.

CATARACTS

Cataracts are assumed to be hereditary, except when a specific cause, such as diabetes mellitus or trauma, can be determined. A cataract is a dense opacity of the lens, which may affect one eye or both and may involve the lens partially or completely. The mode of inheritance is dominant with incomplete penetrance. Affected dogs should not be used for breeding. This includes both partial and complete opacity of the lens. One eye or both may be involved.[3]

CONTROL OF HEREDITARY EYE DISEASES

It is very sad when an owner of one of the most attractive and useful breeds is faced with the unhappy situation of coping with a blind dog. It is regrettable that this happens, but since the blindness is hereditary and can skip generations, it can come as a complete surprise. The average dog owner should investigate carefully the background of the dog he or she plans to purchase and find out what the breeder has done to avoid the problem.

Eye diseases spread down throughout the breed because transmitting animals, whether blind or carriers which appear normal, leave a crop of affected offspring and carriers who in turn pass on the disease to their offspring. This process is reversed by eliminating from the breed, as much as possible, the suspected animals. Stud dogs not carrying the gene should be appropriately used.

One of the major difficulties of control is the fact that the disease can't be detected for a long time, and in the interim the animal may have been used for breeding. Dr. Aguirre says that in the proper hands examinations using the indirect ophthalmoscope are 100 percent accurate as long as the individual using the instrument is trained and the dog is old enough to show the disease if present. If the dog is too young the retina appears normal. The incidence of the disease can be reduced by having breeding stock examined regularly.

The ERG is the best definitive test currently available for the diagnosis of GPRA. The results of the ERG are considered conclusive by two years of age. Breeders should wait until this test is passed, and their dog has an OFA certification, before using the animal for breeding. Most breeders think their dogs are genetically normal, but the only way to tell is to have the dog pass specific tests; even then, only properly executed test breedings will confirm the real genetic status of the dog, which may not be affected phenotypically, but could be a carrier.

Study a pedigree carefully and if there are no known carriers or suspicious dogs within the past four generations, the odds are good that the grandget can safely be bred. Be aware that a dog can be a carrier and not produce an affected animal for a long time after it has been used at stud, when suddenly a mate will turn up which is also a carrier. This creates a very

---

[3] Animal Health Newsletter, *Cornell University College of Veterinary Medicine,* *vol. 12, number 3, May 1994.*

difficult situation for all the bitches previously bred to such a dog, as once again some of their progeny may be carriers, while others will be normal.

The incidence of the disease can be reduced to a minimum if breeders follow control procedures. Responsible breeders must be on the alert for any abnormalities, and they must be willing to share their information with others. The development of the DNA test will be a welcome breakthrough for dog breeders and owners.

CERF

The Canine Eye Registry Foundation (CERF) was founded in 1974 in cooperation with the American College of Veterinary Ophthalmologists (ACVO) to maintain a registry of purebred dogs that are free of major heritable eye diseases. Only veterinarians who are members of ACVO are certified to give these examinations.

There is no minimum age for examination, but usually the dog should be at least eight weeks old. The result is good only for one year. To remain current the dog must have its eyes examined by an ACVO veterinarian annually, at which time it may be re-registered with CERF.

CERF is affiliated with Purdue University's Veterinary Medical Data Base (VMDB) which compiles information submitted from over 25 veterinary schools in the United States and Canada.

AKC now includes CERF and OFA data on pedigrees of only normal dogs. The data are printed on blue forms, registration certificates, and three- and four-generation pedigrees. Because a CERF entry is good only for a 12-month period, it will be automatically deleted unless the dog is recertified.

RECENT RESEARCH

Dr. Aguirre's work on PRA has successfully developed a test for Irish Setters, so hopefully he will soon have one for Labrador Retrievers. Regarding PRA in Irish Setters, Dr. Aguirre reports that "the gene defect is now identified (1994) and we have developed a test which will unequivocally identify normal, carriers, and affected animals. This test will be based on a small blood sample, and will permit the use of any genotype (affected, carrier, normal) in mating as long as the dog to whom they are mated is genetically normal. In this way, it will be possible to always produce clinically normal dogs, and the progeny will be identified as being carriers or normal by using the DNA test."

The Genetics Committee of the American College of Veterinary Ophthalmologists has prepared a book, *Ocular Diseases Proven or Suspected To Be Hereditary in Dogs,* describing inherited eye diseases in 127 dog breeds. Specific genetic diseases are documented in each breed along with other possible disorders under current investigation. The volume gives a series of guidelines for breeding.[4]

---

[4]*Available from CERF (AVCO Book), 1235 SCC-A, Purdue University, W. Lafayette, Indiana 47907-1235. The cost is $29.95 plus $5.00 shipping and handling. Indiana residents only add 5% sales tax.*

chapter 9

Joint Ailments and Bone Diseases

Orthopedic soundness is essential for the Labrador Retriever to perform any work or if it is simply a family pet and companion. There are diseases which affect the dog's joints and cause lameness of varying degrees. In some cases surgery will alleviate the condition, depending on the degree of severity and the location of the problem. Conservative medical therapy is also available. The causes are partly hereditary and partly environmental.

Gerry B. Schnelle, VMD, VmDHC, Chief of Staff at the Angell Memorial Hospital in Boston for many years, was the first veterinarian to describe, in reports in 1935 and 1937, the peculiar changes in the hip joint involving shallow hip sockets and bony or irregular overgrowths of the femoral head in the dog's thighs. At that time hip dysplasia was called "congenital dislocation." About this time also, x-ray machines became available, helping to identify reasons for lameness due to a previously undetected skeletal abnormality. However, a program of pelvic radiology to eliminate hip dysplasia was not even considered.

FEEDING YOUR LABRADOR

A fast growth rate and allowing unlimited access to food can cause orthopedic problems. Fattening a young dog for the show ring, or overfeeding for any reason, is harmful. Puppies should be fed a food that offers a complete, balanced diet without supplements. However, they don't need foods that promote rapid growth. Slower weight gain, by keeping your dog lean, is essential. On the other hand, food should not be restricted to the point where a dog does not reach its growth potential. Dog-food companies usually list amounts of food to feed according to a dog's age or weight. These are general guidelines only and may not be exactly correct for each dog. By observing your dog's physical condition and rate of growth, you can adjust amounts fed to get desired results.

Avoid foods (especially canned) with a large percentage of calories from fat. In 1994 the Association of American Feed Control Officials (AAFCO) passed a new regulation requiring manufacturers to include the caloric content of foods on the label. There is also a requirement for a nutrition statement to indicate the purpose of the food, whether it is for the dog's entire life cycle, growth, maintenance, or high performance.

Study the ingredients, listed in descending order by weight. This can be misleading because the moisture content of ingredients can vary from 8 percent to 80 percent water content. Ingredients must be 70 percent of the product, unless there is a modifier like "banquet" or "dinner," when they can be as little as 10 percent. The difference in prices of foods reflects this as well as a number of other variables. Not each food is best for all dogs, but with intelligent study of the label, you should be able to choose the correct food for your dog.

Pet foods vary tremendously in fat and moisture content, making comparisons between them difficult. You can compare pet foods by making a comparison of the percentage of calories provided by protein, fat, and carbohydrates. There are new developments in the pet food industry all the time. Astute owners will have to learn to read and interpret the labels.

The latest research shows that:

> Reducing the concentration of positively charged electrodes in the diet and then in synovial fluid results in less joint laxity and less hip dysplasia in growing dogs. The synovial fluid contains sodium and potassium, so diets that offer reduced amounts of these and increased amounts of chloride are beneficial.
>
> The new report, from Cornell, the Universities of Pennsylvania and North Carolina, the Ralston Purina Company, and the Swedish Laboratory for Comparative Pathology in Farentuna, Sweden, adds another item to the list of environmental factors that can influence the expression of the hip dysplasia gene in susceptible puppies. Just as slowing the weight gain in the early months of life has been shown to delay the appearance of the disease or reduce its severity and even prevent its expression, reducing synovial fluid volume and changing the balance of sodium, potassium, and chloride in the fluid, as this study indicates, can also influence the disease process. Practically speaking, a diet such as recommended by this study would use ingredients low in sodium, potassium, or both, but high in chloride to achieve a proper balance of electrolytes. Rice and corn gluten meal are, for example, a better balance than meat and bone meal. . . . Even though dietary changes can influence the development of hip dysplasia . . . efforts

to reduce the incidence of the disease by selective breeding practices should continue.[1]

WHAT IS HIP DYSPLASIA?

Hip dysplasia is a specific disease of the hip joints which occurs in young dogs (mostly the large breeds except Greyhounds). At birth the hip joints appear normal, but the disease begins shortly thereafter when the bones of the young dog are still cartilaginous (elastic). Hip dysplasia means a badly formed joint; there can be varying degrees of the condition.

Genetically, hip dysplasia is a hereditary disease of polygenic character. This means that the trait appears in a dog's offspring with no specific pattern of inheritance. Strict selection for breeding of dogs with normal hips, along with heavy pelvic musculature, is important toward solving the problem.

The dog's hip joint is a ball-and-socket arrangement with synovial fluid acting together with the joint capsule to prevent coxofemoral subluxation. A round ligament and muscle forces are part of the stability factor. Looseness in the joint between the femoral head and the acetabulum is the key to the problem. By detecting this looseness at a young age, affected animals can be removed from the breeding pool, and not used for work requiring sound hips.

Subluxation occurs in varying degrees according to how much displacement there is of the femoral head. Complete luxation occurs when the femoral head is entirely dislocated out of the acetabulum, or socket. Degenerative joint disease (osteoarthritis, exostosis, or osteophyte formation) may occur later in life as a result of the unstable joint.

Severely afflicted dogs will show an intolerance for exercise and a reluctance to engage in normal puppy activities. Treatment will not cure the disease but it can make the dog more comfortable. In extreme cases surgery can be performed; in milder situations, analgesics may be given. Joint pain associated with dysplasia is usually treated with buffered aspirin. Prevention of obesity is also recommended to reduce the weight carried by the damaged joint.

Restricting exercise during periods of spontaneous remission, typically from the ninth to the eleventh month, may help to prevent a worsening condition later in the dog's life. Microfractures in the acetabulum will be healing during this time, so light exercise may help to prevent worsening of the arthritic condition.

A promising new drug therapy is undergoing tests. Adequan (Luitpold Pharmaceuticals, Shirley, New York) may effectively ease the pain of hip dysplasia for dogs that are not candidates for surgery. Luitpold is helping to

---

[1] "A Dietary Change Can Lessen the Risk of Hip Dysplasia," Animal Health Newsletter, Cornell University College of Veterinary Medicine; vol. 11, no. 9, Nov. 1993.

finance research at the University of Florida College of Veterinary Medicine, Oklahoma State University, Cornell's James A. Baker Institute, and at private veterinary hospitals. The drug, glycosaminoglycan polysulfate (brand name Adequan), lessens the changes caused by osteoarthritis in stifles, so it well may help dogs with hip dysplasia because they invariably get osteoarthritis in their hip joints. Treatment with the drug may reduce signs of early hip dysplasia when administered at six to eight months, the time during the dog's growth period when the animal will have changes due to hip dysplasia.

Because the hip laxity can be detected before six months of age, it would make sense to x-ray young Labradors and treat them with this drug if there are indications of joint laxity, as well as the slight changes that will be visible to an educated eye on the radiographs. This drug has been used successfully to exercise a protective effect on cartilage in horses. Hopefully researchers will soon learn the proper dosages and time of use for dogs. It is too soon to tell if the drug will have a long-term beneficial effect on the development of the bone or the muscle tissues or on both.

Other factors being analyzed by veterinary researchers working on the development of hip dysplasia are estrogen metabolism, collagen levels, and the effect of increased amounts of synovial fluid in the joints.

Surgical treatment may be used in moderate to severe cases to relieve pain and restore normal function in the leg as much as possible. A variety of surgical approaches have been developed to meet the diverse needs of affected dogs. Veterinary evaluation is essential to determine the best course to follow.

Puppies will appear normal at birth. Extremely severe cases have been identified in puppies from two to four weeks of age. In the worst possible cases the hip joints are absent. In milder cases there may be no visible manifestation of hip dysplasia. The dog may move soundly and be able to perform in shows, trials, or the hunting field. The disease may not have clinical symptoms. Proper muscle tone will assist in stabilizing the hip joint. Usually hip dysplasia will be obvious in the dog's first year. All primary changes will have manifested themselves by eight to ten months of age, but the disability may not be apparent unless the dog is subjected to hard work. Many dogs will recover from the acute stage if left alone. Some dogs learn to live with it with relatively little discomfort.

Dogs with hip dysplasia should be allowed to choose their own level of activity. Moderate exercise to promote good muscle tone is beneficial, but jumping and strenuous activity should be avoided. Some dogs with dysplasia can enjoy being hunting companions, but are not suitable candidates for field training. Affected dogs should not be used for breeding. It is best to have them spayed or neutered. They should be provided with warm, draft-free living quarters, and should be kept trim because excess weight puts a strain on the hip joints.

Have your veterinarian perform an orthopedic exam as part of your dog's annual physical. The goal is to detect orthopedic problems before they become chronic with arthritic changes, so that the dog can be treated before it experiences unbearable pain or uncorrectable arthritis.

OSTEOCHONDROSIS (OCD)

The Labrador Retriever is one of the breeds affected by OCD. Osteochondrosis is a developmental disease that results from a disturbance in the endochondral ossification or cartilage formation of a joint. The cartilage is susceptible to damage (fissures or cracks) if the dog engages in rough play or strenuous exercise. Excess weight in dogs fed high-protein diets and the mechanical stress of rough exercise are the triggers which set the disease process in motion. Flaps of cartilage develop as a result of fissures in the bone below the cartilage.

The lesions primarily affect cartilage and secondarily bone, and can occur in the canine elbow, shoulder, hock, and/or stifle. When the condition is associated with inflammatory joint changes it is known as osteochondritis dissecans (OCD). Two other forms of osteochondrosis are ununited anconeal process (UAP) and fragmented coronoid process (FCP). When any one of these conditions occurs in the elbow, it is referred to as elbow dysplasia.

OCD is characterized by thickened areas of cartilage that are prone to trauma because they don't have support from the underlying bone in the early stages. Before the cartilage has formed a flap, rest and diet restriction can be effective treatments.

Fragments of cartilage (joint mice) may become loose in the joints, causing arthritis or a degree of lameness. The joint mice may lodge in the tendon sheath, leading to pain and lameness. There can be slight or severe lameness in one or both forelegs. An affected dog will shorten its stride. The lameness may be intermittent, or possibly more apparent in damp weather. Atrophied muscles may result. Exercise exacerbates the condition, with resulting lameness.

Fluid buildup in the joint is another sign of osteochondrosis. This is easier to detect in the hock than in the shoulder.

The exact causes of OCD are still under investigation. Rapid growth, overfeeding, and excessive weight gain contribute to the development of the disease. Traumatic episodes could initiate the changes. Hormones could play a role. Genetic influences have not been ruled out. Certainly poor, upright shoulder conformation is a factor; thus dogs with poor shoulder conformation should not be used for breeding. Straight stifles are also a fault that should be avoided by breeders, as this type of conformation is susceptible to osteochondrosis. OCD usually develops at six to seven months of age.

Multiple radiographs are used to diagnose the condition because it may appear bilaterally, affecting several joints. If a joint is abnormally swollen the veterinarian can do a joint tap to evaluate the fluid to rule out infection or autoimmune-related diseases. A Lyme disease titer should also be analyzed because Lyme disease will manifest itself in lameness and swollen joints that may go from one leg to another for no apparent reason. If blood work, radiographs, and joint fluid analysis are not conclusive, exploratory surgery can be performed.

OCD can be treated by surgery or conservative medical therapy. Treatment will depend on the age of the dog and severity of the condition. Medical therapy with analgesics may be chosen. Use of corticosteroids and nonsteroidal anti-inflammatory medications may reduce the pain and lameness, but they do not cure the problem and there may be undesirable side effects. It is possible that anti-inflammatory drugs may slow the healing of the cartilaginous defect. Adequan reportedly inhibits damaging enzymes and stimulates chondrocyte production of proteoglycans, the loss of which are characteristic of OCD.[2]

The prognosis for surgical patients with OCD of the humeral head is good when surgery is performed prior to degenerative changes, although some occasional mild lameness may occur. The advantage of surgery lies in addressing the problem before permanent arthritic changes can set in. Actually, the surgeon's removal of loose or abnormal pieces of cartilage stimulates the growth of new, normal cartilage in the affected area. The post-operative prognosis for dogs with OCD has been very good in operations on the shoulder. Hock and elbow surgery may not be as successful but it does lessen the degree of lameness.

The elbow is probably the most common site of OCD in the Labrador. The most common lesion, sometimes produced by trauma, is a fragmentation or fissure of the medial coronoid process. Lameness is usually intermittent and can be mild or severe. Affected dogs are usually stiff upon rising, and exercise makes matters worse. The dog will exhibit a shortened gait, and there may be some soft tissue swelling. Conservative therapy is usually indicated. However, surgery after early diagnosis may be successful.

OCD of the hind limbs is less common than OCD of the forelimbs. OCD of the tarsocrual joint may be bilateral. The tarsocrual joint is relatively unforgiving and frequently suffers secondary degenerative joint disease. Leaving a cartilage flap in the joint increases the chances of degenerative joint disease developing.

In many cases, OCD of the stifle will be undetected and lesions will heal spontaneously, although some progress to severe osteoarthritis. Some will not have secondary changes. The peculiar gait associated with hip dysplasia may be confused with OCD of the stifle, as the type of lameness associated with OCD is often nonspecific. Dog owners should consult a veterinary specialist

---

[2] *Wagenhauser, F.J. Basic Medical Treatment of the Anthrodesis, Basel, Switzerland,* 1976.

if they suspect a problem.

Swimming is a great postoperative exercise for canine patients. Many Labradors who live in cold climates, or do not have access to ponds or rivers, swim in indoor equine swimming pools.

There are two things an owner can do to prevent osteochondrosis. First, be careful of the kind of exercise your dog is allowed to have so that trauma will not happen. Young dogs like to run at top speed and can crash into something very hard. This often happens when younger pups are allowed to play with adult dogs. Also, when the adult dog gets tired of being harassed by the puppy, it can slam the youngster to the ground.

Second, feed it a proper diet. As with hip dysplasia, rapid growth and excessive weight gain are contributing factors. OCD occurs at sites that receive the greatest stress from weight bearing. Fast-growing dogs like Labradors are very susceptible, especially if they are fed a high-energy, high-protein diet with an excessive intake of calcium and phosphorus. Imbalances in vitamin and mineral intake, along with excessive consumption of food that accelerates growth, induce hormonal disturbances. A dog owner can definitely reduce the incidence of OCD by selecting a dog of good conformation and then using a normal diet to slow the rate of growth and gain.

Genetic factors may influence the growth rate that leads to OCD, but biomechanical studies have indicated that OCD site damage is primarily due to trauma. So far the exact cause of OCD is unknown. If there is a strong family history of osteochondrosis, animals from that line should not be used for breeding.

HYPERTROPHIC OSTEODYSTROPHY

Hypertrophic osteodystrophy (HOD) is a disease of rapidly growing breeds that affects the metaphyseal region of the long bone. Symptoms are lameness, fever (as high as 106 degrees), lethargy, and anorexia. Spontaneous remission may occur or HOD may progress into permanent bone deformity. The cause is unknown, so only the symptoms can be treated to relieve pain and reduce fever. Males are more apt to get HOD than females.

A dog with HOD will exhibit mild to moderate painful swelling in the long bones just above the joints, especially above the carpus or tarsus (hock). The disease is in the bones, not the joint. Be alert for misdiagnosis followed by inappropriate treatment if your veterinarian decides the pain is in the joint, rather than in the bones. Even without treatment, the dog will probably recover in several days or weeks. It is always nice to relieve the pain and reduce the fever.

It is suspected that over-nutrition with calcium may be a cause. Diets should not be over-supplemented, especially with minerals and fat-soluble vitamins.

LIGAMENT RUPTURES

A torn cruciate ligament can cause sudden lameness with the dog refusing to put weight on its hind leg. The cranial cruciate ligament is the major ligament that provides stability to the knee or stifle joint. Rupture of the cranial cruciate ligament, which is a disabling injury, is common in older dogs, while younger dogs get this condition for no apparent reason, other than trauma. It is usually associated with chronic degenerative changes inside the ligament. If dogs are overweight, the extra pounds increase the load on the musculo-skeletal structures, which could accelerate degeneration of the cruciate ligament.

Consult your veterinarian, and if surgery is suggested, a second opinion from a specialist is in order. Surgical repair is the treatment in most cases.

The prognosis is good, depending on the size of the dog and the length of time since the injury was sustained. During recovery the dog will need a fairly long period of cage rest, followed by restricted exercise. The surgery will not reverse arthritic changes that have already taken place, but the dog will usually be able to return to normal activity. The dog's overall physical condition makes a difference. Owners should keep their dogs physically fit with good muscle tone and definitely not obese.

Purdue University has a great deal of data on the incidence of cranial cruciate ligament ruptures in its Veterinary Medical Data Base. More than 10,000 dogs are listed in this study.

PANOSTEITIS

Lameness can also be caused by panosteitis, which is a wandering type of lameness affecting young dogs of large breeds, mostly males, usually from five to 12 months of age. It is an inflammation affecting the bones of the dog's leg. ("Osteitis" means "inflammation of the bone.")

The cause is unknown, but usually the disease tends to run in families. The signs are varying degrees of lameness and pain shifting from one location to another, such as hip to hip or foreleg to foreleg over a period of several months. The lameness may be intermittent. The degree of lameness and pain varies from slight to severe. The dog feels pain when pressure is put on the affected bone. Muscle wasting and lethargy are other signs of this disease. Unlike other bone diseases, panosteitis causes neither swelling nor fever.

Most dogs will recover spontaneously in several weeks or months, although in severe cases they may not recover full muscle strength and condition. During the period of lameness dogs should have their exercise restricted and be given plenty of rest. Aspirin or anti-inflammatory drugs (such as Azium) may be given to relieve pain.

chapter 10

Selecting Your Labrador Puppy

Analyzing each puppy in a litter and estimating in your own mind how it will develop physically is the greatest challenge a breeder will face. An experienced person with a talent for studying conformation and movement, and who knows the breed Standard, should be able to do this rather successfully after many years of breeding. The novice breeder will not find it easy to rate a litter. A very uniform litter will make it difficult to decide which puppy has the best conformation.

In a Labrador puppy the shape of the head and tail represent the breed characteristics. One must look carefully at the width of the skull, the set of the ears and eyes, the amount of stop, and the muzzle length. Tails should be otter-shaped, short, and thick. The puppy should stand foursquare, have good angulation of shoulder and hindquarters, and move properly at the trot.

Eye size and placement have a bearing on expression. Eyes must not be too close or too far apart. They should be diamond-shaped, not round. Eye color may be hard to evaluate in a puppy, so check the eyes of the parents.

Ear size and placement are important. If the puppy has long, houndy ears hanging abnormally low on a narrow, peaked skull, there is little chance for improvement. At the other extreme, small neat ears in a puppy may be set too high in the adult dog. Ear size and placement play an important part in the dog having a classic Labrador head.

Good heads will show chiseling under the eyes and a definite stop. A female's head can be lighter than a male's, but in no instance should it be weedy. The head should have a definite stop but too much stop is incorrect, as is a shallow stop or Flat-coat silhouette in profile.

Puppies should have good bone, not thin, spindly legs. A fine-boned puppy will be too light in frame when mature.

Wolfe's Sugar Badenov, CD, JH (Can. Ch. Southwyck's Boris Badenov ex Madison Lindsay Wolfe CD, WC) with her first litter, 1992, sired by Ch. Jaynecourt The Professor. Owned by Sandra G. Wolfe.

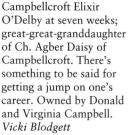

Campbellcroft Elixir O'Delby at seven weeks; great-great-granddaughter of Ch. Agber Daisy of Campbellcroft. There's something to be said for getting a jump on one's career. Owned by Donald and Virginia Campbell. *Vicki Blodgett*

The difference between a bench retriever that wins in the show ring and a working field retriever is not so much in their conformation, which should be nearly identical, but in the latter's invisible qualities.

In choosing a puppy make sure that the prospective litter was bred with the goals that interest you in mind. Try to see the sire and dam and when possible, grandparents. If the litter is a repeat breeding, see the older dogs produced by the sire and dam. Inquire about the health programs used by the breeder. The sire and dam should have normal hips and elbows, preferably with an OFA number, and eye clearances. Ask the breeder about hereditary diseases in their bloodlines.

Bench titles do not always indicate that a dog has quality. Breeding to a dog because of its wins in the show ring is not always the way to breed a good litter. In Helen Warwick's *The New Complete Labrador Retriever,* she says:

> Bench titles, although signposts outwardly pointing in the right direction, may be deceiving to novices and are not to be taken for granted. Everyone is aware of the downfall of many a staunch gundog variety because breeders ignored the cardinal principle of giving their dogs some natural work. One must candidly acknowledge that bench interests on both sides of the Atlantic have extinguished the original natural gifts of many sporting dogs to such a degree that the abyss between show and work is insurmountable. So far it has not become thus with our honest, rugged Labrador. It is to the credit of most Labrador breeders, whose interests lie more in evolving perfection of type, that they realize that "improving" a breed does not end with the stacking up of show wins. Countless among them work their bench dogs here in "fun trials" and sanctions, and abroad in modest stakes and Working Tests, and even beyond.

Originally the same Labradors were winning in the show ring and in the field. Dual champions were admired because handsome dogs of excellent conformation could perform well in a working environment. As field tests became more and more competitive, the field dogs took on racy builds for speed. Conformation faults were overlooked, and were bad enough so that the field dogs could not place in conformation competition. Heads in the field dogs narrowed, the otter tail shape was lost, and other faults that actually impeded sound movement became established.

In the show ring, fads were seen from time to time that did not help the breed. The most recent example is the breeding of shorter dogs with short, stuffy necks, and shorter bodies and incorrect shoulder and hip assemblies. Many of these animals had lovely heads, coats, and otter tails. However, these correct attributes of the breed were hanging on the wrong frame.

For many years field dogs have not gone to the show ring, while conversely, show dogs have been worked in the field. Now that we have Hunting Tests, more and more show dogs are working and doing very well. These are the dogs that have the potential to become dual champions if their owners have the time to put into their training. In the future we would hope that those breeding for the field pay more attention to conformation. The reason for sound conformation is better performance. This is true in the show ring as well as in the field. It doesn't do a show dog any good to wear a great coat, head, and tail if it can't move properly.

Kelly McCarthy and a
Shamrock Acres puppy.
*Photo Sally McCarthy
Munson collection.*

Four-week-old puppies
by Golden Sun of Wigten
ex Spenrock Wirraway,
bred by Maureen Wade.

Chilbrook Rockafella at 10 weeks. He became a Specialty winner and had Bests of Breed by one year of age. Owned by Diane Whitaker. *Debby Kay*

An all-chocolate litter bred by Mark Jones, sired by Highlands John Ross.

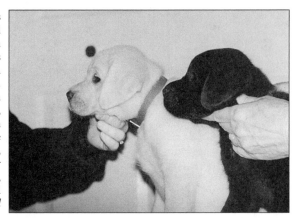

Eight-week-old puppies wearing color-coded collars and tags with an ID number. The litter is sired by Majestic Saxon ex Spenrock Wirraway. When choosing between two puppies in a litter, compare them from the front and from the side: correct head shape, angulation to shoulder and hindquarters, top line, and proper front are all evident. *Jan Churchill*

Many people who are looking for a puppy say they want an "English" type Labrador. This is confusing because even though they are associating the expression "English" with a broad rather than a narrow head, in reality one will find Labradors of both types in England as well as the United States. Americans may think of English Labradors as being heavier in body, but if you travel about England you will see that type as well as a lighter build. For

Ch. Lobuff Missouri
Breaks at eight weeks
of age.

Ch. Lobuff Missouri
Breaks at three and
one-half months of age.

Ch. Lobuff Missouri
Breaks at 16 months.

Oceanview Windjammer,
six weeks old.

Oceanview Windjammer,
seven weeks old.

Oceanview Windjammer
(Spenrock Philip ex
Lobuff's Thyme Piece),
here as an adult, bred by
Lisa Weiss Agresta and
Catherine and Philip
Lewis, owners.
John Ashbey

years after World War II, some English breeders were producing a lightly built, racy sort of Labrador which was atypical looking and described by knowledgeable English breeders as "houndy."

The Labrador breed was originally a hunting dog, and that is still its primary purpose. The main change over the years has basically been size or height. The consensus of opinion over the years added a few inches to the height of the very early Labradors. In selecting a puppy, determine the size of the sire and dam. They should not be too large or too small.

The best age to make a choice is at six to eight weeks. Hopefully the breeder will have taught the puppy to stand quietly upon a table covered with a non-slip surface. In this pose you will check the stance and evaluate the proportions. Each puppy in the litter should be checked for a correct scissors bite, and in males for two testicles. Next check the puppy's movement. If the puppy hasn't been leash-trained, you may want to sit and just watch for a long time while it plays with its littermates.

The puppy's coat should be thick with a harsh outercoat and softer undercoat. A thin, shiny coat in a puppy probably means that the dog will lack undercoat when grown. The best otter tails have the least feather; instead the hairs curl slightly around the tail bone and meet underneath. Long, thin tails are incorrect.

Ask the breeder what goals he or she has in mind for the litter. Do the sire and dam complement each other? Ask the breeder to explain this to you. Dogs and bitches with common weak points should not be bred to each other. The goal in breeding should be to improve the quality of the offspring over the parents. Have the breeders used a stud dog that can correct weaknesses or faults in the bitch?

The prospective owner may be trying to select a puppy that is far above average in all respects. An average sire and dam will usually produce one outstanding puppy while the rest of the litter is ordinary. These average

Canadian Triple Ch. Whistlewings Kitty McGee, WCX (Am., Can. Ch. Monarch's Black Arrogance, CD, WC ex Can. Triple Ch. Kenosee's Jim Dandy, CDX). As a puppy she won Best Puppy at the Labrador Retriever Club of Saskatchewan Specialty show. *Mikron*

puppies can make wonderful pets and give their owners great satisfaction working in obedience or in the field. Better-than-average parents should pro-duce litters with excellent quality in depth.

After checking type, conformation, breeding, and general health of the puppy, you will need to evaluate temperament. Color has nothing to do with temperament or hunting ability. A puppy's personality will be shaped not only by hereditary factors, but by the way it has been handled since birth. The puppy should be well socialized, come when it is called, and be willing to pick up objects thrown for it. The natural retrieving instinct should be evident in an eight- to ten-week-old puppy. Labrador puppies should not show aggressive/dominant behavior if there are small children in the family.

The largest puppy is not necessarily the best. Puppies change rapidly and as a general rule, the size of the parents will indicate the growth potential of the puppy. A puppy with a really large head may be coarse when grown. Small-headed puppies usually don't mature with a decent-sized head.

From the Judge's Point of View

Breeder/judges who have spent years raising Labradors and studying the breed should earn the respect of exhibitors whenever those judges officiate. There are also individuals from outside the breed who do very well judging Labradors because they have spent time with the good breeders, asking questions and learning what is important in the breed. Competent judges should always be able to select the most representative dogs.

Each breed has a Standard that describes the ideal dog and a judge will use the Standard as a guide when evaluating dogs in the ring. Each animal in competition is compared in the judge's mind with what he perceives to be the ideal Labrador. A judge must have studied the historical development of the breed and should be acquainted with the great dogs of the past.

Memorizing the breed Standard alone will not make a good judge. In fact, if the points in the Standard are all a judge knows, he will end up "fault" judging, which is an unsatisfactory, negative approach. A novice may fault judge because it is easy to recognize faults. Experience is required to be able to put faults in proper perspective while balancing them against the correct breed points.

If a judge has seen only average-type Labradors over the years, a dog that is superior will not be one that he is accustomed to. A generic sort of Labrador can win easily as a result of mediocre dogs in the classes and judges who do not have a good "eye" for the breed. A really good Labrador will approach the model for the breed, both in looks and in movement.

At a Specialty show the quality will usually run deep throughout the classes. At all-breed shows the dogs may be mostly mediocre, and the judge is lucky to find a good representative of the breed.

Ch. Breton Gate Cairngorm, CD, JH, WC takes a "victory lap" around the ring after winning Best of Breed at the Denver Specialty following the National. She received a Judge's Award of Merit (JAM) at a field trial the day before the show. Owned by Donald and Virginia Campbell. *Berger*

Two years after the victory scored in the above photograph, Ch. Breton Gate Cairngorm, CD, JH, WC was still making his presence felt in the Labrador ring. Here as a veteran he is shown cool and at ease with the help of a damp towel, as he waits at ringside with Virginia Campbell for yet another call to action. *Berger*

Ch. Spenrock's Bohemia Champagne (Ch. Lockerbie Goldentone Jensen ex Int. Ch. Spenrock's Banner, WC), BOS at the 1973 National Specialty under judge Mrs. Helen Warwick. Bred by Janet Churchill, this bitch is found in many Labrador pedigrees. Owned by Diane Pilbin. *Shafer*

Ch. Chucklebrook Black Irish at one year of age (Ch. Lockerbie Brian Boru, WC ex Ch. Spenrock's Bohemia Champagne). Owned by Shirley Kaiden. *Gilbert*

JUDGING A CLASS

At AKC shows, time is of the essence. Upon arriving at the ring, the judge will meet the steward; check the judge's book, which lists each class and the number of each exhibit; and look over the ring. The layout of the ring will determine how the judge will arrange the dogs. At outdoor shows, if the weather is hot or rainy, shelter from the tent is over part of the ring and the judge's table. In extremely large classes, the judge may divide the dogs into two or three groups so that each group will have sufficient room for a free trot. The lead dog should not overtake the end of the line as the dogs move. None of the dogs have a fair chance to gait freely if conditions are crowded.

Once the dogs are in the ring, the judge will check armband numbers against the numbers listed in the judge's book. Absentees will be marked. By then each handler will have the dog set up or standing freely in its best pose.

Ch. Barbaree's Daisy Duke, CDX was Winners Bitch under Anne Roslin-Williams at the 1989 LRC of Potomac Specialty. At the 1976 National LRC Specialty, Anne's mother Mary Roslin-Williams gave Daisy Duke's Sire, Shookstown Solo Smasher WD and first place in a large American-Bred Bitch class to her dam, Springfield's High Barbaree. Both Roslin-Williamses were fascinated when they saw the pedigree, but not surprised—they have an eye for a certain type. Owned by Nancy Beach. *Chuck Tatham*

When judging I like to stand back and look at each dog's outline, comparing it in my mind to a picture of the true Labrador. Before going over the dogs individually, I like to have them trot around the ring once. First impressions are important, so this is a good time to get the outstanding dogs in the forefront of your thinking, bearing in mind that individual examinations are yet to come.

Each dog will then be examined and moved individually. In examining the dog, the judge has a chance to look right into the dog's eyes for a gentle expression. The "bite" or placement of the teeth is checked. The judge's hands will check for shoulder placement, musculature, strength of upper thigh, and undercoat. The length of the tail can be checked by making sure it does not fall below the hock joint.

Merely by looking at the dog, a judge who really knows movement will have a good idea of what to expect before the dog moves. The judge will indicate the pattern to be used, such as a triangle or down and back. The best pattern is one that allows the judge to see the dog move directly away from him and directly back, and then along one side for side movement. I like to see the dog trot around the entire ring as well to check for fluid, balanced movement and proper use of the hindquarters.

In a large class it is wise to use a grading system. In horse shows, judges use a card with each entry's number and spaces to mark each item that counts. Unless a judge uses some written system, he or she has to memorize things that are no longer visible when the dog is standing.

When the judge has moved all the dogs, the exhibitors will have them posed, and at this point the judge must remember all the things observed about

Ch. Follytower Singalong
(Secret Song of Lawnwood
ex Follytower Augusta)
bred by Margot Woolley in
England, owned by Diane
Pilbin, winning BOS at the
LRC Potomac Specialty.
Gilbert

each dog when it was moving. Teeth are no longer in view so any problems in the mouth must also be memorized or noted.

Then, as the dogs are standing, the judge must sort out the best conformation and type and add observations on soundness. I have judged many classes where none of the dogs moved really well. When this is the case, movement *per se* does not have anything to do with the placements.

Judges with years of experience judging horses or cattle have an advantage. With horses, one must understand movement, and when judging cattle one must be prepared to announce to the audience the reasons for all placings.

Judges who keep notes on their judging of dogs will better remember the reasons for their placings. Exhibitors may ask why a dog was third, or what a judge didn't like about it. The judge can always suggest that they bring the dog back so he can refresh his memory, and then refer to his notes. If a judge is to write a critique, he will need those notes.

Picking Best of Breed and Best of Winners does not require as much note-taking because the best of each category is being selected. In a very large Best of Breed class, it is still wise to make a list of the six or eight most outstanding exhibits before narrowing the selection down to Best of Breed.

The average time allowed for a judge to view each dog is a little over two minutes. This means that the handlers must know what they are doing and present each dog to best advantage with a minimum of fussing. A superior handler will minimize a dog's faults and keep it on its toes, showing itself off. A superior handler can make an average dog appear just a little better than it really is. Many times a handler takes a dog to Winners and having won the necessary points for the day, allows the owner to handle for Best of Winners. Now the dog is relaxed and may be performing in a sloppy fashion.

A judge concentrates on the dog, not the handler, but the person at the end of the leash makes a big difference. Dogs must be judged on their merit

Highlands Gimme A Cheer and Ch. Highlands Break of Dawn (Ch. Coalcreek's Gimme A Break ex Hennings Mill's Bixby Kate) won the brace class at the 1990 Winnebago Labrador Retriever Club Specialty. Owned by Lillian and George Knobloch. *Smith*

Ch. Meadowrock Fudge of Ayr, WC (Ch. Dickendall's Flip Flop ex Ch. Meadowrock's Angelica of Ayr), owned by Nancy Martin. *Ashbey*

Am., Can. Ch. Lobuff's Sundown at Kerrymark (Ch. Northwood Sandman ex Ch. Lobuff's Tequila Sunrise), by Mollie Weiss and Kevin Acheson. *Stephen Klein*

at the moment. A good handler knows how to make an average dog look better than it really is; he or she knows exactly how to get the utmost from the dog. The animal isn't allowed to assume unflattering poses. The amateur owner can do as well as, and sometimes better than, the professionals, as long as the owner has studied the best handlers and knows what they are doing. With video cameras it is possible to study yourself and your dog and then critique your performance. If you need help, a professional can render an opinion.

JUDGING THE JUDGE

Judging from outside the ring is not easy. First, there are distractions; to do the job, a judge can't be chatting or looking away from the task at hand. People at ringside like to follow along, and a great deal can be learned if they are paying attention, but it is not a good substitute for being in the ring. A knowledgeable audience likes to understand what the judge is doing and appreciates consistency. Good judges are consistent and able to select the dogs that best resemble a true and correct Labrador. This is usually evident in a Winners class where all the dogs should be similar in type. At small shows this may not happen because of lack of quality.

The most important quality in a judge is to know what the ideal Labrador should look like and to be able to sort out a class by comparing each exhibit to a mental picture. A judge must know the most important breed points because any group of sound animals lacking in breed type could be a sorry-looking lot. The Labrador is a working dog, so in addition to the correct shape of head and body, coat and tail, the dog must be faulted for conformation that would prevent it from doing a day's work.

A working gun dog may need to work hard all day in difficult going. My first two bench champion Labradors, Banner and her brother Ballot, also worked as gun dogs. At my Eastern Shore farm, I took men gunning, and Banner retrieved in rough, swampy areas, as well as in the more open waters. Ballot never cared for dog shows. He finished with a five-point win at age five, but he was not the sort of dog who liked to show any animation moving in the ring. At that time I used to go to St. Michaels, Maryland for the best goose hunting, taking Banner and Ballot along. I was really anxious to prove that they could perform in the field in spite of their "show ring" pedigrees.

The owners of Perry Cabin Farm ran a commercial hunting operation, with gunners coming in from all over the world to the Eastern Shore's goose hunting capital. Ballot started working for them and did so well that he moved in with the owners and handled all the retrieving chores for the gunners. He was a true dual purpose Labrador with excellent conformation and soundness that enabled him to work hard for long days.

In those days there were no Hunting Tests for Labradors, only the Working Certificate. To train Ballot and Banner for their Working Certificates I

Ch. Spenrock's Cognac
(Ch. Lockerbie
Goldentone Jensen ex
Ch. Spenrock's Banner,
WC), at ten years of age
with co-owner Donna Lee
Weiss.

Ch. Lobuff's Gandy
Dancer (Ch. Almar's Bobo
Quivari ex Ch. Spenrock's
Cognac), taking a Specialty
Reserve under Mrs. Mary
Roslin-Williams,
owner-handled by Lisa
Weiss Agresta. *Sheri*

kept several dozen mallards. After their initial training was completed, I released the mallards in a suitable wildlife area. I used to go to the Waterland Retriever Club and run the dogs in picnic trials occasionally. I purchased a field trial—bred bitch as a mate for Ballot, as I intended to produce

Ch. Campbellcroft Elixir O'Delby, CD, JH, WD (Ch. Andercroft Mijan's Bravo ex Ch. Breton Gate Cairngorm, CD, JH, WC), was BOB at Rose City LRC Specialty, 1991. Owned by Vicki Blodgett. *Callea*

Ch. Clemson of Killingworth (Eng., Am. Ch. Lawnwoods Hot Chocolate ex Stonewood Killingworth Katie) was the first chocolate to win BOB at Westminster. (He was the dog conceived behind a hangar at the Oxford, Connecticut airport). *Gilbert*

good-looking, correctly conformed dogs that could perform well in field trials. This bitch was sent to field trial trainer Jay Sweezey for training. My project failed because the bitch refused to work with dummies—she wanted birds, which were too expensive for the amount of training required of a field dog. When she turned out to have hip dysplasia, I had her spayed and used her as a gun dog.

COLONEL JERRY WEISS (USMC-RET.)

In 1965 I met Col. Jerry Weiss at the Labrador Specialty show on Long Island. Several years later he admired my Ch. Spenrock Cardigan Bay, another great gun dog from the second litter I bred. Col. Weiss soon acquired Cardigan's sister, Ch. Spenrock's Cognac, who became the foundation bitch for his kennel and exerted through her offspring a tremendous influence on the breed. Col. Weiss eventually took up judging and now judges about forty shows a year.

I asked Col. Weiss what he thinks about when he goes in the ring. Col. Weiss replied:

You have to have a single-mindedness of purpose and the ability to concentrate on the exhibit you have in front of you at the time. I think that at times my mind is computer-like . . . that when I start looking at the exhibit I file away in the "core" the things I like and don't like about each exhibit. Eventually what my mind is actually doing is running up a score, and without my consciously knowing it I'm saying to myself, the second one is better than the first one because the head is better, the top is better, it has better angulation of shoulder; most of the things I'm looking for are better in exhibit two than one. Then you go to each dog down the line. You have to be able to have a good-sized "core" because if you are judging a class of 15 to 20 dogs, you are going to have to remember that #14 was better than #20 but that #32 was best of all.

What I do, now that I am older, is to keep a paper and pen in my pocket. I have the dogs come in the ring in catalog order. I write the numbers down and make a line through the number if the dog is not good. Then, after I have gone over the class, I see which numbers I did not put lines through. It's an aid I use in judging large classes, not that I am eliminating the poorest exhibits—that would be fault judging—but I have circled the ones I think are really outstanding and the ones I want to spend a little more time with. Then I excuse the other dogs and work with these. I keep at least six or seven in and look for the points I really want.

In Labradors the main thing I'm looking for is a balanced dog with good substance. I want an otter tail. I can't stand a Labrador with a tail way over its back; it really bothers me. I had several recently in the northwest where I also had many silky coats. I don't know why—it's not a congenital thing. They had undercoats, but their coats felt like a setter's.

I want a nice topline and of course the head. Some heads are not typical Labrador. I don't want big, floppy ears hanging down. When I see a head, I see your Banner (Ch. Spenrock Banner, W.C.) or my Banner (Ch. Lobuff's Seafaring Banner).

If the shoulder is not laid back, the dog can't work in the field. I judge all my dogs for the purpose for which they were bred. They have to be able to go in the field and retrieve. Labradors have to be hunting dogs.

Straight stifles drive me up the wall. I can't stand them. Also troubling is not enough second thigh. All that goes with strength in the rear and the ability to drive. The second thigh, the turn of stifle, and the hock—if it is too high—it isn't any good either. You have to understand the different breeds. The Labrador is a driving dog and you have to have that turn of stifle and it's got to be able to drive; therefore the legs have got to be able to come off the ground a bit.

Ch. Spenrock Tweed of Windfields (Ch. Eireannach Black Coachman ex Ch. Spenrock Winds Aloft) winning BOW under Mrs. Helen Warwick, handled by Bonnie Threlfall, owner-breeder Janet Churchill. *Ashbey*

While looking at movement my "computer" (where I have already filed away the type, quality, and substance) is working as I judge this important second factor. I can't put up a dog that is not sound. I don't care how beautiful he looks—if he isn't sound, I won't put him up. By the same token, I'm not going to put the soundest dog up no matter what it looks like. So, there is where my computer comes into work. You're looking at the dogs and you've decided which ones are the best-looking; now you are going to decide which

Ch. Highlands Country Preacher (Ch. Scrimshaw Another Deacon ex Highlands Egyptian Queen), owned by Lillian and George Knobloch. *Klein*

are the best-looking and also sound. My little computer is figuring out which dog looks the best and moves the soundest.

Limping is not the only thing I can't reward. I can't abide a dog that moves too close behind or one that moves wide in front. Thirty years ago I learned two sayings from Joan Read and Anne Carpenter; Joan Read admonished against the dog so wide coming at you that you could drive a truck through his legs, while Anne Carpenter used to say the dog looks like he has two sticks coming out of the same hole. If the dog coming at me moves very wide, I don't like it any more than the legs too close together.

In the rear a dog that moves wide cannot drive and loses any strength. A dog that moves a little too close in the rear can still drive. A too-wide front is not as bad as a too-wide rear, nor is too close in front as bad as too close in the rear. You still have to balance all these things out.

While judging you have to be able to concentrate to the exclusion of everything else going on around you. If something happens to distract my attention, I will stop judging completely, walk away, and then turn back and start over. I get back to that mind-set I had been in so I can concentrate exclusively on the dogs that I have in front of me. I feel very strongly about my second, third, and fourth places; I work just as hard getting all these places right as I do on the first place. Also, my Winners class is judged as a whole new class. Many judges automatically put up the open dog for Winners. I want to look at them all over again, and I judge as if I had never seen them before.

I couldn't care less about the handler. I pay no attention to methods of handling. If they don't do what I like, I ask them to change. If they can't stack the dog, I'll stack the dog. Not that a dog really has to be stacked, but sometimes a neophyte handler will leave a dog looking straight-stifled, when all you have to do is go over and move the legs and then the dog has really nice angulation. Sometimes they need a little help. Really good handlers can hide faults on you. They will show the best parts of the dog off better than anyone

Ch. Chucklebrook Danmark (Ch. Beechcroft's Dover ex Ch. Chucklebrook Fannie Farmer), owned by Diane Pilbin. *Tatham*

else. I try very hard to see through all that. I don't think anybody can always see through that because really, the good handlers are very skillful at what they do. I recognize that.

The side gait is very important. That's where you see the reach and the drive. A narrow front disturbs me because it means that the dog has no chest and therefore no strength. I put my hand between the front legs. I must be able to wiggle my hand. If the front is a little too wide, it is just aesthetically a little worse looking.

Our Standard does not say so, but I believe that a Lab, like a Golden Retriever, is supposed to single track. The faster they go, the more the legs tend to converge under the center part of the body, which is the case in most all true-moving dogs. Dogs in the water swim like a single tracker.

LISA AGRESTA

Col. Weiss's daughter, Lisa Agresta, also a judge, learned to handle at an early age. She exhibited in the breed ring as well as in junior showmanship. A real student of the breed, she learned a great deal from many Lab people. She established her own successful breeding program, carrying on with dogs in her parents' kennel.

Commenting on judging, Lisa said:

The total dog is more important than its parts. I give every exhibitor the same amount of time to make a picture, to put all the parts together and get the dog doing what they want it to do. In my mind, I decide if this is the right picture, that the dog is balanced, has a double coat, the correct head, tail set, angulation, and that this one is better than that one.

Someone can't just read the Standard and start judging. You can't say that the Lab is a head breed or a tail breed. The total dog is very important. You can't just memorize the key points as there is so much between the head and the otter tail. It takes time to understand the expression. You want the diamond-shaped eye. You see so many almond-shaped or round eyes, which are incorrect. You don't want eyes that are too close together. You are looking for a warm, brown eye. Yellow eyes are bad and so are ink-black eyes. In yellows the eye shouldn't be lighter than the coat color.

Learning what is the correct expression for the Labrador, or about the breed in general, is something that you only learn by looking at hundreds and hundreds of dogs and watching them as they grow. Too many shows are judged by people who didn't breed a lot of dogs and watch them mature. I think you only learn structure by your failures over the years. You learn structure and conformation by watching your puppies grow.

THE JUDGE'S OPINION

Several years ago Julie Brown, well known for her directories of Labrador pedigrees, published *The Judge's Opinion*. The consensus of the judges was that the Labrador should be strong, athletic, and powerful. Its greatest assets are retrieving instinct, temperament, adaptability, and desire to please.

Loss of athletic ability is a major problem. Upright shoulders with steep upper arms are faults to avoid, as well as wide fronts causing dogs to be out at the elbows. Judges prefer well-laid-back shoulders. Too many exhibits lack broad, deep chests and prominent breastbones. Necks are too short and thick, and balance is upset with short legs and cobby bodies. Rears lack well-bent stifles with a good second thigh and good, muscular hindquarters. Low tail sets are also faulty.

Judges see too many dogs that are overweight, flabby, and carrying excess bone. The dogs should have substance without being coarse. Single coats are also faulty. Undercoats and otter tails are usually found together, while dogs with single coats have Pointer-style tails.

The judges felt that heads are getting too strong, i.e., wide in the skull and short in the muzzle. Exaggerated stops are faults along with too-wide skulls and lacking enough length and depth in the foreface. Thick, apple cheeks are faulty. The opposite head, which is long, weak, and plain with no stop or depth of muzzle, is also faulty. Light eyes with hard expressions are also faults cited by the judges. Eye color and shape are important. The eyes should not be round.

Temperament in the show ring should not be nervous, hyper, or excitable. The majority of judges commented that stacking the dog and holding tight leads detract from what the exhibitor is trying to present. Judges want to see a natural stance to determine balance and type. Many handlers stretch the hindquarters back too far. They make a dog look worse than it is.

Fads and fashions are promoted by the show fancy. Just because judges put up poor movement and weak conformation doesn't make this acceptable. Titles and performance in the show ring are man-made influences.

chapter 12

Obedience and Other Training

Labradors like to be trained and to perform tasks. With their quick, intelligent minds, they approach jobs eagerly. They can be trained for formal exercises in the obedience ring, the field, or in some other working capacity, or perhaps just taught good manners for a family pet. Each dog is an individual and not all Labradors will react the same way to training. Their breeding will, as a general rule, influence their aptitude for some things. There are Labradors that don't like to swim, others may not enjoy retrieving, and then there are those, no matter what the pedigree, that will do whatever is asked of them.

The Labrador is more than a "dual purpose" dog. It is a generalist capable of success in many fields. Dogs bred for the field usually have more aptitude there, just as dogs bred to be guide dogs excel in that service. However, there are exceptions to all rules of thumb. The owner must decide what he wants to accomplish and then give the dog a chance to learn and succeed.

Early lessons in obedience are the foundation for successful completion of advanced work. As training continues you will meet more challenges. You must learn what you are supposed to do so you won't confuse your dog. Remember that intelligent dogs get bored with repetitive training. Work in various places and seek valuable help from trainers and experienced friends.

Obedience titles are the result of many hours of devotion and work, as are hunting titles or field trial points. If you don't wish to do those things, the Canine Good Citizen award is a gratifying goal (see Chapter 19).

Obedience dogs compete in Novice, Open, and Utility classes for the degrees Companion Dog (CD), Companion Dog Excellent (CDX), Utility Dog (UD), and Utility Dog Excellent (UDX). In the 1970s the AKC initiated the

OT Ch. Millgrove's Special Amy, WC, Can. CD (Ch. Spenrock Heatheredge Mariner), was #1 Obedience dog (all breeds) in 1979, the only Labrador ever to be awarded this honor. Amy won numerous Highs in Trial and High Combined awards and was a four-time winner of the Obedience Dog of the Year given by The Labrador Retriever Club of the Potomac. She was owned and trained by Vicky Manyette Creamer. *Gaines*

Obedience Trial Champion or "OT Ch." title. Dogs that already have a UD compete for points by placing first or second in utility classes until they earn 100 points with at least three placements to earn the "OT Ch." title.

"Sit and Stay" demonstrated by littermates Ayr's Real Humdinger, JH (left), owned by Nancy Martin, and Ch. Ayr's Real McCoy, CDX, JH (right), owned by Nancy Martin and Joanne Summers. The dogs are by Ch. Dickendalls Ruffy ex Ayr's Mollywog of the Sea.

"Down and Stay" demonstrated (l. to r.) by OT Ch. Chilbrook Keepsake, Am. Can. UD; Belquest Something Special CD; and OT Ch. Millgrove's Special Amie, WC, Can. CD. *Debby Kay*

In 1994 AKC instituted a new obedience title called "Utility Dog Excellent" or a "UDX" title. This title does not require a dog to place in a class but rather to gain qualifying scores consistently in Open-B and Utility-B classes at the same show. To gain this title a dog has to earn a qualifying score in both classes, which is called a "combined score," at least ten times at ten different shows.

Match shows, which are informal shows using similar rules to AKC shows, are excellent opportunities to practice with a young dog before entering a regular show. No points are given towards AKC titles. In obedience a sub-novice class is offered where dogs can perform the obedience exercises while remaining on leash.

OTCH. Highlands Uptown Girl UD, WC, Can. CD (Sir Keith of Kimvalley ex Highlands Just Jesse). Quinn was #1 obedience Labrador Retriever (High Combined) in United States, 1991. Owned by Lillian and George Knobloch. *Gilbert*

WORKING AND OBEDIENCE TRIALS IN ENGLAND

Many Labradors in the United States have British dogs in their pedigrees. Debby Kay, an experienced trainer, gives some insight on English Working and Obedience titles.

In England working trials and obedience trials are two different events with titles representing different types of work. In the working trials there are five levels of competition starting with the CD level, then progressively moving on to UD, WD, TD, and PD. The "ex" designation after any of these titles is not a different title, like many other countries, but rather distinguishes

Chelons Frosty Morning
Mist CDX, WC, CGC,
owned by Margie Douma.
Lindemaier

dogs which have earned marks of 80 percent overall and not less than 70 percent in any one of the sections for that title. In English titles, the designation appears as a lower case "ex" after the upper case letters of the title.

There are 16 championship working trials held each year throughout Great Britain, so making up a WT champion is a difficult feat at best. The process is complicated, requiring a dog to win certain titles before going on to compete in the classes required for the championship. Three of the English titles may look familiar to American competitors but that is where the similarity stops. The English tests are a bit more involved and all the scent

Highlands Sunkissed Molly UD, WC, Can. CDX, winner of many awards including Highest Scoring Labrador at the Mid-Jersey LRC, 1986. Owned by Lillian and George Knobloch. *Kernan*

discrimination exercises are with a stranger's odor, not the handler's. Once a dog qualifies through the CD, UD, and WD stages with a minimum of 80 percent of the total scores, then that dog is eligible to enter the championship stakes.

There are two types of championship stakes, the TD and PD. The highest scoring dog in the stake is awarded a working trial certificate similar to the breed Challenge Certificates. A dog has to win two of these WT certificates to become a WT champion.

In the TD stakes, a dog must achieve 80 percent of the available points in each of four sections which include tracking, search, control, and agility. Tracks are similar to American TDX tracks. Search exercises include finding four tiny objects in a grassy area within five minutes. The dog does not see the objects being placed and the objects do not have the dog's handler's scent on them. The handler cannot enter the search area but may encourage the dog from the perimeter. Control and agility exercises include heeling, out-of-sight stays, barking on command, clearing a three-foot hurdle, six-foot wall, and nine-foot broad jump, drop on recall, send away, and signals.

The Police Dog Stake (PD) is quite unlike any event offered by AKC; it is more like the tests offered by the Schutzhund USA Club. All the TD stake's sections are run with a two-hour-old track. Additionally the dogs must do basic "man-work" requiring the attack and hold of an agitator. Many readers may be appalled to think of Labs doing "man-work," but from my own experience in training Labradors to do this, I have found that they rather enjoy the "game" of it. I have not encountered a Lab that took this training in any other light. All my personal detector dogs are trained to disarm anyone attacking me and to bark and hold at bay anyone they are told to. This has proved to be very useful training when out with my dogs doing police work.

Ch. Ahilo's Igloo Iggy UD, a BIS Labrador, demonstrates perfect form retrieving a dumbbell over a jump. Owner-handled by Elaine Brock.

On several occasions I credit them with saving me from potentially danger-ous situations. It is important for readers to note here that Labradors trained to do this "man-work" are not by any means vicious, hyper, or high-strung dogs. They are loyal working companions of their masters and do their job out of a willingness to please, not out of a desire for blood!

In England the early Labrador qualifiers in the Police Dog Stakes were Lady Simpson's Foxhanger dogs, who also served with the local police force. In more recent times the only Labrador I could uncover that won a PD stake was a yellow male, Hill Billy Boy, owned by Mr. P. Lewis. It obviously takes a great deal of handler dedication and one fantastically talented and athletic dog to make an English working trial champion.

Mrs. Mason, who uses the Linnafold prefix, has had tremendous suc-cess in the past 30 years with Labradors at working trials, having made up three WT champions from her breeding. Her foundation and first WT cham-pion was a black bitch, Karadoc Zanella, from Whatstandwell breeding. A most notable daughter of Zanella was WT Ch. Linnafold Blarney who won an incredible seven open stakes, possibly a record for the breed. Many of the current Linnafold Labradors have earned awards at the trials; I am sure sev-eral more from this outstanding kennel will be crowned with the coveted title over the next few years.

Susan Scales started in Labradors with foundation stock from the Foxhanger lines of Lady Simpson; her first bitch being Manymills Lucky Charm, WDex, UDex, CDex, sired by Foxhanger Mascot, PDex, TDex, UDex, CDex, WDex, out of Lisnamallard Peggy. From this bitch descend all the current Manymills Labradors including WT Ch. Manymills Tanne (by Eng. Show Ch. Sandylands Tandy). Mrs. Scales has always attempted to maintain

Ch. Winterset Major
Marker UD, JH, WC
practices scent discrimination at a match show.
Owned by Enid Bloome.

a balance between conformation, type, and working ability, and many of her dogs have awards from championship shows. In 1991, a son of her Manymills Drake, CDex, Eng. Ch. Abbeystead Heron Court, won Best of Breed at the Labrador Retriever Club annual Specialty show, thus proving that judicious crosses of working, field, and show lines can produce good-looking and effective working dogs. Heron Court, in addition to this win, has a total of five CCs, one reserve CC, and several awards from field trials. He regularly picks up at shoots and is a registered therapy dog.

In English obedience trials there are three levels of tests with only the winners of the top level being eligible to earn the Kennel Club Obedience Certificate that is needed for the championship title. Three certificates are needed for the championship and no more than ten points may be lost during the competition. No titles are awarded other than the obedience trial champion title for any of the wins leading to this. When you see CD or UD on a foreign pedigree, this is only for working trial competitors and not the obedience trial competitors.

The tests themselves are more involved than Canadian or United States tests but essentially include the same exercises as our utility classes plus a few more. Retrieving exercises do not use a standard-size dumbbell, but may use any object not injurious to a dog. Scent discrimination involves the judge's scent on the article, not the handler's, an interesting concept. The precision required to win this competition is about on a par with our "super-dog" trials and is dominated by Border Collies. It seems that the consensus of Labrador folks abroad, as here, is that this type of repetitive routine is too boring for the active, challenging minds of eager Labradors; hence, as here in the United States, few Labradors are found to compete.

Ten Labrador Retrievers have earned the title of working trial champion in England. Only two obedience trial champions have been made up in the breed. They are:

NAME	OWNER
OTCh. Amerber Sunlight	Mr. Lord
OTCh. Wanda of Tankersley	Miss Ogle
WTCh. Frenchcourt Ripple (the breed's first, 1949)	Lady Simpson
WTCh. Foxhanger Maze	Miss Gowlland
WTCh. Karadoc Zanella	Mrs. J. S. Mason
WTCh. Linnafold Blarney	Mrs. J. S. Mason
WTCh. Linnafold Mason	Mrs. J. S. Mason
WTCh. Manymills Tanne	Mrs. S. Scales
WTCh. Clevedale Fawn of Lumsbank	Mr. D. Lumsden
WTCh. Linnafold Black Magic	Mrs. S. Wood
WTCh. Linnafold Witchcraft	Mrs. J. S. Mason
WT Lumsbank Cherokee (1989)	Mrs. J. Culter

SHOW CHAMPIONS

It is much more difficult for a dog to earn the title of champion in England than in the United States. To become a champion a dog must win three CCs (Challenge Certificates). Only a select number of shows are designated "championship" shows where CCs may be awarded. The other shows are "open shows." The competition is keen because dogs that are already champions compete in the same open class as the non-champions. It takes a dog of exceptional quality to consistently win CCs.

In the United States, dogs compete against other class dogs (non-champions) to gather points, which means that they can eventually be champions without necessarily defeating any better-than-average dogs. A dog that wins its majors (three points or better) at a large Labrador specialty has defeated many quality dogs, whereas a dog could win the same number of points by defeating only ordinary dogs at smaller shows. This means that when evaluating pedigrees and counting the number of American champions in that pedigree, you need to know what sort of dogs were defeated en route to the title. Perhaps someone will come up with a computer program which could grade the shows, with the specialty shows being more heavily weighted, then the supported shows, and then the regular shows. This sort of system is used with Thoroughbred race horses grading stake races, because wins of important races deserve much more recognition than winning a small stake at a minor racetrack.

TRAINING YOUR DOG FOR CONFORMATION SHOWS

There are many ways to train your dog for the show ring. Your Labrador should stand foursquare and look at you without being strung up and stretched out. The tail should wag gently and the dog should use its ears well to demonstrate a kind expression. When gaiting, the dog should move on a loose lead at a brisk, moderate trot. If you use a one-piece lead, be careful where you let it fall as you may detract from the dog's profile. A video of your efforts may help you refine your technique.

Set weekly goals for a conformation class dog and don't go on to the next one until the goal you seek has been accomplished.

WEEK 1

Pat the dog all over to get it used to being inspected. Have strangers go over the dog. Check the bite and get a helper to play "judge" and check the bite. Accustom a male dog to having the testicles checked. Get the dog used to having its tail felt by another person. Practice gaiting and moving in a straight line. Do turns and halts, and keep the dog alert while it is moving. Don't jerk

Barbaree's Rooster Cogburn CD (Ch. Groveton's Lucky Lindy ex Springfield's High Barbaree Am. Can. CD, TD) loves to jump. He was bred by Linda Oldham and owned by Nancy Beach.

the dog around or string it up in an unnatural fashion. Study the breed Standard and learn your dog's faults and good points to minimize the former and capitalize on the latter.

WEEK 2

Stop while gaiting and teach the dog to stand and stay and look at you attentively. Practice gaiting with your dog, not you, in line with the judge. Start the dog with a few slower steps before a full trot so as not to start the dog off at a gallop. Some Labradors will pace; you must recognize this at once and correct the dog so it will trot.

Practice stacking the dog's front end. Standing over the dog, slide your right hand down the dog's right shoulder to the elbow and place the foot directly under the shoulder, not out in front of the dog. Your knee can, unobtrusively, keep the dog's weight on that foot. Then set the other leg, again from the elbow. Tell the dog "steady," which means remain motionless.

WEEK 3

Stack the rear after first stacking the front. Hold the front steady with a little tension on the lead. Run your hand under the dog's body to set the outside rear leg first (because this is what the judge will see first) by lifting the rear leg above the hock and setting the foot on the ground so that the rear pastern is perpendicular to the ground. Set the inside leg. Never reach over your dog to set the rear legs; always reach from under the dog. If your dog is straight in the rear you may have to set the legs a little further back so the dog won't look high in the rear. Make your dog stay in position for about ten seconds.

In the show ring, keep your dog set up just in case the judge looks your way. (In large classes you may not do this, to give the dog a chance to relax and not get tired. When it is hot, relaxing under the tent is important when it is not your dog's turn.) Always keep the dog between yourself and the judge. If the judge does look your way, be sure the dog looks good. Get your dog used to having you stand on either side or in front of it. Gait your dog in a triangle using a focal point so you will move straight. When returning to the end of the line always use the greatest distance available back to the end of the line to give the judge the longest view possible of your dog. Try to stand away from your dog and look at it, conveying to the judge your admiration for this dog.

WEEK 4

Practice gaiting and changing sides if the judge asks you to move in a "T" or "L" pattern. Think about ways to show off your dog's good points and disguise its faults. Keep the leash curled up in your hand and out of sight. Keep one eye on the judge and always move out of his or her way. If the judge lines up the dogs to look at rears, you stand at the dog's head. If the judge goes down this line to look at heads, you stand behind your dog. If your dog has a really good front you may want to set the dog up angled slightly toward the judge so he notices this most. But beware of what this does to the hindquarters. As a handler, you should always look at the best part of your dog, the part you want others to notice. Some handlers will run their hands over the best part of the dog, hoping to attract attention. As a judge I don't like this, but it may be helpful in certain situations.

If your dog has a weak top line, scratch it under the flank to encourage it to straighten up. If you have a short-necked dog, keep the collar all the way to the base of the neck or all the way up behind the ears. A collar in the mid-section of the neck will make it appear shorter. Many of the Labradors shown today are too short in neck for the proportion of the body. If your dog has a proper-length neck, you may wish to use a contrasting color collar to emphasize this good point. A matching color will not draw attention to that area and better suits the shorter necks. The same is true of what the handler wears. If your dog has a nice topline, wear a contrasting color; with a poor topline, you need a subdued color.

WEEK 5

Practice in front of a mirror and if possible have someone take videos of you and your dog. Have a friend pretend to be a judge. Practice gaiting your dog and having it stop and stand naturally in front of the judge. Stand away from your dog but towards the judge. Use a little bait to perk the dog up and allow the judge to see its intelligent expression.

A good Labrador show dog will stand and gait with great ring presence. The dog is always "up" for the occasion. Labradors get easily bored, so don't overdo baiting and feeding liver and treats. The great show dogs have an appreciation for an audience. They may not know why they are being looked at, but they do sense the extra attention and importance of the occasion. The great show dogs love applause and move out with marvelous, springy steps. A dog that is a natural showman will set itself up. However, judges can't put dogs up just for flash alone. It takes a very good judge, especially one who has not hunted with a Labrador or shot over one, to sort out the showy dogs from the true but quiet, excellent type.

chapter 13

Competition in the Field

I n the 1930s and 1940s, trials were held only in the spring and fall. During the off-season owners wishing competition went to dog shows. In those days trials were essentially like the walk-up shoots of British trials. Dogs didn't mark as they do today. The dog heeled and did not see the bird fall; after the bird was shot, the dog was sent downwind to pick up the scent and work out the problem. Since the dogs didn't mark the falls and simply hunted, and since the handlers did not assist them, they had to be good game finders on their own.

When shore blinds were first used, the retrieve was as far as a man could throw a duck. Decoys were used and often the luck of the wind direction and tide influenced the outcome.

EVOLUTION OF MODERN FIELD TRIALS

By 1938 walk-up shooting was eliminated and thrown birds were used. In 1937 there was an important change in the field trial rules. There could be no sticks and stones used on blind retrieves. Up to that time dogs would sit in a blind (a structure that kept the dog from seeing a bird fall, similar to what would happen in the hunting field), and the handler would throw stones in the direction of the fallen bird. A three-stone retrieve meant that it took a handler three thrown stones to direct the dog to the fallen bird. The dog would swim as far as the first stone and then be directed farther by the next stone and so on. Sticks were used similarly in the field.

Dave Elliot, the Scottish gamekeeper, started competing in the Long Island trials in 1935 using whistle and hand signals in the same manner that Border Collies were handled in Scotland. Elliot was the first to introduce blind retrieves with these handling methods, rather than throwing stones and sticks.

Further Innovations

In 1935 bird boxes were introduced with spring-loaded trap doors to release the birds. This way more dogs could be entered and the element of chance was removed. Dogs that broke or had hard mouths were disqualified.

Field trials became more artificial by the 1940s as more dogs were entered. Trials were no longer merely the by-product of shooting, but had become a sport in themselves. With the increased number of dogs entered in trials, the tests became more demanding in order to find a winner. After seven years of war in England, the trials there went through a transition from professional handlers to a large, successful owner-handled section. Labradors dominated the trials. Small-scale breeding became the norm. Dual-purpose Labradors were the goal of many breeders as they combined good looks with working ability. The first dual champion in the United States was Michael of Glenmere, owned by Jerry Angle of Nebraska. This dog was born March 24, 1935, and was sired by Ace of Whitmore (Tad of Whitmore ex Lilly of Harwood) out of Vixen of Glenmere (Decco of Glenmere ex Vamp of Glenmere).

By the 1950s, the trials became a demonstration of a hunting obedience test in the field and in many test series there was no semblance of hunting conditions. Distances were lengthened and tests were made more difficult to sort out winners. Even a minor mistake would eliminate a dog. Control became more and more important. Soundness of dogs was not a factor, and as long as a dog could run a test, no premium was placed on conformation.

Emergence of the Amateur

In the United States the Depression and World War II changed the social order. As people from all walks of life entered field trials, the professionals no longer dominated the sport. The tests became more demanding. Handlers had to spend more time training each dog, but professional handlers could not do this as readily with large strings of dogs; this gave the diligent amateur owner an opportunity to compete on a professional level.

Paul Bakewell III was the first successful amateur. He beat the pros at their own game, winning seven nationals between 1939 and 1949. Bakewell worked his dogs every day, fed them himself, and kept them in his house in the evening so they would bond to him.

Distinctly American

While the British did not change their hunting methods or field trial tests, their system became Americanized in the United States. One of the first definitive American books on the subject was *Training Your Retriever,* written by James Lamb Free in 1949. As competition became keener, emphasis was placed on training. Tests became more artificial to make competitive scoring of the dogs possible. The natural ability of the Labrador was not stressed as precision became important for scoring purposes. To keep the tests fair, every dog had to be given the same test. Cripples, actually the most important part of a retriever's work, were called a "no-bird." Cripples and runners were also time-consuming and so had no place in trials with large entries. Dave Elliot and T. W. "Cotton" Pershall, another of the best trainers, were both concerned with the fact that tests were mechanical and eliminated the natural ability of the dog.

While the British trials emphasized the cast-and-hunt method, the Americans went to straight lines, more water retrieves, and longer legs.

Cotton Pershall of Arkansas worked for Paul Bakewell in the 1940s (in addition to a stint during World War II training K-9 Corps dogs). Even while he was training war dogs Pershall kept his field dogs nearby and trained them, too. It was Bakewell who taught Pershall, a former horse groom, how to train retrievers. Pershall left Bakewell after the war and worked for several other people. By 1951 he was working for John Olin at Nilo Kennels. Early in his competitive years Cotton Pershall introduced white coats to the trials so that dogs could see arm signals better.

FIELD LABRADORS TO REMEMBER

John Olin's King Buck (Timothy of Arden ex Alta of Banchory), one of the greatest field Labradors of all time, was trained by Pershall. King Buck was not a large dog but he had style, precise responses, and perseverance. He had been ill with distemper as a puppy, which probably affected his size. It never mattered. During his years at Nilo, King Buck ran 75 series in seven consecutive runnings of the National Championship Stake, completing all but two as he won the National in 1952 and 1953. At the age of nine, competing with much younger dogs, he qualified for the National and almost won it, completing 11 out of the 12 series.

King Buck was also a great wild duck hunter's dog in spite of his intense field trial training. In 1959 King Buck appeared on the federal duck stamp holding a mallard in his mouth. This painting of him by the premier artist Maynard Reese was the first time a dog ever appeared on a United States stamp.

Three times National Champion Shed of Arden was another of the early outstanding dogs in the United States. Shed was a dual champion bred by Tom Briggs at Averell Harriman's kennel. Dual Ch. Shed of Arden was sired by Ch. Raffles of Earlsmoor (Thatch of Whitmore ex Task of Whitmore by Toi of Whitmore) ex FT Ch. Decoy of Arden (Odds On ex Peggy of Shipton by Ronald of Candahar). Shed's great-great-granddam was an interbred bitch, Jubilee Daisy.)

Shed was sold, on approval, to Paul Bakewell because he wouldn't enter the water for a second retrieve. Bakewell worked with Shed every day and overcame this problem. Bakewell gave the dog affection and appreciation for correct work and the dog responded, winning his field trial championship very quickly. In 1942, Bakewell got leave from the Navy and went to Wisconsin to run Shed in a trial that was held in below-zero weather. That day the water was very icy but Shed did not refuse to enter, as did many of the other dogs. Shed was one of two dogs called back for the final series and the other dog refused to enter the water. While waiting for his turn it was so cold that ice formed on Shed's coat and gray muzzle. When his turn came he took his handler's line, broke the ice, and made his retrieve.

Because Shed of Arden was a nice-looking dog, Bakewell had Hollis Wilson show him to his bench championship. During Bakewell's service with the Navy in World War II, Cotton Pershall kept Shed in training. Shed was an American champion, Canadian champion, American amateur field champion, American field champion, and National retriever champion in 1942, 1943, and 1946.

Bakewell and Pershall asked a great deal more of the dogs during training than they faced in the trials, both on land and water. Pershall was the first to start lining his dogs a great distance. As the trials became more difficult, the training methods had to change and adapt. Bakewell and Pershall trained with long triples in all types of cover and terrain.

Field trials are held all over the United States; some are for Labradors only, but the Nationals and retriever clubs are open to all breeds of retrievers and Irish Water Spaniels. Starting in 1936 the Labrador Club offered trophies to encourage amateur handlers. The Amateur Trophy, presented by Jay F. Carlisle, was for the dog winning the amateur stake at the Club's annual field trial. The first winner was Mrs. E. Rolland Harriman with Cinar's Gladglen of Kenjockety (Kinpurnie Kelly of Kenjockety ex Kenjockety Nellie). The Vivian Challenge Cup, presented by Col. Lord Vivian, was awarded to the amateur best handling a dog in any stake at the Club's annual field trial. Best handling meant the handler displayed quiet control, avoiding unnecessary disturbance of ground. J. Gould Remmick was the first winner in 1937.

The Hill-Wood Challenge Cup, presented to the Club by the Hon. Mrs. Hill-Wood, was awarded to the best dog handled by its amateur owner, provided that the dog had not been trained or run by a professional trainer within three months before the date of the trial. To win the trophy the dog must be awarded a certificate of merit or better. The first winner in 1939 was Mrs. Morgan Belmont with Echo of Arden (Drinkstone Pons of Wingan ex Babe of Arden by Duke of Kirkmahoe—Peggy of Shipton). James Lamb Free won in 1940 with his Freehaven Jay (FT Ch. Glenairlie Rover ex Spot of Barrington).

Many other special trophies were presented. One of the most significant was the Hiwood Mike Trophy presented to the Labrador Club by Mrs. John S. Williams. It was awarded at the discretion of the Field Trial Judges to the

August Belmont and FC/AFCH Super Chief (FC/AFC Paha Sapa Chief II ex Ironwood Cherokee Chica). *photo courtesy August Belmont*

best-looking and best-working Labrador in any stake at the Club's annual field trial. In 1948, with the approval of Mrs. Williams, this award was changed so that the trophy was awarded to the winner of the field trial class at the Club's annual Specialty show. The first winner, in 1942, was Mrs. Morgan Belmont's Dual Ch. Gorse of Arden by Ch. Raffles of Earlsmoor

(Thatch of Whitmore ex Tee of Whitmore) ex FT Ch. Decoy of Arden (Odds On ex Peggy of Shipton). English and American FT Ch. Hiwood Mike was an import by Pettistree Dan (by Dual Ch. Banchory Painter ex FT Ch. Quest of Wilbury) ex Pettistree Poppet (Cedars Michael ex Cransford Flapper).

To achieve top honors in field trials on a national level, a dog must be outstanding. Time and dedication are demanded of the owner/handler or professional trainer. Mr. and Mrs. August Belmont made some great records with their retrievers, the best known being FC-AFC Super Chief. August Belmont won the National in 1968 with Super Chief, the first amateur to win since Bakewell. August Belmont was dedicated to working with his dogs, as was his wife Louise. The dogs and the Belmonts were trained by Rex Carr, the well-known California trainer.

Rex Carr was the "father" of the electronic collar, which he used to great advantage to train the dog and owner as a team. Carr never raised his voice at the dogs, only at their handlers. He trained the handlers with such good results that the amateurs began beating the pros regularly.

Carr believed in using the dog's natural instinct. He never handled his dogs in trials; he trained the owners to handle. Mr. Belmont said, "He used to give me hell." Carr was innovative in various training techniques. He developed a method called "two steps back," which was a way to teach a dog not to pick up the first dummy thrown, but to go past it to get the second, retrieve it, and then return for the first.

Super Chief was bred by Wilbur Goode of Rapid City, South Dakota. Louise Belmont had bought a puppy from Mr. Goode by FC-AFC Paha Sapa Chief II (FC Freehaven Muscles ex Treasure State Be-Wise). She tried to train him but he was always lame. Two years later Mr. Goode called her and said he had another litter by Paha Sapa Chief (out of Ironwood Cherokee Chica by Dual Ch. Cherokee Buck ex Glen-Water Fantom by FC-AFC Cork of Oakwood Lane), and she could have first choice to replace the other puppy. The Belmonts were careful with this puppy, as Louise knew he was special. August Belmont decided "this would be my dog because since he had the responsibility of going to work he wouldn't have time or be tempted to train him." Belmont recalled "Soupy was just part of the family. He slept in the ashes in the fireplace in the summertime. He just lounged around and no one threw things for him."

Around Christmas time, they sent the young dog to Rex Carr to be trained. After Carr had had him five or six weeks, he called the Belmonts and said, "Send me more Soupys . . . He makes the sun shine brighter." By the following February the Belmonts went to California to train with their dog and had a great time with him. He was no machine even though he worked equally well for Carr or the Belmonts.

The Belmonts went on the field trial circuit with Super Chief. When August Belmont had to work Saturdays, Louise Belmont handled the dog. Mr. Belmont said, "My wife had to handle my dogs and train them too."

Louise handled Super Chief herself for his amateur and field trial championship. She won the amateur national championship two years in a row.

The schedule was intensive, with the Belmonts spending 22 to 24 weekends away from home. Mr. Belmont said, "We were very gung-ho." It was a tremendous time commitment. Eventually, when Mrs. Belmont had physical problems, she handled the dog using canes for herself.

When Soupy was at home, he lived in the Belmont's home near Easton, Maryland. Dogs that are highly trained are not spoiled by kind treatment. We recall that in England the Earl of Malmesbury did not banish his dogs to some kennel at night. They slept in the bedroom and enjoyed little games and conversations with their master. The most successful owner/handlers are the ones who show their dogs affection and appreciation for their efforts. Kind words are the dog's best reward.

THE NATIONALS

The National Field Trial Championships have been held under the auspices of the National Retriever Field Trial Club since 1941. Until recently, only one dog, Shed of Arden, was a three-time winner, and he was a dual champion as well. The dogs who have won twice are: NFC-FC King Buck in 1952 and 1953, NFC-FC Spirit Lake Duke in 1957 and 1959, NFC-FC Del-Tone Colvin in 1961 and 1963, and NFC-FC Whygin's Cork's Coot in 1966 and 1969. The National Amateur Retriever Club has sponsored a National Amateur Championship since 1957.

A black Labrador bitch, NFC-AFC Candlewood's Tanks a Lot, owned by Mary Howley of Wisconsin and Randy Kuehl of Iowa, joined record holder NFC-Dual Ch. Shed of Arden in 1993 by winning the National for the third time. She first won in 1990 when she was the youngest titled dog in retriever field trial history to win the national crown. Handled by trainer Mike Hardy, "Lottie" won again in 1991, setting another record as the youngest bitch to claim the NFC title twice. By the time she won in 1993, Lottie was the only bitch, as well as the youngest retriever, to accomplish this feat in the 53-year history of the National Championship Stake.

Originally 81 dogs qualified for the 1993 National Retriever Club championship stake, which was held in Statesboro, Georgia. To deserve her crown, Lottie entered the tenth series of the trial with 13 other retrievers. In poor visibility she retrieved a difficult triple, a land-water combination on each of three marks, with the first, or memory bird, a pheasant thrown by a retired gun against a tree-lined backdrop. This was a dark bird against a dark background in poor light.

Lottie is all the more remarkable because she whelped large litters each year from 1990 through 1992. She cared for her puppies for eight weeks each time and then returned to the rigors of training, winning two consecutive Nationals just months after weaning her puppies. Her sire, NFC-NAFC-FC

Dual Ch. Pelican Lake Toby. Note reach of neck and proportionate length of leg. *Debby Kay collection*

FC/AFC MD's Cotton Pick'n Cropper (FC/AFC Candlewood's M.D. Houston ex Krugerrand's Honey Bee), owned by Newt Cropper.

Candlewood's Super Tanker, a black male bred by Mary Howley and owned by Joyce Williams, won the National in 1992.

PRESENT-DAY FIELD TRIALS

Retriever clubs all over the United States put on field trials and sanctioned matches. There is a trial somewhere every weekend starting down south and in California at the beginning of the year and running well into November. The National Open and National Amateur are the ultimate wins. The Nationals are held in a different time zone and area each year. Dogs have to qualify each year to run in a National by winning at least one first place and two or more additional points at a licensed trial. Basically this means that to qualify, the dog has to complete the same requirements for a field championship each year, even though it already holds a title.

FC Eskay's Loulou from LSU (Howley's Folly ex Tina of Evergreen), owned by B. J. Thompson, was among the top ten bitches in the United States for many years. Her best year was 1979 when she won five open stakes and an amateur stake.

The Nationals run a series of ten tests, but more can be used if necessary. Retrievers must complete each test successfully to continue in the competition. The dogs are judged on their ability to retrieve fallen game on land and in water. Consideration is given to marking ability, courage, perseverance, willingness to please, and the ability to respond to the commands given by the handler.

The tests are combinations of marked land and water retrieves, where the dog sees and remembers the falls of up to four birds, retrieving these birds to its handler. There are also blind retrieving tests where the dog does not know the location of the bird. The dog is expected to run or swim to that bird at the direction of its handler. Blind retrieves can be asked of the dogs at distances up to 300 yards over all sorts of terrain and through all sorts of water situations. Average retrieves are 100 yards.

Three judges officiate at the National level, calling back after each test series only those dogs which, in their opinion, remain in serious contention for the National. Testing and elimination run over a number of days during which time the weather can change and add to the degree of difficulty.

Over the years requirements and tests have changed. In the 1940s judges were impressed with dogs that could be handled with a side cast around a bush or trees, whereas today, this maneuver is considered a correction. By the 1950s the emphasis shifted to lining a dog. Great precision became a prerequisite for success, and the trials became a super-obedience game. To separate the dogs the judges developed more demanding tests. The trainers rose to the occasion and the dogs learned whatever was the current idea of the competitions.

AKC rules stipulated that the tests were supposed to simulate hunting conditions. However, to have a competition where one dog would emerge the winner, more and more difficult tests were used. The handler must have the dog under complete command. The judges look for the dogs which have taken the most precise lines, run with style, taken a true cast, all with the fewest whistles and signals from the handler. Birds must be delivered to hand.

At each trial the judges select the section of the field to use for a test and set it up taking terrain, wind direction, and cover into consideration. Each dog tested will run the same test. Usually a noncompeting test dog is run first. Guns (shooters) and bird boys place the birds as directed by the judges. The tests use combinations of dead and live birds. If a bird flies out of the prescribed area, the judges may call it a "no bird" and allow the dog a rerun.

Dogs are called to the line (starting point) one at a time. When the dog is sitting quietly at the handler's side, the handler signals the judges for the birds. If the dog breaks, it is eliminated. When the dog has finished his retrieves, the judge may ask it to stay on the line to honor or observe the birds that are shot for the next dog. The honoring dog must be steady and stay put.

Many books and videos cover field trial training in great detail. Field trial work is very demanding and time-consuming. To participate you need a place to train and people to assist with throwing and shooting, as well as birds and a variety of training grounds where shooting is allowed.

You also need the right dog. Many field-trial-bred dogs will not make it to the top competitions for a number of reasons. This is also an expensive sport if you plan to have a dog on the circuit, either with a trainer or with yourself. Not many duck and goose hunters have the time or money, or even the interest, to train on this level. The average Labrador owner may not aspire to a National championship, but they may wish to hunt or train their dogs. Most Labradors, if given a fair chance, will retrieve. However, many will not take the degree of training necessary for a super trial dog. By the same token, many dog owners never learn all the techniques and nuances that would make their animals decent field trial dogs.

As trials became more of an obedience game than a test under hunting conditions in the 1970s and 1980s, informal gun dog stakes began to take place among average hunters. Clubs and associations were formed to hold these events. Participants had a good time and learned a great deal from fellow hunters. The gun dog stakes were designed for retrievers not quite up to the precision performances demanded of serious field trialers. These dogs were hunted and handled by their owners.

THE NORTH AMERICAN HUNTING RETRIEVER ASSOCIATION (NAHRA)

NAHRA was based on the principle that many hunters had never seen excellent retriever work and did not know the potential of their own dogs. These tests would give the hunter a structure within which to train his dog and evaluate it during the off season. Tests would demonstrate the dog's accomplishments. A registry of dogs that passed the tests would be kept so that hunters would be able to choose breeding stock from proven hunting retrievers. The first NAHRA trial was run in 1983.

Enid Bloome and Nell accept their NAHRA ribbon from judge Sue Lassey.

Dogs are tested in four categories based on ability and degree of training, rather than age: Beginner, Started, Intermediate, and Senior. For the first time in retriever trials a noncompetitive system was established. The dogs competed against a standard on a pass/fail basis. A passing grade is 80 percent. If a dog passes all the tests in its category, it is awarded points toward its title.

The Started dog must display natural retrieving ability on land and in water. Points are accumulated toward a Started Certificate. The Intermediate dog works for a title of Working Retriever (WR) in both upland and waterfowl work. A dog at this level has enough training so as not to embarrass a hunter on any kind of game in any part of North America. The Senior Dog works for points toward the title of Master Hunting Retriever (MHR). This is the top of the line, and these dogs can run for Grand Master Hunting Retriever.

There are many retriever training clubs all over the United States. For many years owners could train on a local level and run their dogs in sanctioned matches, but this was still competitive. This new approach brought many more hunters out to work and train together in an atmosphere where they could cheer for all the dogs to pass the noncompetitive tests.

The Northeast Hunting Retriever Association instituted judges' workshops and seminars long before the AKC climbed on the bandwagon. At these seminars the differences between field trials and hunting retriever tests were explained and demonstrated. According to Enid P. Bloome, a participant,

> Aspiring judges were given a chance to set up a test which was critiqued from the standpoint of a hunting situation. Gunners were hidden, walk-ups were prevalent, trailing and quartering came into Senior tests, and an honest attempt was made to make the test as close to a hunting scenario as possible. The judges were required to give a scenario to the handlers before the start of the test. Some judges did call upon their own hunting experience, a sense of humor, and an honest attempt to make it seem like we were really out there hunting, working the field, when suddenly the birds came in from over there and we got one down. Then another shot by our buddy fell over the rise and we were asked to send our dog for that bird. It became more realistic, distances were shortened, and the dog was really required to hunt, use its nose, display its desire and perseverance.

AKC HUNTING TESTS FOR RETRIEVERS

Following the acceptance by hunters of NAHRA, the AKC decided to establish its own hunting tests for retrievers. In contrast to field trials where judges set up tests designed to eliminate dogs, hunting tests would determine how many dogs on a certain day are working satisfactorily at the level they have entered. The appeal would be a noncompetitive event in actual hunting situations that would truly represent the retriever's accomplishments. The hunting tests evaluate the suitability of the retriever as a hunting companion. Dogs are expected to retrieve any type of game bird under all conditions.

Dogs are tested at three levels of retrieving ability: Junior, Senior, and Master. The goal is uniformity in tests and uniformity in judging. Judges, who are selected from people with broad and extensive retriever experience in the hunting field, set up tests and evaluate the dogs. Judges must agree that a dog should qualify. Judging is not an exact science, but rather an understanding of the rules and qualities that are being judged. The retrievers must get birds to hand as quickly as possible, in a pleasing, obedient manner, without hurting the bird. The more experience a judge has, the better, because he or she is scoring the dog against a mental standard.

The judges must score the dogs on:

1. Their natural abilities including marking (memory).
2. Style.
3. Perseverance or courage.
4. Trainability as evidenced in steadiness, control, response, and delivery.

Qualifiers at Black Creek HC hunting retriever test (l. to r.): Janet Suranna with Ch. Balnamore Keeper Texas Oil, JH; Winterset Mark Me Well JH, CDX; her son Wayside Firemark with owner Barbara Lindsay; and Enid Bloome with Flame finishing her JH.

Field trials and hunting retriever tests are held several times a year on the north side of the Chesapeake and Delaware Canal. The configuration of this pond allows various tests to be set up according to the wind conditions. *Aerial photo by Jan Churchill*

The dogs' abilities are scored against an established standard with a numerical score from 1 to 10. To qualify, a dog must receive an overall average of seven (7.0) for the entire test and must not have an average score in any one ability category below five (5.0).

The hunting test promotes retriever training not only for hunting people, but also for show dogs. The same dogs can do well in both areas; after all, working dogs need good conformation and sound structure, as well as hunting instincts. Hunting tests are good for the breed, but they do not measure stamina. A good gunning dog is able to work day in and day out under difficult conditions. The hunting tests are a better measure of hunting ability than the original Working Certificates, although both have had their place in the history of the breed. The hunting tests are making people look closer at their breeding programs.

Junior Hunter

To be recorded as a Junior Hunter (JH), a dog must be individually registered with the AKC and must have acquired qualifying scores in the Junior

Larry Wharton's Labrador retrieves a water series. Note that the dog returns in a straight line. *J. Churchill*

hunting test in four AKC licensed or member club hunting tests. In the Junior tests, dogs are tested on four single marks, two on land and two on water. Retrieves usually do not exceed 100 yards. Dogs must be steady. They must retrieve to hand.

Senior Hunter

To be recorded as a Senior Hunter (SH), a dog must be individually registered with the AKC and must have acquired qualifying scores in the Senior hunting test at five licensed or member club hunting tests. If the dog is a Junior Hunter (JH), only four qualifying scores are needed.

Senior dogs are tested in a minimum of four hunting situations, which include one land blind, one water blind (which may be run as a double blind on land and water), one double land mark, and one double water mark. Retrieves do not normally exceed 100 yards. Dogs must be steady and retrieve to hand. A dog must honor a working dog at least once. A diversion shot is used. Dogs that switch cannot receive a qualifying score.

Master Hunter

To be recorded as a Master Hunter (MH), a dog must be individually registered with AKC and must acquire qualifying scores at six AKC licensed or member club hunting tests, or if the dog is a Senior Hunter, in five AKC licensed or member club hunting tests. Dogs are tested in a minimum of five hunting situations as follows: multiple land marks, multiple water marks, multiple marks on water and land, land blind(s), and water blind(s). Diversion birds must be used at least once. Master dogs must honor. They may not switch. They must be steady and deliver to hand. Judging standards are more stringent.

In all hunting tests the ability to mark accurately is of primary importance. A dog that marks the fall of a bird, uses the wind, follows a strong cripple, and takes direction from its handler is of great value. After delivering a bird (unhurt) to its handler, a dog should stand or sit close to its handler until given further orders. When told to retrieve, a dog should proceed quickly and eagerly on land or into water to marked falls, or on the line given it by the handler on falls it has not seen. The dog should not disturb too much ground. The dog must pay attention to whistles and signals given by its handler. A dog is considered an intelligent and reliable marker if it runs past a bird, recognizes the situation, and returns and hunts the area systematically.

Style is reflected in the dog's way of going about its work. Eagerness, alertness, aggressive search, and speed on retrieves are some of the traits that are considered as the dog is marked on a pleasing performance.

Perseverance is the dog's willingness to get the job done no matter what conditions it encounters. The dog must face difficult going and icy water

Delivering the bird to hand, Wharton's dog approaches the handler and circles into a sit beside the handler. *J. Churchill*

Campbellcroft Black Hawkeye CDX, SH, the first Golden Gate LRC "Do It All" challenge winner, for the highest scoring dog on the bench, in the obedience ring and in the field. Breeder and co-owner, Terri Herigstad; co-owners and field trainers, Jim and Linda Fulks.

In the Junior Hunter test the dog does not have to be steady on the line. Deborah L. Musgrove holds Ransome's Kruise Control M (Solberg's Giddeon By Choice CD, MH ex Ransome's Perpetual Pursuit, CDX, MH, bred by Bernadette Brown). *J. Churchill*

Echo Road Redstone, SH (FC, CFC, CAFC Sugarfoot's Rocky Road ex Sugarfoot's Uptown Girl), a three-year-old Labrador, Qualified All Age, retrieving a mallard as a test dog at a hunting test at the Del-Bay Retriever Club grounds. Owned by Vicky Lane Trainor. *J. Churchill*

Retrievers must not disturb decoys while working. A chocolate dog, Mount Hope's Winston Cup (Ayr's Toast to the Max ex Rip Van Winkles Maggie Mae), bred by Steve and Diane Craft and owned by Robin and Lisa Quann, retrieving at a hunting test at the Del-Bay Retriever Club. *J. Churchill*

without hesitation. The dog cannot give up and switch to another bird somewhere else.

The final attribute evaluated by the judges is trainability. These are traits acquired through training such as steadiness, control, response, and delivery. The level demonstrated will differ in the various levels of hunting tests.

The AKC publishes *Regulations and Guidelines for AKC Hunting Tests for Retrievers and Field Trials for Retrievers*. These publications explain, in detail, general regulations, qualifying scores and the awarding of titles, instructions to judges and committees (hunt tests or field trials), standards for all tests and titles, test requirements, and other important considerations. Anyone interested in working in the field should acquire copies of these booklets from AKC.

Misconduct, either at the test or trial grounds, or at social events connected with the tests, is not allowed. This includes anything prejudicial to the sport or AKC. A person guilty of misconduct will be suspended from all AKC privileges. This is not the same as a rule violation.

XLT Squash Blossom of Winroc (FC/AFC Highest CC Waterback ex Winroc XLT Onyx Injun, SH), bred by Terry and Mike Borg and owned by Mr. and Mrs. A. L. Foote, retrieves at a hunt test for Mr. Foote. *J. Churchill*

chapter 14

Training Your Dog for the Field

Assume that you have been a spectator or volunteer at some hunting tests and field trials, you have selected your puppy, and you have great expectations. Basic obedience for a young puppy is essential no matter what your plans are for the dog. The best way to learn and get involved is to join a club or amateur training group. Invaluable advice and assistance should be available from experienced participants and trainers that you will meet. There is also the possibility of working with a professional trainer.

If you are new to the sport, it is very important to work with people who can train you, the handler. It is not fair to expect consistent work from a dog if you don't know what you are doing. A novice handler who hasn't taken the time to study and watch the experts is looking for trouble. There are no short cuts in training a good working dog. While a retriever will bring back birds by instinct, to perform in the tests or just to give you the utmost in efficient retrieving takes time and training. Many hunters do not appreciate the capabilities of their dogs until they join training groups. There are many books and training videos available to supplement what you learn during group sessions or working individually with a trainer.

HANDLING SKILLS

The dog is only half of the team. The handler is the other. The handler needs to develop the skills and techniques necessary to work well with the dog. A successful team will consist of a dog that is under control and shows a willingness to be handled, and a handler who understands how to work with his or her dog in a variety of situations. Basically, the handler wants to encourage the dog's natural hunting instincts while keeping the work enjoyable.

Eng., Am. Ch. Lawnwoods Hot Chocolate demonstrating a retrieve for four of his get at the Bohemia River on Maryland's Eastern Shore. *Jan Churchill*

Handlers must exercise voice control, think deliberately, and know how to make instant decisions. When training a dog, you must be able to think ahead and know how to relate to the dog what it is you want it to do. There is no set formula because every dog is an individual and must be treated as such. A handler must be patient and be aware that while not every dog is field trial material, most dogs can be fine hunting companions and make a good showing in hunting tests. It is important for handlers to control their tempers.

Dogs are very sensitive to mood and tone of voice. They can read you like a book, so if you are feeling down for whatever reason, your dog will sense this at once, and it may affect its performance. For example, a slow dog will move even slower. The mood you are in may cause you to lose patience, resulting in a setback for your training program. Successful trainers and handlers are aware of their own frames of mind, as well as observing the same in the dog. Good trainers who have dog intuition know how to get on the dog's wavelength.

THE RIGHT GROUNDWORK

Until the puppy is seven months of age, a primary task is socializing, which means taking it to a variety of places where it gets used to many people, strange sounds, and varied situations. In decent weather the puppy should be

High Peak Honey, six months of age, exhibits an enthusiastic water entry. Owned by Ed Katz.

swimming. Your dog must have a good foundation of basic obedience that you will build on. The basic things to learn are sit, stay, heel, and come. The puppy should be doing short single retrieves and developing marking skills. Make all the exercises upbeat and friendly. You want the puppy to have a good time. Don't go through the basics too fast. Allow each puppy to progress at its own speed—they won't all be the same.

Play games with a very young puppy—throwing a rolled-up sock, ball, or toy a short distance. Make a big fuss when the puppy brings it back. Don't do it so much that the puppy gets bored and goes off. The puppy should not be allowed to play retrieving games with anyone except the person who will train it for field work. Family members can play different types of games with the puppy. Never give the puppy a training dummy as a play toy.

Yard drills will be introduced to your young dog for the practice of obedience training and to keep your dog sharp. As the training becomes increasingly difficult, it should be more interesting and challenging to your dog. Labradors are very intelligent and can become bored quickly, so they really enjoy challenging exercises which are presented to them in a meaningful way. Exercises will be basic to almost all field work and good line habits. Yard drills help to reinforce what a dog has learned. Praise is the most essential element because Labradors have a tremendous desire to please. Working with these exercises creates an excellent one-on-one relationship between handler and dog.

Don't demand too much from your puppy. It needs time to have fun and grow up. Puppies need lots of association with people and other dogs. Keeping a puppy in a kennel run most of the time is not a good idea. Short lessons, several times a day, are better than long sessions for a youngster. Teach your dog what you want before you apply pressure. Show your dog the drill and practice in stages so you will build confidence. End on a good note so that you and your dog will feel successful.

TRAINING EFFECTIVELY

Remember that dogs think like dogs, not humans, so the handler must be able to get in the dog's head and see the situation from its point of view. Whenever a dog has problems you should go back to basic obedience, give the dog commands it knows well, and then work towards the problem area. Do not overtrain the dog or expect too much too soon. Praise your dog with a simple "good dog" rather than exciting phrases.

Training is a long-term proposition. Inexperienced trainers must guard against overtraining their dog or cramming by waiting until a few days before a test and then overworking the dog. Things learned over a period of

Chilbrook Gullah with handler Allan Spense shows how to introduce a six-month-old puppy to simple water retrieves. *Debby Kay*

time in an intelligent manner are retained well by the dog, rather than attempting to cram too much just a few days prior to a hunting test.

Training carefully over a period of time should aid the handler in not being nervous when test time comes. Keep yourself calm and make all your motions deliberate. A handler has to learn what bad habits lead to problems, such as creeping, so they can be avoided. It is much easier to prevent the dog from developing bad habits than it is to retrain the dog. For example, do not allow a dog to creep in the first place because this is a very difficult habit to break. Head swinging is another bad habit which can develop when you train your dog on too many doubles too early in its development.

Dogs are like top athletes. They must be kept in top physical condition by jogging with them or allowing them to swim on the days you don't train. If they are fed properly, kept parasite-free, and at the proper weight, they will perform better and be keener in tests or competitions. Give your dog a light meal the night before the test and no food at all the morning of the test. Monitor the water intake carefully. Exercise the dog so that it can eliminate; most dogs will take care of their needs when released from their crates. After that, don't keep taking it in and out of the crate, but wait until it is time to compete. If you have a black dog, remember that the coat absorbs heat, so train it when the weather is cool, and at competitions, keep it in the shade until its turn comes.

When you are ready to enter a hunting test you will have high hopes and expectations. Concentrate on your dog. There is a tremendous amount of handler error at tests, so whatever you do, do not punish your dog for your own mistakes. Do not take failure personally. Learn how to handle yourself when your dog doesn't pass. Realize that some dogs just have bad days.

When your dog doesn't pass a test or do as well as you think it should, make a realistic assessment of the factors contributing to the poor performance. Judge yourself as well as the dog. Many people think they can do hunting tests without the work involved in regular training sessions.

As your dog's work gets better, you will progress to Master Hunter or even field trials. You will have to keep your dog's skills sharpened and use a variety of environments to train. Time management between handler and dog becomes a priority, as there may be limited windows of opportunity to train. At trials a tremendous amount of luck is involved. You can get a bad break, and it can be crushingly disappointing at times. Once again, don't take your personal disappointment out on your dog. Some degree of equanimity is important—you must win humbly and lose graciously.

JUDGES

Judges are volunteers who have a thankless, tiring job in whatever kind of weather the day brings. They may have traveled a great distance to give you and your dog their time. Be courteous and thank the judge when you leave the line. Whether your dog has done well or poorly, and no matter what your personal opinion of the tests, be respectful to the judges.

The Del Bay Retriever Club, which holds hunt tests and field trials in Delaware and Maryland, has adopted the practice of inviting new judges to judge along with an experienced judge. The Club wants to bring new judges to the sport and is willing to fly them in from other areas to accomplish this aim.

The grounds of the Del Bay Retriever Club, near Chesapeake City, Maryland, with the ponds designed by Larry Wharton. *Jan Churchill*

A field trial at the Del Bay Retriever Club's pond. The black Labrador is in the holding blind, which prevents the dog from seeing the test, waiting for its turn. *Jan Churchill*

IDEAL TRAINING GROUNDS

Larry Wharton, President of the Del Bay Retriever Club (one of the oldest in America; it held its first field trial on October 20, 1945) has developed excellent training grounds near Chesapeake City, Maryland, just north of the Chesapeake and Delaware Canal. The main field of 13 acres contains a large pond, which is a technical masterpiece of about three acres with multiple swim-by ponds, 3½ to 10 feet deep, spread out all over the field. There are also several 40' × 9' rectangular ponds surrounded by tightly mowed grass. The area is such that tests can be set up properly no matter which way the wind is blowing. There are high mounds so that handlers can watch the dogs work. At no time is a point of land more than a foot high; it is important for the terrain to be relatively flat so the dog can be seen, enabling the handler to make a fair correction when necessary.

WORKING CERTIFICATE

In the early years of the Labrador Retriever Club (LRC), field trial dogs, handled by field trial trainers, supplied the entries for field and show events. The same names were found in pedigrees for both bench and field competitions. However, it wasn't long before it became obvious that two strains were being developed. In 1939 the Club's constitution added Article VII, which stated that if a member's dog won a bench championship, it could not use the title "Champion" (Ch.) until it received a Working Certificate or better at a field trial. Section two of this article permitted a dog to be entered at a Club trial for the purpose of obtaining a Working Certificate. The dog did not have to compete in the trial classes, but did have to satisfactorily complete both a land and water series in the same trial, or place in an AKC-sanctioned trial.

The Working Certificate requirement is limited to LRC members, but the Certificate is available to all Labrador Retrievers that have completed AKC championship requirements. However, since the Certificate is not an AKC title, it does not appear on AKC registration papers. The program is open to the entire Labrador community (LRC directors set a fee of $25 for each Certificate).

The Working Certificate test can also be administered by any director of the Club, or anyone who has judged licensed field trials. Any dog receiving a JAM (Judge's Award of Merit) or better at an AKC-licensed or AKC-sanctioned trial qualifies automatically for the Working Certificate.

(The English Kennel Club requires a working ability test for any dog that finishes its bench championship but does not hold a field title. A "full champion" in England is a dog that has won the required three Challenge Certificates for its bench championship and has passed tests demonstrating field ability. The English Kennel Club uses a special title of "show champion" for dogs that have a bench title but have not passed a field test.)

The Working Certificate is designed to demonstrate the natural retrieving ability of a Labrador, which is an important part of the breed's heritage. These simple tests make it possible to assess the individual dog's willingness to work and to demonstrate that it is not gun-shy—qualities that are essential in animals to be used for breeding.

Larry Wharton with a favorite sporting partner. FC Rebel Cody's Mischief (FC, NAFC Trumarc's Zip Code ex FC AFC MS Mischief Magic Marker), linebred to FC AFC Super Chief. *Kenneth Andrews*

An enthusiastic water entry at a hunting test. Campbellcroft Sentinel CDX, JH (Ch. Jaynecourt Ajoco Justice ex Campbellcroft Bristol Cream, UD, JH), owned by Terri Herigstad. *Berger*

Formal training is not necessary but elementary retrieving lessons are recommended. The dog does not have to be steady and can be held on the line. Line manners are not marked. The dogs do not have to retrieve to hand, but they must return the bird to the immediate vicinity of the handler.

Birds used for the tests can be pigeons or pheasants on land and ducks on water. The tests include a single retrieve on land of about 40 yards in light cover. The water test is a "back-to-back" single to show willingness to re-enter the water. The goals are simple, and owners will find it fun and challenging to train their dogs in the field. It is more relaxing than obedience classes, but it won't adversely affect a dog's performance in the obedience ring.

A Labrador can be awarded a Working Certificate by the Labrador Retriever Club, Inc., when it has demonstrated the skills and qualities required at a licensed field trial or hunt test in the following:

1. A back-to-back land and water series.

2. A land and a water series.

3. Has achieved one leg on Senior or Master Hunter title.

4. Has achieved a Junior Hunter title.

5. In some other way demonstrates that it has satisfied the requirements.

Details may be obtained from the Labrador Retriever Club, Inc.

Preliminary Training for a Working Certificate

The equipment you will need is a collar and leash. The collar can be nylon or leather. If you use a metal choke, be sure that it has no more than two inches of slack in the chain, and do not leave it on the dog after the training session.

The dummies can be canvas or plastic. Later on you will want to practice with live birds so your dog won't encounter them for the first time at a trial. White dummies are easier for the dog to see. For the same reason handlers should wear a white shirt or jacket.

To accustom your dog to the sound of a gun you can use a starter pistol (a .22 blank) or a shotgun. A shotgun will be used at a trial. You don't have to know how to shoot, but you should have someone who can fire a gun for you. A whistle should be used for communicating with your dog.

Early work can be done with canvas dummies. Have an assistant walk a short distance away from you and shout so that the dog looks his way as he throws the dummy with an underhand motion causing it to arc high in the air. As soon as the dummy falls, send your dog to retrieve it.

For water work, have your assistant throw a dummy while standing a short distance down the shore from you, but be sure the dummy lands in front of the dog so the dog will not run along the bank before entering the water. If you have access to a narrow body of water, your assistant can stand on the opposite bank and throw towards the dog.

In the working test, you can hold the dog by the collar as you signal the judge. A duck call will sound as the bird is thrown and a gun fires. You will send your dog and hope it returns the bird to where you are standing. For the water test the procedure is similar, with a line near the water's edge. No decoys are used.

Work your dog in as many different locations as possible. Try to find different bodies of water. After your dog has learned the "drill," try to find a group to train with so your dog will learn to work with all the distractions and excitement that will be found at a trial.

You must introduce your dog to birds after it has learned to retrieve dummies. You would not want your dog to meet a duck for the first time at a trial and refuse to retrieve it. By the same token, do not start the dog with birds unless you can afford to use birds all the time. A dog accustomed to birds may refuse to work on dummies.

Working Certificate Excellent

This advanced Certificate requires satisfactory completion of a double on land and "back-to-back" singles in water. The dog must heel off lead from the last holding blind to the line. It must be steady and deliver to hand.

You wait for your turn in the holding blind where you can see what is happening, but your dog is sitting behind the blind and thus cannot see anything. When the judge calls "dog," you remove the lead and command "heel" as you walk to the line. You signal the judge that you are ready. The throwers and gunners are hidden. A duck call goes off, a bird is thrown, and a gun goes off while the bird is in the air.

The dog must mark the fall of two birds in different places. You send it to the first bird, which it delivers to your hand by sitting in front of you while holding the bird; the dog then circles to heeling position, and you line it up for the second bird to be retrieved.

For the water test the dog also heels from the blind to the line, which may be some distance from the water's edge. Two birds are thrown and shot. To reach the birds the dog may have to go through reeds, swim to an island, run across, enter more water, and swim to the bird. The second mark may be in open water, in which case it is nice if the dog makes a diving entry.

Generally, dogs are more interested in water retrieves, as birds are somewhat easier to pick up in the water. Some tests may use shackled ducks, which are capable of quacking, so be sure to train your dogs with these, as well as shot birds.

Enid Bloome signals "ready" while Flame (aka Winterset Light My Fire) marks the water "mark" in a WCX test.

Regional Labrador Club Tests

Some Labrador Retriever clubs have their own tests and awards. An advanced test could require heeling your dog off lead to the line for back-to-back singles on land. Usually the handler can choose which mark to retrieve first. After getting the first bird, your dog must be sent immediately for the second bird. Typically the gunner and thrower will be hidden. Various kinds of terrain will add difficulty to the test. Delivery in advanced tests will be to hand, which means the dog sits in front of you holding the bird for you to take it. The dog must not drop the bird or offer it to another person.

Advanced water tests usually use decoys and islands to test the dog's ability to travel straight no matter what the distractions. Gunners and throwers are usually hidden, or they may be in a boat.

Dogs need to practice to maintain their skills. You will train more often during the learning phases. Fairly regular sessions in various locations will keep your dog interested, enthusiastic, and ready should you want to enter competitions.

OBEDIENCE AND GUN DOG TRAINING

A hunter's dog will perform all the exercises learned in novice obedience: sit, stay, heel, and stand. The more advanced obedience dogs will have mastered retrieving and jumping with an object in their mouths. These lessons are easily transferred to the field, especially if the dog has been worked in a variety of places so it knows how to perform when there are distractions. After your dog has learned some hunting basics, you are ready to think about hunting tests. Contact AKC for the names of hunting test or field trial clubs.

There are a number of good books and videos on training gun dogs and AKC has an excellent video on hunting tests. You must educate yourself before you start to train your dog. There is also a two-hour video step-by-step training guide called *Richard A. Wolters Trains Retrievers,* describing a training method that uses almost no force. The program helps your dog become a skilled retriever by age one.

ELECTRONIC COLLARS

Many advances in technology have improved electronic collars since Rex Carr started to use them. Carr stressed that the dog must understand its mistakes before corrections are made. Carr used the electronic collar to be able to correct mistakes within a half second of occurrence. In those days there was a lot of misuse of the collar by imitators of Carr. Carr considered the psychological makeup of the dog and used the collar to get precision.

However, it is well recognized that a natural training system is sufficient for a top-flight hunting dog. A hunter's dog doesn't need precise training, such as that required by a competitive field trial dog.

Anyone interested in learning about various training methods should contact a professional or good amateur trainer. Training methods should not abuse a dog. Training aids such as electronic collars in the hands of an ignorant and impatient person are very unfair to a dog and can be more abusive mentally than physically. The art of training has progressed a great deal in recent years, but those who use the electronic collar for a quick fix are ignorant. There is no substitute for a proper training course for a dog.

Tri-Tronics has a one-hour training video, *Step By Step Basic Training Video* (1993), that teaches a humane manner for using Tri-Tronics collars. Jim and Phyllis Dobbs give training seminars, and they have written a book, *Tri-Tronics Retriever Training,* which is a complete guide to electronic collar training in all retriever sports. It is comprehensive, covering everything from how to pick a puppy to mastering advanced retriever skills.

The remote training collars have become very sophisticated, offering the opportunity to correct or discipline your dog at a great distance. Hand-held transmitters offer eight to fifteen levels of stimulation, depending on the unit used, and range up to one mile in an open field or 200 to 400 yards in thick cover. The units consist of a hand-held transmitter, a collar worn by the dog, and additional accessories that allow you to adjust the level of electric stimulation the dog receives. They are not complicated to use and all come with an instructional manual to supplement the training books and videos.

Tri-Tronics collars offer "continuous" or "momentary" stimulation. Different dog trainers have different goals, and these goals require a specific type of electronic stimulation. Low levels of continuous stimulation are most effectively used to guide your dog into obedience. Your dog learns how to turn off stimulation by following commands. Continuous stimulation at higher levels of training is designed for overcoming resistance or distraction in training, once the dog has learned to shut off stimulation. You need flexibility with the collar so you can instantly match it to the degree of distraction.

Momentary stimulation is of short duration. It starts as soon as you touch the button, but automatically turns off almost immediately. Each stimulus is over almost before it starts, much shorter than using manual tap-and-release buttons on a more conventional remote trainer.

Reasonable training methods make the Tri-Tronics collar a viable training tool. However, it must be kept out of the hands of abusers. An educational process must teach people to recognize when they are being abusive. Many so-called dog trainers don't recognize that they are abusing a dog, and when they don't care, that makes matters even worse. Unfortunately, training with this sophisticated tool requires capable instruction, which is not always readily available. Used correctly the electronic collar can be a tool to motivate positive responses and really fine-tune a dog's performance so the animal is well satisfied that it has pleased you.

Tracking

Tracking is a challenge not offered in any other type of training. Tracking is the ability of the dog to follow a specific scent at the will of the handler. The AKC awards two titles, Tracking Dog (TD) and Tracking Dog Excellent (TDX). A dog must earn a TD before it can compete for its TDX, which is a very high honor due to the difficulty of the course. The TDX course will be on more difficult terrain, of greater length with cross tracks, with several articles placed on the track.

Because there are many more dogs trying for these titles than there are competitions available, dogs must first pass a qualifying test and must be at least six months old. AKC regulations specify a track of 440 to 500 yards. There is a stake at the start of the track and another stake 30 yards into the track to show the direction of the track. These stakes are the only indicators of direction and track. If your dog makes a poor start, you are allowed to restart once, provided your dog has not passed the second stake. The track must be at least 30 minutes old and no more than two hours old.

AS A PARTICIPANT SEES IT

Margie Douma from Monmouth, Oregon, started working on tracking with the Luckiamute Dog Training Club. She explains:

Tracking tests require about five acres of land for each dog entered. Most tests are limited to fewer than 10 dogs because of the space requirements. Most clubs only hold one test per year. Tracking tests do not make money and require two judges, several track-layers, and a great deal of work. Needless to say, there are many more dogs ready to be tested than there are available tests. Entry into a tracking test is by drawing. Entries are collected until

Winterset Marks Brigadoon, owned by Enid Bloome, completed a Tracking degree at just nineteen months, with proof to show for it.

the closing date, then thrown into a hat for a public drawing. Dogs are listed as they are drawn, up to the entry limit. The rest of the entries are drawn for "Alternate" numbers.

Many people travel great distances to participate in a tracking test. In order to help ensure that these limited spaces are not taken by dogs that are unprepared for the test, AKC requires that each dog must have passed a certifying track. The certifying track must be equivalent to a regular test track. However, you need only one judge, who must be a licensed AKC tracking judge, and you can schedule the test yourself—as sort of a private test. The judge plans the test and if your dog successfully completes the track, you receive four original certifying letters indicating that your dog has passed a track. The letters are good for one year. If your dog fails four tests in that time, or if the year passes without getting in tests, your dog will have to be recertified.

The track-giving club usually provides food for judges and exhibitors and passes out awards. In a tracking test, there is no score, only a pass or fail.

Teaching a Labrador Retriever to track is an excellent stress reduction sport for both handler and dog. Labradors have a natural talent for following their noses and need only a little guidance and encouragement to become experts. Training for tracking generally consists of helping, encouraging, and rewarding your dog. Naturally, they love it. It's a game you and your dog should enjoy.

A dog's sense of smell is tremendously better than yours. Once your dog understands his job, he enjoys finding that glove you so carelessly dropped out in the park or field. Every time your dog successfully maneuvers a corner, finds the article, works a track at a run, you will be amazed at this ability to follow a scrap of scent and distinguish that scent from all others in an open field. This is a great activity for young puppies, the immature dog that's not ready for show, a stressed-out show dog, an older dog that's retired but still active, and every dog in between.

AKC tracking tests require a dog to follow a human trail for between 440 and 500 yards for a TD. The track-layer must be a stranger to the dog. The track will be over fairly open ground and must have at least two turns. At the end of the track, the dog must find and indicate an article (such as a glove or wallet of a dark color, but no smaller than wallet size) that the track-layer has left. The track is laid one-half to one hour before the dog begins working and cannot be more than two hours old. There is no time limit as long as the dog continues to work.

No guiding of the dog is allowed at any time during the test. The handler must work the dog on a lead no less than 20 and no more than 40 feet in length. Acute angles and crosstracks are not allowed.

Labradors are excellent trackers—and excellent hunters. You will need to work to teach them to follow the trail instead of relying on their hunting ability to "air-scent" their way to the article. Also, Labradors tend to quarter so much that they lose the track, especially at corners and in windy weather. A tracking dog must *follow the track* so that, if used in a real situation, it does not miss clues/evidence left along the way. In tracking, the means is as important as the end.

The most difficult task in tracking is teaching yourself to trust your dog. In tracking, the judge and track-layers have maps. There are no indicators for the handler on the track except a start flag and a direction flag set about 30 feet down the track. Past the start, the handler has no idea where the track goes. Many tracks have been nonqualifying because the handler pulled the dog off the track. Train well and always remember who has the better nose.

Each dog is different, has a different style, and progresses in a different way. Ms. Douma said:

I have a bitch that progressed from a straight track to multiple turns at a dead run on her first day out tracking. My younger bitch did only straight, double-laid tracks the first couple of sessions and did not appear to be actually tracking until the third session. Don't worry if the dog doesn't seem to "get it" the first time out. Believe me, it *will* get the idea, and once it does, you'll probably be getting your exercise trying to keep up. But take heart; even a fast learner will slow down as the tracks become harder and you extend the "age" of the track. Slowing down will help the dog's accuracy and your heart and lungs.

The most important rule to remember in tracking is that BOTH YOU AND YOUR DOG SHOULD BE HAVING FUN! So go out, and let your dog take you for a walk.

In tracking, as in any other performance event, there are a dozen things that can go wrong, from handler error to a dog having a bad day. My dog and I didn't pass our first tracking test, probably due to both of those factors. But we're learning. And it is fun. FUN? Jogging through a rough field, with standing water six inches deep, for 500 yards—does that qualify as fun?

TRUST YOUR PUPPY

Your puppy understands scent from its earliest days in the whelping pen. It uses its nose to locate its dam and places such as a toilet area. You can make tracking an interesting game for your puppy, which will instill confidence in it as well as in you. You can break the elements of the lessons into small sections. Make up a lesson plan for each item to cover, so you can be consistent and orderly in what you ask of your dog.

Each lesson plan should specify equipment needed, the objective, and what must be done. Write down items that make each lesson satisfactory or unsatisfactory. Keep a file of lesson plans and make notes about what happens each time.

Puppies two to three months old can begin to learn a word such as "glovie" while playing with you indoors. Toss the glove around until the puppy associates the word with the object it will later be asked to find in the field. Since you may also plan to do retrieving with your puppy, tug-of-war games with the glove are not suitable.

Next get your puppy used to a nonrestrictive harness. At this point your puppy has not had any obedience training, so it should be happy to pull you around a field. Lay short tracks and use little bits of food as rewards. Gradually add corners, one at a time. Keep the lessons short, but repeat the important elements to encourage correct behavior. Do not have the tracks too old or too long for a young puppy. Make a game of it, and keep the puppy enthusiastic with lots of praise.

Most puppies that have not been exposed to obedience training will concentrate on a track dotted with food tidbits far longer than they would pay attention in obedience lessons, where their attention span is short. The puppy will learn that you are pleased with its ability to think for itself.

A puppy will use its nose naturally, so actually you are just guiding it to do so in a way that will eventually pass a tracking test. First your dog will learn that it must follow a specific scent, which leads to a reward. A puppy will delight in finding food, while an older dog will get satisfaction from pleasing you. The puppy must learn that the scent can make turns, which, as time goes on in the training sessions, become more acute angles.

Until a puppy is six months old, tracks should not be longer than 300 yards. Train during early morning hours or whenever scenting conditions are optimum.

The dog must learn to cast about an area if it loses the scent. *Casting* is moving back and forth in a sort of semicircle so as to cover all possible grounds on each side of the last-known positive scent. The handler must not get in the way, nor do anything to distract the dog when it is casting.

An adult dog with previous obedience training may be reluctant to get out in front of its handler and look for a track, and it may not want to pull on the tracking line. Adult dogs that have been taught through obedience training (or from field training hand signals) to look to the handler for signals when they aren't sure what to do may worry about doing something wrong, making mistakes, and getting corrections. The dog must learn to make independent decisions and work independently, as it will in advanced obedience scent discrimination and advanced hunting situations.

The tracking dog is taught to follow a track when he thinks it is right by pulling on the leash. A handler/trainer shouldn't second-guess his dog and must never make a correction unless he is absolutely certain the dog is in error. The dog needs your encouragement, so you will always go with him when he is right. There is a saying in tracking that "it is always better to go with your dog when he is wrong than to refuse to go with him when he is right."

A puppy gains great confidence as a result of the handler following it around and believing in it. This bond, which is developed between puppy and handler, will be with them for the dog's lifetime. Believing your dog is the foundation of all dog work. It is up to the dog's handler to train consistently and thoroughly to encourage reliability. The handler himself must be trained to recognize what the dog is doing and never to correct the dog when it is the handler's fault that something has gone wrong. Do not put your dog in a situation that will have a bad ending. All training sessions should end on a positive note, especially if there have been some areas of failure.

A six-week training session for a puppy would include teaching the puppy to follow a specific scent the first week. The second week the puppy learns that following a specific scent leads to a reward. In the third week, teach the puppy that the scent can change direction—keep it simple with one-turn tracks. In the fourth week teach the puppy that the scent can go in any direction—two-turn tracks. In the fifth week teach the dog acute angle turns and to work all around the handler in case the scent is lost. In the sixth week, work on progressive track aging and add another turn. After that you will work on "reading" your dog and vary the conditions and terrain more and more. You will now add problems of wind, temperature, time of day, and rain. A good tracking dog must be trained in all sorts of conditions. Those that will be involved in search and rescue will be called out in the worst of weather and field conditions.

Training scenarios should become more and more difficult, not only to challenge the dog and maintain its skills, but also to make tracking tests seem

Chilbrook Hurricane Heather, CD, owned by Debby Kay, worked on the Douglas Point Research Project (NERF funded) locating "Hunting Box Turtles." *Debby Kay*

easy to the dog. You and your dog will have mutual confidence because you have practiced in every conceivable situation. This is the one area where you are entirely dependent on your dog's ability and intelligence. You must not let your dog down by being the weak member of the team, nor should you interfere with the dog when it is working. A delicate balance and understanding are crucial. Verbal praise from you at the right time means everything to your dog. Whatever you do, don't lose your temper or patience.

EQUIPMENT NEEDED

For tracking you will need the following equipment:

1. A non-restrictive harness, made of nylon or leather, which does not interfere with the full fore and aft movement of the dog's legs.

2. A 40-foot tracking line (maximum length allowed by AKC). It's best to use ³/₈" nylon rope with a decent snap on the end. Nylon web lines aren't as suitable, as they flap around in a heavy wind. If you use a wide, web line in calm weather, switch to a lighter tracking line in windy or wet weather. Strong winds will whip a heavier line around, giving unwanted jerks to the dog. You might want to tie a knot 20 feet along the line, as that is the minimum distance at which you are supposed to work the dog unless it comes up to you.

3. Articles to be found usually include a pair of cloth gloves and a pair of leather gloves. Gloves will be used in the test, but it's a good idea to have something else along, such as a wallet, so in the event you have to terminate the track, you can allow the dog to be successful in finding something you value.

4. Marking flags, such as wire surveyor flags.

5. A log book to record all actions of your dog. Include weather conditions in your observations as well as time of day.

WEATHER AND FIELD CONSIDERATIONS

You must learn how weather conditions affect scenting conditions, and you must be able to identify upwind and downwind. If it is extremely hot, do your tracking very early in the day to get the best scenting conditions. Some dogs, especially older animals, are unable to perform well in extreme heat.

Generally, moist conditions make tracking easier. A light rain, after a track has been laid, may even freshen the track and make it easier for the dog to follow. However, a torrential downpour will make the task more difficult.

Cold weather does not affect scenting ability. Dogs can detect articles even under snow. Remember that well-trained Labradors can find avalanche victims under 70 feet of snow.

You can use light snow to your advantage in training because you can actually see where the track is. Since you can see turns and curves, you can see exactly how your dog handles them. If your dog has become "flag-wise," you can train it in snow without flags. Cross-track training is also easier in snow or heavy frost. The handler gains confidence in these conditions from knowing where the track really is located.

Tracking in heavy snow is quite different, and dogs that do this well may have to be retrained when working in heavy vegetation in warm weather because of the difference in sounds and smells emitted from crushed vegetation. Dogs may track with a sense of hearing, as well as smell, as they can hear sounds of distress from injured or disturbed micro-organisms and plants on the track line.[1]

Dogs' senses are very acute and they may switch from ground scenting to wind scenting. The older the track is, the more difficult it is for the dog to follow. Also, as the amount of vegetation declines, it is more difficult for the dog to track. There are fewer surfaces for scent to adhere to and fewer micro-organisms and plants to sustain telltale damage. Pavement (or any extremely hard surface) is one of the most difficult surfaces for tracking.

Ground cover will affect a test's passing rate, as will wind and weather conditions. Scent adheres better to some things than others; for example, an overgrazed area will cut the pass rate probably in half. Track-layers have to be well versed in types of vegetation and article placement. In addition, they also need to have actually trained (or helped to train) a tracking dog to be well qualified to lay a TDX primary track.

Handlers have to learn how to "read" their dogs. This means that any given dog has its own way of letting you know it is on the trail, or has found the object. Your dog's body language will indicate if it is on track, working to find a track, or on the wrong track. Handlers also have to let their dogs do the tracking and not interfere with the direction indicated by the dog.

---

[1] *William G. Syrotuck.* Scent and the Scenting Dog, *Arner Publications, 1972.*

Handlers must believe in their dogs, just as blind people believe in their guide dogs. Actually, dogs can learn to follow scent with very little training, whereas it takes much longer for a handler to learn how to "read" his/her dog. The handler has to recognize each individual dog's signal that it knows where it is by signs such as a certain earset, a twitch of the tail, or a tug on the line. Once a handler and dog have this bond, there is no limit to what and where they can track successfully.

Dogs must be trained so that they will be consistent and reliable. The ability, intelligence, and decisiveness of the dog make it successful in a way that is a tremendous confidence builder. One can see how the same qualities that make a Labrador an excellent tracking dog make it excel in related endeavors, such as search and rescue and guide work.

chapter 16

Labradors as Detector Dogs

Labradors are well-qualified to perform as detector dogs because of their inherent trainability or willingness to please, intelligence, agility, endurance, and tremendous scenting powers. Picking up game falls in this category, but additional services performed by Labradors to assist their owners or handlers include leading the blind, aiding the deaf, drug detection, explosive detection, arson detection, and search and rescue work at all types of disasters.

The dog's ability to use its nose sets it apart from humans. The canine nose is many, many times more sensitive than a human nose. We have five million olfactory cells compared to a long-nosed dog's two hundred and twenty million.[1] A dog's olfactory system allows it to discriminate between very minute amounts of similar odors. Dogs can sense temperature changes, thus allowing them to find still-living humans covered by avalanche, earthquake, or tornado debris. Dogs also breathe in such a way as to rapidly exhale stale scent so as to clean off their receptors (chemoreceptors, vomeronasal receptors, and infrared receptors which sense temperature differences), after which fresh scent can be inhaled and analyzed.

The Labrador has the brain to back up its scenting ability. Once the Labrador understands what scent you want detected, it will search for that particular scent. A detector dog can be imprinted for any particular odor. Labradors can be cross-trained for more than one scent.

Labradors begin to use their scenting powers as newborns. Even little puppies can be imprinted with a specific scent at five or six weeks. However, normally detector Labradors would not begin serious training until they are between one and two years old.

---

[1]*Robicheaux, Jack.* Basic Narc Detector Dog Training, *Mrs. Vitas Droscher, 1991.*

Debby Kay and K-9 Dingo (Chilbrook Mandingo), 1989, the first toxic waste detection K-9. Dingo was also a certified narcotic dog.

EARLY DETECTOR DOGS

World War II was the turning point for Labradors being introduced into service. "Dogs for Defense" was a volunteer program incorporated in January 1942, with David L. Elliot of the famous Wingan Kennels on Long Island, New York, as director of training regulations. During both World Wars dogs, mostly German Shepherds, performed messenger service or served as sentry dogs. There was also a need for "point dogs" for alerting to the presence of the enemy. One small group of "M" dogs was trained for mine detection work, and some Labradors did perform this task during the invasion of Sicily and Italy.

Labradors were responsible for detecting the mines on the roads to Cassino, Italy. Patrols were suffering losses, and it was the uncanny ability of the Labrador to locate the mines that had been placed around the castle that helped the mine recovery soldiers accomplish their mission. Mine detection dogs go on maneuvers with the military. Dogs have detected buried explosives and weapons up to four feet below the ground surface as long as one year past the time of burial. Labradors proved their worth in Vietnam not only because of their excellent nose and trainability, but because they were able to adapt to the harsh climate and experienced no adverse foot conditions (which plagued other breeds). Labradors have a tough constitution and do not mind working in bad weather.

Fairfax Downey's book *Dogs for Defense* cites the Labrador as "more numerous in the U.S. than any of the other Retriever breeds. Highly favored by the British Army, he is noted for his nose, ability in the water, and endurance."[2]

During World War II the ability of the Labrador to detect complicated scents of items other than game was not commonly known. In Vietnam Labradors were used for tracking in combat situations. It was not until the 1960s that the Labrador was generally accepted for use in law enforcement as a detector dog.

Chief Cahill, who had worked at Scotland Yard, promoted the Labrador when he was with the Washington, D.C. Metro Police Department. Using a dog named "Narco," Chief Cahill demonstrated the valuable work of the Labrador in detecting drugs, which at that time were becoming a prevalent problem.

The U.S. Customs Service began using Labradors in 1970 in its detector program. Today, Labradors serve the military and police and other law enforcement groups, where they have earned a place of respect.

Most dogs used by the U.S. Customs Service are rescued from pounds and humane societies. The Narcotic Detection School at Front Royal, Virginia, sends out procurement teams to visit animal shelters looking for promising dogs. Labradors are sought after because, according to Tom Iverson, a District K-9 Supervisor, "We want a dog with a strong drive to search, and we can build on that if the dog has a strong desire to retrieve. We want the type of dog that will retrieve and play and never quit."[3]

Other uses of Labradors as detector dogs include the specialized jobs of evidence searches; finding cadavers, toxic waste, chemicals, gas pipeline leaks; biological detection, which includes unusual jobs such as detection of the peak estrus cycle in cattle for accurate artificial breeding; gypsy moth egg detection; and various target species detection.

Debby Kay, president of International Detector Dogs, Ltd. (IDD), turned her hobby of detector dog training into a full-time occupation early in the 1980s.

---

[2]*Downey, Fairfax*. Dogs for Defense, *1955, p. 30.*
[3]Dogs USA Annual, *1992, vol. 7, no. 1, p. 215.*

Ms. Kay has been actively involved in dogs for more than 30 years, successfully training and breeding obedience dogs, field trial dogs, and bench show winners. She also participated in the Seeing Eye, Inc., breeding program during its reorganization stages in the 1970s, both as an expert consultant on Labrador Retrievers and in supplying foundation breeding stock. She has also supplied breeding stock for Guide Dogs for the Blind (California) and Leader Dogs for the Blind (Michigan).

Her most challenging work has been in the field of detector dogs. When Ms. Kay began this work she told me:

> I have shared many rewarding hours working with Labradors over the years but perhaps the most interesting of all my experiences has been training Labs as detector dogs. The Labs chosen for this work are indeed a unique lot—what most breeders and show people would consider rejects. To the people whose lives they touch, though, they are very special.
>
> Good drug detector dogs are very strongly, intensely driven to work—that is to say, they are hyperactive. They constantly want to play and retrieve and will pester you incessantly to do so. The training is based on this through a process of association. The dog learns that when, and only when, he finds the desired substance, he gets to play. At no time are the dogs ever addicted to the drugs they are to find.
>
> For the explosives and accelerant detection dogs, a slightly less hyper dog is chosen, and a reward of food is more often used. The dogs I get for detector training are those that have not worked well in other situations, such as dogs that chew, bark, climb on things, can't be housebroken, are stubborn, etc. They range from one to five years.
>
> Working with one bad dog is difficult enough, but imagine living and working with as many as eight bad dogs at one time. It will definitely keep you alert. With patience and persistence, though, all bad habits can be redirected and channeled into good working habits; in about four to six months a polished working dog emerges. The key is working every day, repetition, and lots of praise.
>
> Working for a private firm gives me the opportunity to travel and work in a variety of environments. I most often travel with a two-year-old Lab, Sam, who was donated by Mary Baker of New York. Sam is trained to find concealed weapons and explosives. He loves his work so much, he continues to work even when 'off duty,' which has led to some interesting experiences.
>
> On one occasion, while waiting for a West Coast flight, Sam started sniffing a row of carry-on bags that passengers had lined up near the ticket counter. To my astonishment he became alert to an attache case. Before I had time to fully react, the case was picked up by a gentleman who later turned out to be a sky marshall. There was a concealed weapon in that attache case.
>
> Another time at a New York airport Sam's inquisitive nose nearly blew the cover of a plainclothes policeman on stakeout. Fortunately our plane was boarding and I was able to get Sam, who was intently staring at the

unnerved officer, out of the area quickly. There is no doubt the dogs thoroughly enjoy their work; they even take the constant travel in the easy stride for which the Labrador is so well-known.

ARSON DOGS

The Federal Bureau of Alcohol, Tobacco and Firearms (BATF) worked with the Connecticut State Police to promote the use of Labradors as accelerant detection dogs for use during fire investigations. The BATF had determined that dogs could be conditioned to respond to an accelerant odor. Dogs were found to be an invaluable tool, saving time and money by assisting investigators in determining the origin of suspicious fires.

At a suspected arson fire scene, samples must be collected and tested for the presence of flammable material(s). This is often a time-consuming and tedious job. Hundreds of suspected samples are taken and tested, costing thousands of dollars and many man-hours. Virtually every sample indicated by the dog becomes positive evidence as determined by laboratory tests. As a result of the dog's work, better samples are obtained in a shorter time.

Mechanical sniffers are not as sensitive as the Labrador. Field accelerant detection instruments may give false-positive indications because many classes of compounds are formed by fire, which chemically alters synthetic materials. Because of the complex chemical reactions, all evidence found by mechanical detectors has to be submitted for further analysis by gas chromatography. This puts a burden on crime labs, whereas K-9 samples are fewer and most often (but not always) test positive. Using a dog also results in sending the right samples to the labs. If many samples are picked up at the scene of a fire, they will be taken inside and lined up. Only those that the dog alerts to will be sent to the laboratory.

In 1986 Maryland State Fire Marshall Rocco J. Gabriele learned that the BATF was working with the Connecticut State Police in training a dog to detect accelerants. Fire Marshall Gabriele assigned John H. Farrell, then Chief Deputy State Fire Marshall, to further investigate the possibility of using dogs for arson detection in Maryland.

At the time a black Labrador named Mattie was being trained by the Connecticut State Police using a concept developed by BATF forensic chemist Richard S. Strobel and BATF canine trainer Robert Noll. These men found that a dog can be trained to detect the difference between the odors of accelerants and other similar chemical gases normally found at fire scenes. Dogs that are "conditioned" to respond to accelerant odor have far greater sensitivity than field accelerant detection devices and forensic laboratories. Dogs are trained to identify accelerants from the three categories that start fires: petroleum-based, chemical-based, and natural (such as turpentine).

Mattie was the prototype for an arson dog. She became the model for all accelerant detection dogs. Mattie and her handler, Trooper Douglas Lancelot,

Arson dog Mya with the Kentucky Fire Marshall's office on a fire scene. These dogs can locate any one of 17 flammable liquids in concentrations of less than one part per million. *Photo courtesy International Detector Dogs, Ltd.*

were part of the BATF National Response Team, ready to respond to fires when requested by a local agency. Mattie was trained to detect a scent and sit quietly. When asked to confirm, she would put her nose on the exact spot. Mattie was able to alert to a scent buried under many feet of debris.

Chief Farrell had a big black Labrador that he had purchased for goose hunting. On Maryland's Eastern Shore, Farrell learned of a seven-month-old untrained pup for sale at a local farm and went to look at the dog. The owner clapped two pans together to call the dog. The big black pup came running and Farrell put his hand up toward the dog. The pup didn't cringe so Farrell determined it hadn't been beaten. The dog then retrieved a stick for Farrell. "His eyes followed me as we worked," recalled Farrell. He bought Barney on the spot.

Chief Farrell, after spending time with the Connecticut State Police, began training Barney for arson detection work. Part of Barney's training consisted of using a carousel, a device with four-foot arms extending from a center post about six inches off the ground. A one-gallon can containing burnt material was placed on each post. The burnt material was also placed on the ground around the carousel. By using constant repetition, Barney was able to determine which can contained the charred or burnt material that had been contaminated by the accelerant.

Barney's training for arson K-9 also included conditioning such as running and swimming, retrieving, obedience training, and socialization, as well as disregarding distractions. The conditioning program helped to relieve the stress placed on the dog by the demanding parts of the program, thus making a better adjusted animal for the job. Barney was desensitized to distractions in crowds, elevators, and airports, and from vehicles such as helicopters and fire engines.

Chief Farrell experimented with various training methods, and as a result, Barney was trained in all the detector dog fields of expertise: arson, bombs, and narcotics. Chief Farrell says, "A single-purpose dog is better,

Chief John Farrell and Barney at the fire detection training wheel. A substance that could start a fire is in only one of the cans. The dog is trained to sniff and alert the handler by sitting close to the suspicious can. *Jan Churchill*

Find a needle in a haystack—that's exactly what it is like for a detector dog at a fire scene. During this exercise K-9 Nikki is shown zeroing in on the location of a single drop of hydrocarbon liquid. The detector dog's ability to do such fine discrimination is one reason these dogs are such valuable tools to investigators. *Debby Kay*

but not all law enforcement agencies can afford such dogs, so the dogs are cross-trained."

Farrell selects arson K-9 dogs only if they respond to him. He will not train with the electric shocking collars used by some field trial trainers. "If the dog doesn't work for me, I get another dog," says Farrell. "I want to see that dog happy, with his tail up."

Barney was the second dog in the world to work as an accelerant detective. One case that made Barney famous was a fire that claimed the lives of three children. Early the next morning after the deadly fire, Barney and Chief Farrell arrived at the scene and began an examination of the two-story wooden home. Barney alerted in three separate areas in the home, confirming the findings of investigators that a suspected flammable liquid had started the fire. Then Barney went to police headquarters, where he picked the suspect out of a five-man lineup by detecting kerosene on the man's clothing. Charged with three counts of murder in the first degree by arson, the suspect pleaded guilty and was sentenced to life without parole on all three charges. Barney and Chief

Farrell reenacted this case for the filming of a "True Detective" TV segment dealing with the effectiveness of dogs in arson investigations.

Barney has demonstrated that Labradors' noses are far more sensitive than arson laboratory equipment. A controlled test was set up by Atlantic City, New Jersey, where accelerant samples were placed in open containers and allowed to evaporate. Each week, samples were checked, and when their crime lab could no longer detect flammable vapors, but their dogs could, the samples were sent to the New York State Fire Marshall. The dogs in New York alerted to the samples but their lab could not detect any flammable vapors. The samples were then sent to Chief Farrell at the Maryland State Police Lab, which could not detect a flammable vapor. A year after sensitive laboratory equipment could no longer detect the accelerants, Barney still 'alerted' on the samples. According to Chief Farrell, "We are not talking about parts per million here; it could be parts per trillion."

In addition to his detecting duties, Barney goes hunting, not only for geese, but he also flushes and retrieves quail and pheasants. Chief Farrell works him hard enough to burn some calories every day to keep the dog in excellent shape.

BOMB DOGS

Labradors were brought into bomb detection when bomb threats in airports, courthouses, and other places posed a threat. Bomb scares on airplanes can be investigated by dogs trained to sniff out bombs. Trained dogs were used in conjunction with a military program about 20 years ago, with 18 teams strategically located so that if a flight encountered a bomb scare, within 30 minutes it could land at an airport that had a dog team. Eventually the Federal Aviation Administration (FAA) enlarged the program so that now approximately 80 teams are available across the country.

Training is done at Lackland Air Force Base in San Antonio, Texas, during a three-month course. Retrievers learning detector work get training with obedience and agility work first, after which they progress to scent work. When the dogs are finally on real duty with their handlers, they look forward to "work." Sniffing for bombs is fun and these dogs are eager to go. When there are no real threats, the handlers set up training problems to keep the dogs on their toes.

The FAA certifies each team once a year over a six-day evaluation period. A high pass rate of 92.6 percent is required for searching large planes, small planes, luggage, warehouses, terminals, and motor vehicles. Dogs must perform very carefully. They can't make an aggressive response, such as touching a box or barking, in case of a hidden switch or a voice-activated bomb. The dogs "alert" with a sit and expect a food reward. Because bomb threats are very serious, usually two dog teams will work an area to make sure a handler doesn't miss a dog's quick reaction, which could go unnoticed since it is a passive response.

Bomb detector dogs are usually chosen from calmer animals, whereas narcotic dogs need aggressive behavior, as well as great confidence and drive. Bomb dog training takes a week or two longer than narcotics training to make sure the dog will perform with a passive response. The bomb dog must hunt with intensity and then be willing to sit quietly and look in the indicated direction just in case any movement or word might explode the device.

SELECTION AND TRAINING OF LABRADOR DETECTOR DOGS

The selection process is a learned skill in which the handler considers the conditions under which a dog will work and by which method it will be trained. There are two basic training methods, one that uses a play/praise as a reward and the other, which uses food to reinforce the desired behavior. In both methods the dog learns by repetition and reward that if it performs according to the handler's wishes, it will get its favorite reward. Each dog must be analyzed as an individual, because the reactions of any dog to given circumstances may not be the same. Dogs do not think or reason like humans, so it takes an experienced trainer to comprehend or "read" the dog's responses to given situations.

Unlike guide dog schools, law enforcement agencies do not have breeding programs. Many of the dogs they get are "throw-away dogs" from SPCAs or Labrador rescue programs. Mattie was a reject from a guide dog school.

The selection process, according to trainer Debby Kay of IDD, is limited to one- to two-year-old dogs. The dog must have enjoyed its puppyhood and be beyond the teething stage. By one year of age, the trainer can get a pretty good idea of the dog's general disposition. Another reason for starting with a young dog is so that, after it is fully trained, it will have a good many years of working life ahead of it for whichever police department or agency invests in the trained animal.

Several tests are given to potential detector dogs before they are chosen for training. The place for the testing, as well as the tester, is unfamiliar to the dog. The area chosen must have an open, grassy field, a building with a variety of floor coverings, and a few simple obstacles. The dog is not fed on the day of the test.

Debby Kay [4] says that there are a few simple tests that all detector dogs must pass. The dogs must demonstrate that they are sociable, both with other animals and with people. Dogs that are too animal-aggressive will be easily

---

[4]*For more information, see* The Complete Guide to Training Accelerant Detector Dogs *by Debby Kay.*

Detector dogs must be very self-confident in difficult situations and curious by nature, as every place needs to be examined at a crime scene. Shown here is K-9 Nikki with handler Pat Brandenburg during a training exercise. *Debby Kay*

distracted, which makes them less effective as detector dogs. The candidate should be willing to go anywhere with a stranger and do so in a happy and confident manner. "You have no idea how many dogs I evaluate that flunk out on this point, especially Labradors."

The dog candidates are tested on all types of surfaces to show that they are not afraid of anything, including ceramic tile and open grating. Kay says, "If the dogs in any of these tests panic, they are rejected and not subjected to any further testing."

Detector dogs travel a great deal, so any dog that gets carsick is rejected; because of time restrictions, problems like this are not worked out. The same is true for noise shyness, as the detector dog must have a rock-steady set of nerves. General health is also considered. Dogs with allergies, joint problems, skin problems, eye conditions, or any health problem that would interfere with working are not accepted for training.

The dogs that pass the above criteria must now pass a test to evaluate their scenting acuity and drive. This involves a great deal of educated interpretation on the part of the tester. Kay says, "I can only explain the general procedure, as it is difficult to put the rest in words. For the play/praise method, a rolled-up towel is introduced to the dog in the open, grassy field. The tester tries to get the dog excited about the towel. The more wildly excited the dog gets about the towel, the better. When the towel is thrown a short distance the dog must retrieve it with enthusiasm. When the dog returns with the towel, if he fights to hold on to it, so much the better. Actually, the best a dog can do on this test is to make a mad dash after the towel and run away, refusing to give it up under any circumstances. In other words, he claims it for himself, which ends the exercise."

This is contrary to what a field retriever is asked to do. Dogs in the field are expected to bring a bird directly back to the handler, deliver it to hand, and give it up gently without injury to the bird. A dog going into training will be working in his specialized area. An intelligent Labrador knows the difference between detecting and sport-type bird hunting, and if given the opportunity for a day's gunning work, this Labrador will make retrieves to hand in the manner expected of a dual-purpose Labrador.

The next step in testing for a potential detector is to check his desire to find and intensity of search by throwing the rolled-up towel into tall grass in the field so that it is hidden from sight. As the dog searches for the towel, the tester evaluates the intensity with which the dog searches and its ability to use its nose. Marking ability is not graded at all. The exercise is repeated several times to check the length of the dog's attention span. Finally the towel is thrown under a vehicle, and then inside a vehicle, to see if the dog will search out these places willingly.

For the food training method, the tester wants the same intensity as in the retrieval method, but with the dog's interest directed toward food. The best candidate is a dog that would do anything to get food, regardless of the distractions or obstacles. These dogs are tested by placing food in places that are difficult to reach or hard to find.

Following the selection process, the selected dogs are paired with their handlers. Normally the dog will work with one handler with whom it will spend the rest of its life. Kay says, "Rarely will a dog be reassigned to a new handler unless the handler suddenly dies before the dog has reached retirement age. Detector dogs lead a wonderful life. They are well cared for and loved and most importantly, perform a very necessary and useful job."

The training program takes from 12 to 16 weeks. It always takes a minimum of three weeks for imprinting to commit to a dog's long-term memory. Imprinting is a process of association based on Pavlov's experiments, which demonstrated how conditioned reflexes could be developed by associating a desired response with a reward. It starts with a particular scent, an accelerant or certain chemical compounds. In the early stages of imprinting, the dog gets a reward—food or a favorite toy. The most direct method is to use food. For the toy reward, the dog needs a strong urge to retrieve, as the toy will be thrown for the dog's pleasure in retrieving. There are limits to this sort of training, as dogs that do this may overrun objects. Also, not all Labradors have a strong desire to retrieve.

Imprinting works through play, praise, or food, but methods have changed as trainers now know that some clever dogs will lie to get food. They will give false indications or alerts by sitting just to get extra tidbits. Even the dog that loves to play may "lie" just to get the ball or toy reward. In these cases, verbal praise rewards are best. Labradors can be extremely intelligent and outsmart their handlers unless the trainers are aware, very early on, of what the dog is doing. Trainers have to know how to "read" or interpret all the dog's actions and to understand the dog's thinking ability. Dogs that work demonstrate much more intelligence than dogs that lie around all day. Labradors that are "couch potatoes" become very dull, "like robots," says Chief Farrell.

TRAINING MUST BE REINFORCED

K-9 dogs must be retrained and evaluated (in writing) every 30 days even though the dogs are fully trained and on call 24 hours a day with their respective handlers for response to possible arsons. The written reports are used when the officers go to court to prove that the dogs are tested regularly and are in top working condition when used to detect evidence at a fire or crime scene. If the agencies didn't have written reports of testing and training, they would have nothing to go back to. In court the agency will be challenged to prove that the dog is working regularly. Written records help the officer prove that dogs are worked and training is on a strict scheduled basis.

To reinforce training procedures, the dogs travel to fires that have been determined to be accidental. With the owner's permission, the dogs walk around the premises to get them used to actual odors of burned items. The handlers can also set up tests at these fire scenes by placing drops of gasoline or some other accelerant to reinforce the dog's ability to seek and find.

Scenting conditions will affect a dog's ability to work. Some target scents are easier to detect during the cooler evening and night temperatures, while others may be more readily found in hot air. Air movement both inside a building and outside must be considered. Scenting conditions should be taken into consideration during practice sessions to give a dog a chance to work under all conditions.

The arson K-9 handler will work the dog systematically at the fire scene in a clockwise direction from the outer part of the building to the center. Hand signals are used to indicate to the dog where it should look. The dog is given

During field training exercises, accelerant detection dogs learn to track arsonists from the scene of a fire, often locating valuable evidence. Here K-9 Nikki finds a can outside a fire scene and will track the arsonist from the crime scene, taking the scent from the gas can used during the crime. *Debby Kay*

the command "seek." When the dog locates an accelerant it "tells" the handler by sitting in the area where the odor originates. The handler may then ask the dog to "show me" the specific area of the odor, at which time the dog puts its nose on that spot. Investigators then take a sample to submit to the forensic laboratory for detailed analysis.

In addition to the fire scene, the arson dog will also search vehicles and alert to those which may have transported accelerants. They will search the clothing of suspects and will also alert to suspicious people who may be in a crowd at a fire scene.

Chief Farrell says, "The smaller dog is better for our work as the dog may have to be carried up or down a ladder by holding the dog up over your shoulders (like a shepherd's lamb) in case stairs are burned out or unsafe." Weak floors are always a hazard at fire scenes.

Arson dogs live with their handlers and are part of the family, which is important in the bonding process. The handler is the only person who feeds, grooms and cares for the dog. However, in those departments where a dog has two handlers, it usually favors one even though it will work for both. "It's sort of a personality thing," observed Chief Farrell.

Even though the dogs live at home, they maintain a working posture at all times. They aren't allowed to run and play with the neighbors' dogs. During obedience and agility work, they have been trained to perform five to six feet away from other dogs without being distracted. They can't even turn their heads to look at the nearby dogs. They have to learn not to be distracted by other dogs that may be around fire scenes or wherever they are working.

Actually, the training enhances the natural ability of the Labrador to hunt until it finds the assigned quarry, be it ducks or bombs. The Labrador wants to please the person who praises it and really enjoys working for a purpose. Chief Farrell, after many decades of training Labradors, feels that Labradors lose their natural ability in three generations if they don't train and work regularly. Unfortunately the popularity of the breed has forced the backyard breeder into the business, which, says Farrell, "will lead to its downfall—Labradors are too good at everything—it's in their genes to be quiet and sociable."

Fire marshals take their dogs to work every day. It is important to have the dog lie down when it travels. If it stands when the vehicle is in motion, it puts too much stress on the joints, which over a period of time does damage. The safest way for a dog to travel is in a crate where it is not only lying down, but also has some protection in case of an accident.

Summing up the program, Maryland Chief Fire Marshal Farrell stated, "A trained arson canine will not conclusively prove arson. It is an investigative tool, not a final conclusion. Establishing arson requires extensive fire and police investigation into the origin and circumstances of a fire. However, the canine accelerant detection program has become another useful weapon in an investigator's arsenal to combat arson, saving time and supplying more accurate evidence."

Since the inception of the Arson K-9 program, many state and local law enforcement agencies and fire departments, as well as the BATF, are using trained dogs. Labradors have been the outstanding performers since this work began. Some of the Labradors have come from unknown bloodlines while others have well-known pedigrees. The first yellow Labrador detector dog, Nellie, was a great-great-granddaughter of Ch. Spenrock Heatheredge Mariner, one of this writer's favorite dogs, which she imported from England. Mariner's name will be found behind many guide dogs for the blind, and he was also sire of Vicky Creamer's Ch. Milgrove Special Amie, the first Labrador to become the highest ranking obedience dog, all breeds.

NARCOTICS DOGS

A narcotics dog must be bold with an intense desire to retrieve. These dogs learn to detect four basic types of odors:

1. Marijuana and hashish (the latter being a derivative of the former).
2. Cocaine.
3. Heroin.
4. Chemicals, such as those used in methamphetamines.

Additional odors are introduced depending on current drugs of choice in an area. Drug owners try to disguise the scent of the drugs to fool narcotics dogs by adding adulterants such as sugar, laundry detergent, pepper, or coffee. Anyone who has trained a dog for scent discrimination will understand that this doesn't work. The dog still can identify the substance it is seeking.

Narcotics dogs must be incredibly accurate as they search all sorts of places to find contraband. Generally a narcotics dog works on a leash. Initially it may have conducted a presearch by doing a run-by just to get familiar with the area (arson dogs do this, too) before doing the detailed search. Accurate records must be kept with every find noted, as well as every failure.

Law enforcement agencies prefer an aggressive alert except when dogs are sniffing out drugs on people, such as visitors at a penal institution. In the latter instance the dogs will alert to the presence of drugs in a passive manner, usually by sitting or lying down. In the aggressive alert scenarios, the handler is passive, leaving it up to the dog to be very positive and prove drugs are there by pawing, clawing, or biting.

If the handler encourages the dog prematurely, the dog may sniff the drug from a distance and sit, anticipating its reward. This is not a strong enough response when detailed accuracy is necessary to justify the obtaining of a search warrant. A misjudgement on the part of the handler could interfere with a dog's credibility.

Narcotics dogs are taught aggressive retrieves (not the type of soft-mouthed retrieve used for birds). If they find a suspicious package they are encouraged to pounce and "destroy." The dogs have to learn to concentrate when working in strange places and not be distracted by anything.

Narcotics dogs are certified by the National Narcotic Detector Dog and the North American Police/Work Dog associations after successfully demonstrating their ability to locate various drugs in a variety of situations.

THE LABRADOR POLICE DOG

Police dogs must be sound, intelligent, courageous, and persistent. A Labrador has all these attributes plus trainability and a willingness to please. A

Labrador is compatible with many situations, and from a practical point of view has a coat that is easy to care for.

Training for police work starts at about 18 months to two years of age. The dogs are trained slowly and carefully, so that each phase is thoroughly understood and learned before a new subject is introduced. If the dog is youthful and exuberant, which are good qualities, the training will probably take eight months, a little longer than the average time.

The dogs learn agility so they can climb or traverse many different kinds of obstacles. They are kept in top physical condition. Their lessons are systematically reinforced so that all phases of training will be stored in the dog's memory, even if they aren't put to use all the time.

Many tests must be passed by the police dog. Obedience exercises off lead (heel, sit, stay, stand, come) using both voice commands and hand signals prove that the dog is under absolute control at all times.

An "article search" demonstrates that the dog can find a human scent (much like the seek-back exercise used in utility obedience work). The dog does not search for a particular scent, but rather for something that may be out of place or suspicious at a crime scene. It could be anything left behind by a suspect making a fast getaway, such as a piece of clothing, a weapon, or even something ordinary.

A very difficult agility or obstacle course tests the dog's ability to traverse all sorts of rough going. It climbs ladders, jumps through elevated open-ended oil drums, crawls through tunnels, walks along horizontal ladders, scales walls, and walks along suspension bridges, just to name a few. This work proves the dog's ability to chase a suspect almost anyplace.

The dogs are tested with gunfire and while handicapped, such as wearing a muzzle. They have to put up with this as well as show that they disregard distractions. In the midst of any situation, the dogs could be ordered back to the heel position.

Dogs that pass this rigorous training may be seen at the side of police officers in their patrol cars, ready for whatever comes along. The Labrador is intelligent and versatile; these police dogs may enjoy their days off doing retrieves in the field.

Early in 1965 the Metropolitan Police in London were faced with a tremendous increase in drug traffic. They decided to train two Labradors solely for the detection of dangerous drugs. Rupert was $3^{1}/_{2}$ years old and had completed two years of duty in London's East End. The other Labrador was Pytch, eight months old and completely untrained. Contrary to accepted dog training principles, the Labradors did not receive any obedience training. Strict control in handling them was forbidden, as the success of the whole venture depended upon development of the dog's natural instincts rather than automatic responses brought about by the use of forced behavior. The dogs were never allowed to find any article that bore human scent alone. Obliterating this association with human scent takes a long time, but as the dogs mastered their tasks over a three-month period, with lessons kept short but interesting, they were finally taught to find drugs concealed in such places as they might expect to encounter in an actual search.

Six months after their training had commenced, Pytch and Rupert were considered ready for operational duties. They were very successful, and thanks to their efforts, the Metropolitan Police Training Establishment was able to continue developing better methods.

Lady Jacqueline Barlow (now residing in Newfoundland) told me about a Labrador she raised as a puppy, from three months to a year old, for the Metropolitan Police in London. She called the dog Pongo, but when he entered police work, he became known as Major 33 as there were 32 other dogs called Major in the ranks. This dog's four sisters were guide dogs for the blind. The litter, sired by Foxhanger Mascot, had been bred by Lady Simpson, wife of Sir Joseph Simpson, the Commissioner of Police. (The Simpson "Foxhanger" Labradors were well known in the field as all-around dual-purpose dogs.)

Major 33 and his handler, Albert Parrack, amassed more arrests to their credit than any other man/dog police team by the time they retired in 1969. Parrack told Lady Barlow, "Labradors made much the most determined police dogs, being a breed that is used to keeping on till he finds what he is after, and who is used to figuring things out for himself." He said Major would give him a look which said, "you do your bit, and I'll do mine."

SCHUTZHUND WORK

Although the Labrador's versatility is well known, the breed is not usually associated with "Schutzhund" work. Schutzhund is a German sport in which dogs are trained in obedience, tracking, and protection. Schutzhund dogs need even temperaments, and because their handlers administer corrections positively, a very confident dog is developed.

Protection work is a challenge for a Labrador, but it can learn it and do very well. Labradors in the United States and Canada have earned Schutzhund degrees. The same Labradors that excel in Schutzhund work will go hunting with their owners and never harm the birds. Labradors are smart enough to know the difference (in fact, some Labradors are smarter than their owners).

CADAVER DOGS

Cadaver dogs are trained only to find dead bodies, as compared to search and rescue (SAR) dogs, which search for both the living and the dead. Dogs react differently to corpses. Cadaver dogs can find either bodies or body parts,

Am., Can. Ch. Chilbrook Solitaire CD, CGC, TDI, "Jetta," is a police detector dog, a cadaver detection dog, a Group winner, dam of Group winners, winner of BOS from the classes at a Canadian Specialty, a HIT Obedience winner, and winner of many *Dog World* awards. Jetta is also a trained Schutzhund dog. Owned by Debby Kay.

and they won't indicate a live person. For training purposes a commercially made scent is used rather than real body parts. Cadaver dogs will sit at the location of the body.

Dogs will become depressed with a great deal of cadaver search, according to IDD trainer Debby Kay, who says the dogs need a change of scene to refresh their mental attitude. The handler can tell when the dog is depressed, as the tail will droop and the dog will lose enthusiasm. It's not the same as finding a lost child.

The Alaska Search and Rescue dogs in Anchorage are the only SAR group using Labradors (which they have rescued from the pound) for cadaver search. These dogs train all year 'round for locating avalanche and drowning victims. The dogs work off leash in very precarious situations, so they must be under absolute control and willing to obey their handlers to avoid danger. They have to travel in all sorts of transportation, especially small airplanes, which are one of the major modes of transportation in Alaska. Diminished daylight and extreme weather make work in Alaska especially difficult.

The world record for the oldest cadaver find was made by a trained chocolate Labrador named "Candy," owned by Bill Tolhurst of the Niagara, NY, County Sheriff Department. They were specifically looking for a grave 147 years old, and the dog accurately located it!

Water searches are usually performed by cadaver-trained dogs because the victims are most likely dead.

TOXIC WASTE DETECTION

The first toxic waste detection dog was Chilbrook Mandingo, owned by Debby Kay. This dog is capable of finding toxic waste buried several meters below the surface. It can locate the remains of buried toxic waste in a dump or in buried 55-gallon drums. If something has a unique odor, the dog can find it, and in quantities less than a PPB (parts per billion) instrument could detect. Labradors are amazing because they can detect a drop of chemical six months after it has been placed three feet below the surface and covered over.

It goes without saying that Labradors excel in all phases of detection work. They are sure of themselves, will go anywhere any time, and do what is asked. Professionals in the field prefer Labradors because the breed is so intelligent and capable of thinking. Labs need to be regularly challenged with new things to learn. Labradors need stimulation and excel when it is provided.

AIR SCENTING SEARCH DOGS

Labradors excel at search and rescue. Their innate desire to please coupled with their scenting talents make them a natural to perform search and rescue (SAR) missions.

Their SAR missions range from locating one lost person on the ground or in water to catastrophic disasters such as earthquakes, where victims may be pinned under rubble. Avalanche victims can also be located.

All humans, dead or alive, constantly emit microscopic particles bearing human scent, which are windborne for considerable distances. Labradors are among the breeds trained to locate the scent of any human in a specific search area. They are not restricted to following a person's tracks and can find a victim long after the track left by that person may be obliterated. Dogs can cover more territory in less time than a ground crew.

Bobbie Snyder, who lives in New Jersey, is a member of Mid-Atlantic Dogs on Ground Search (DOGS), a search and rescue unit made up of highly trained dogs and handlers. She volunteers her time and resources for this work. Each handler is responsible for the cost of training and personal equipment. Mid-Atlantic DOGS responds only to the request of a public agency, and there is no charge for their services.

Snyder's partner in this work is a young yellow Labrador named Katie. Not too long after Snyder and Katie became fully operational, an 81-year-old man with a history of heart attacks and strokes was reported missing deep in the woods of the 3,400-acre Cape Henlopen State Park in Delaware. Daybreak brought no news of his whereabouts. A chilly night had passed slowly and painfully for his family members, who became separated from him during what had started out as a pleasant family walk.

Almost immediately after his family reported his disappearance, helicopters and professional ground searchers systematically spread out over the northeast section of the park. Snyder's unit was called in to participate in the search. The rescue teams included state police, personnel from the Delaware Department of Natural Resources, firefighters, and paramedics, as well as auxiliaries with food.

Alaska Search and Rescue Dogs team member Guy Jones with his chocolate Labrador, Hershey, which is trained to locate avalanche victims. *Debby Kay*

In searches such as this one, the area to be covered is divided into grids for systematic searching. The mission coordinator figures out the area of highest probability based on the last reported position of the victim, and the search teams cover their grids accordingly. The dog and handler teams like to be sent out in advance of the ground teams.

Usually the victim's family is at the search site. In this search Snyder said, "They don't have to say anything—you can see the agony in their eyes." During the search Snyder's voice excitedly repeated over a two-way radio "Status 1, Status 1," a code meaning the victim had been found alive. With no food or fresh water and after 18 hours of wandering through difficult conditions, including waist-deep marshes, darkness, and low temperatures, the man was found in fairly good condition. "The outcome of the search at Cape Henlopen State Park gives the greatest satisfaction of the whole experience," related Snyder. "I know it and Katie knows it."

Bobbie Snyder purchased Katie at seven weeks of age. Snyder attended a Search and Rescue Seminar and "had it in the back of my mind that this was something I would like to do." Snyder had never owned a Labrador so she relied on the breeders to sell her a suitable puppy. A yellow female was selected, and when Katie was six months old, Snyder started her in obedience. Katie earned her CD at 18 months.

At the same time Snyder contacted a Pennsylvania SAR Unit and worked with it for two years, after which she transferred to Mid-Atlantic DOGS in Rockville, Maryland.

SAR training begins at approximately six months of age with "run-aways." Someone holds your dog, and you run away and hide behind a tree. Your dog comes and finds you and receives lots of rewards, both verbal and food. Actually, you can teach this as soon as your Labrador is able to concentrate on where you are. Praise at the time of finding you is extremely important.

The next stage in training is for the dog to learn to find someone else. The owner holds the dog and gets another person to run away and say, "Where am I going, Katie?" Again, the dog is rewarded for finding this person.

The third stage involves hiding the person who is running away from the dog. The distance is about 20 to 30 feet. Once again handlers stress the reward system. It can be voice, food, or a toy the dog really likes. It helps if the dog gets to play at the end of the maneuver. Sometimes the "victim" gives the reward.

Labradors respond very well to a reward system, and because of their high intelligence they soon understand the mission. The training is repeated until the dog knows what "FIND" means and learns to follow its nose and to air scent. As the dog progresses through the training exercise, the problems and distances are lengthened. Handlers must be aware of how much to ask of their dog during any one training session. It's important to end the day on a successful note.

The next goal is to teach the dog a "refind." The dog learns to come back and tell the handler, "I have found this person—you come and look." Snyder explained, "Katie jumps at me—I ask her, 'show me, Katie' and then she takes me back to what she has found." Some handlers like a bark-alert and some prefer the jump. Snyder said, "Katie gets agitated if I don't get to the 'victim' fast enough."

Every handler has to learn how to "read" his or her dog. Each dog has its own particular alert mode. In Katie's case her ears pull forward and her tail has a certain waggle as she goes from a searching mode to a happy finding mode.

Teamwork between dog and handler is extremely important. The handlers must be dedicated to their dogs plus feel a need for helping others. Snyder explains that "essential for this type of work is an instinct for survival and a great commitment. One must brave the extremes of weather, tramp through marshes, get scratched up in thick thorny areas, and slog through all kinds of muck with the possibility of spending the night on the trail."

Dogs can become operational at approximately 18 months to two years of age. The training is very intensive and extensive. Human participants must become proficient in terrain analysis, reading topographical maps, compass use, land navigation, search strategy, radio communications, helicopter rescue techniques, wilderness survival, victim behavior, and advanced first aid with CPR. Training is ongoing. Handlers and dogs keep their skills current with weekend training sessions.

Am., Can. Ch. Chilbrook Solitaire, CD, TDI, CGC during a training exercise preparing her for disaster work in locating buried victims. The alert signal is for the dog to sit and bark. Owner/handler, Debby Kay.

Bobbi Snyder with her search dog, Katie. *Pam & Sherry Pet Portraits*

Labradors learn "agility" to prepare for catastrophic disasters such as a building collapse or earthquake. The dogs must be able to climb up and down ladders and traverse slippery areas or planks. The dogs must be fearless and not feel threatened by noisy machinery. Standards are set by the Federal Emergency Management Agency (FEMA).

During catastrophic searches, dogs do not wear any equipment because of the risk of getting caught in something. The handlers wear appropriate gear including a hard hat. The dog is tattooed for identification purposes.

In a wilderness search the dog wears an orange vest with the letters SEARCH DOG on it. During night searching a glow stick is attached to the vest over the dog's withers, making the dog look like a giant lightning bug!

Snyder's goal is to be named to the U.S. Disaster Team. She keeps her passport current as she could be sent to another country. Certain countries would not be included due to quarantine regulations. Snyder maintains a two- to three-hour response time from her home in New Jersey to Andrews Air Force Base near Washington, D.C.

Snyder says her family is very supportive, which is vital because of the time she commits to training every weekend. She tries to attend training sessions three times a month at locations far from home. Snyder says, "There is no half-way to do it right. People don't realize how important this service is until they see us in action." This is one of the most rewarding activities Labrador owners can enjoy as long as they have the proper commitment to SAR goals.

TRAINING FOR WATER SEARCHES

Even though the dog is the most important part of the team, most of the training for water searches is for the handler. By the time teams are working on water searches, the dog already knows its job. The dog knows what to alert on when human scent is located. The handler must understand wind patterns and scenting conditions, as well as interpreting correctly the dog's body language and knowing his own and the dog's limitations. The handler must not interfere with the dog.

The handler will work the dog downwind of the area to be searched, keeping in mind the horizontal and vertical wind patterns. A dog team can work from a shoreline or a boat. Any handler using a boat for water searches must be trained in basic boatsmanship and related water skills. The dog must be confident of the stability of the boat, or it won't work. Various types of water must be analyzed, and the dog and handler must be comfortable with the conditions, especially in rough water or rapids. Dog handler safety practices are very important. There are many types of hazards that may be encountered on water searches, such as overhanging branches, low dams, or low bridges. Cold weather or water doesn't bother a Labrador, but handlers must be careful working around ice, especially shelf ice along the banks of a river, pond, or lake.

The size and depth of the body of water must be taken into consideration, as well as wind speed and direction. The scent from the victim will rise to the water surface where it may be acted upon by currents, after which, under certain conditions, air currents will take over. If the dog is working from a boat, the alert locations should be marked with a buoy as a point of reference for the divers. Dogs should not swim for this type of detection work unless the handler is sure there are no hazards that present a danger to the dog.

However, there are times when the swimming ability of the Labrador will be of great value. When the air temperature is below 35 degrees Fahrenheit, the scent emerging from the water may not get airborne because of the rate of evaporation, wind force, and barometric pressure acting upon it in the very dense cold air. Because the scent in these conditions will pool at the water surface, it can be detected only by a swimming dog.

As the seasons change, so do the physical characteristics of lakes, ponds, and rivers. Handlers have to learn a great deal about temperature, density, different temperatures in different layers of water, and all the myriad details that affect scenting conditions. When working with divers, handlers must brief them on what to expect from the dog.

After dog and handler are comfortable with swimming (if you swim with the dog, do not let it climb on you—you could be pushed under the water), and basic boatsmanship skills have been practiced with the dog in different types of boats and on various bodies of water, training is divided into three parts. The dog learns to detect human scent coming from under the water from a vantage point on a shoreline, to work while riding in some sort of boat, and to work while swimming in the water.

Any dog trained to locate generic human scent can learn to do a reliable water search no matter what training techniques are used. Once the dog is made aware that human scent can come from under water, it is up to the handler to learn to "read" the dog and not create "false alerts" by encouraging the dog at the wrong moment. The handler must beware of encouragement and reinforcement when he or she does not know what is being reinforced. Poor handling techniques and a lack of understanding by the handler are detrimental to the ability of a dog to do this work. The timing of the reward to the dog is critical for both novice and experienced search dogs.

Most SAR handlers introduce the dog to human scent from under the water with a diver wearing scuba gear. When the dog passes downwind of the scent emanating from the water, it will alert in some fashion (pawing, whining, barking, or trying to jump in the water). The handler immediately recognizes the alert and signals the diver to emerge from the water (or has an assistant who will signal the diver), and together they reward the dog. The handler and the diver reinforce the dog's alert on the human scent coming from the water.

An experienced wilderness SAR dog will pick up this type of search very quickly and will not require as much training as an inexperienced dog.

The process can be taught to novice dogs step by step, starting with a run-away where the diver ends up in shallow water and is visible to the dog.

Next the run-away diver submerges as the dog approaches either by swimming or wading. More difficulty is introduced by using a boat. Each time the reward reinforces the dog's alert as it enjoys success in finding the human scent.

If a dog catches on fast, the handler should not bore it with overtraining. Labradors are very intelligent, and some will give false alerts to get food or just to fool the handler when training is overdone. The handler must create scenarios that will challenge the dog by using various locations and many types of water.

In practice exercises, it is important that the handler always know where the human scent is located. This will prevent the handler, in his enthusiasm to encourage the dog's alert, from doing so in the wrong places. If the scent is not there, the dog will be confused by the handler's urging. Any encouragement and reinforcement by handlers who do not know what they are reinforcing may well result in training a false alert. A handler's lack of confidence in the dog and his lack of experience in reading his dog will result in confusion, which is not fair to the dog. Handlers must not punish dogs or become exasperated with them when the handlers are at fault.

Dogs may require differences in their training according to their job assignments. SAR dogs are trained to work off leash, to be curious, and to work out problems for themselves in hide-and-seek games, much like the hunter's Labrador. The reward for these dogs is play or praise. On the other hand, police K-9 dogs, because of the nature of their work, may not be able to work off leash and indulge in the type of off-lead "play" training given to the SAR dog. Adjustments may have to be made in the training process, but the key element is the reward system. Each handler must figure out which reward system works best for his dog. Labradors are individuals and each will react a little differently to a given situation.

chapter 17

Labradors Guiding the Blind

THE SEEING EYE

Labradors are one of the three primary breeds used by The Seeing Eye in Morristown, New Jersey. This is the oldest guide dog school in the world, founded in 1929 by Mrs. Dorothy Harrison Eustis. German Shepherds were the first dogs to help blind men and women achieve independence and mobility through the use of properly trained dogs. The other primary breed used is the Golden Retriever.

The Seeing Eye has its own scientific breeding program. Information on each dog in the breeding colony is entered into a computer, where a list of physical characteristics and temperament traits is recorded. A guide dog must be intelligent and quiet, and have steady nerves and good character.

Both males and females are used—all are neutered. When puppies are eight to ten weeks old they go to live with volunteers who will raise them through The Seeing Eye Puppy-Raising Program /4H Project. For the next year the children raise and socialize the puppy. Basic obedience is taught as well as good manners. The puppy-raisers show a great deal of love and affection to their charges. The foundation they give the puppies enables thousands of blind people to step forth with dignity and independence alongside their best friend in the world, a Labrador Seeing Eye dog.

Children nine years of age or older who have at least one family member at home during the day may raise a puppy. Retired adults who are at home during the day may also volunteer to raise a puppy. All puppy-raisers must participate in the 4H puppy-raising program. The Seeing Eye pays for veterinary costs and pays an allowance quarterly for dog food.

A great deal of credit goes to the puppy-raisers. From its beginning in 1942, today's Seeing Eye Puppy-Raising Project /4H Program has five staff coordinators who work with approximately 400 families in Delaware, New Jersey, and Pennsylvania. At the 50th anniversary of The Seeing Eye Puppy-Raising Program, Wayne McLeod, a member of the Seeing Eye Board of Trustees, said, "Puppy-raisers volunteer to give our pups love, guidance, and socialization experience that allow them to become competent, confident Seeing Eye dogs. A dog raised in a kennel does not have either the firm foundation of love and trust, or the wide exposure to different daily stimuli like traffic, stores, and people, that a dog has after being raised by a nurturing family in a home."

When the dogs are between 12 and 14 months old, they go back to The Seeing Eye to begin formal training. A sighted Seeing Eye instructor works with the dog, training it about 45 minutes a day. A system of rewards and gentle corrections is used to train the dogs. About four weeks are spent on an initial evaluation, and if the dog is suitable, it is trained for another eight weeks. Each instructor works with about ten dogs, teaching them basic guiding commands and to pull in harness. The dogs are worked in the residential and downtown areas of Morristown, New Jersey.

The dogs must develop a specialized awareness of the world around them. At the end of the training period, the instructor wears a blindfold and the chief instructor walks behind to monitor the dog's performance. By then the dog has developed instinctive responses.

Before the instructors can work with the dogs, they spend a thorough two-year apprenticeship at the school. Instructors work in teams of four, with staggered training cycles, so that while one team works with a class of students, another has dogs in the final stages of training before the next class, and the third has dogs a little less far along.

A trainer working a Labrador at The Seeing Eye in Morristown, New Jersey. *Jan Churchill*

At the beginning of their training cycle the dogs are taught to pull in harness, and basic obedience commands are reviewed. Their reward is most often an affectionate pat, and the correction merely a verbal reprimand from the instructor. The Seeing Eye staff has found that a stiff harness that the blind person holds, as opposed to a flexible handle, gives a more delicate feel and better communication between dog and master. Early in their training, they progress to a residential route in a quiet section of Morristown, where they are taught to pull out and lead in the harness and to stop at curbs. Gradually the dogs progress to busier streets where there is heavy auto and pedestrian traffic. After mastering these situations, the dogs learn "intelligent disobedience," where they use their own initiative and judgment to disregard a command if it would lead to danger.

For example, Lukas Franck, Community Orientation and Mobility Instructor, returned from a visit to a Seeing Eye graduate in Florida with this story:

> It was a few days after a local flood, and our graduate was out for a walk with her Seeing Eye Labrador. She came to a corner where she usually crossed and gave the "Forward" command. The dog refused. She listened, no cars were coming, so she repeated the command. This time the dog whipped around and started home. The woman knew this was unusual, so she followed the dog, as she was trained to do. At home, she told her husband what had happened. He drove to the spot to have a look. When he returned, he was as white as a sheet. It seems there were two alligators, each five feet long, on the other side of the street. Franck's moral: When in doubt, follow that dog!

The dogs learn that when they wear a harness, they are on duty. They learn that they must ignore other dogs. They learn to walk at a fast gait so that a slight slackening in their pace will signal their master instantly through the rigid harness. During training their instructor will make "mistakes" such as a blind person might make, so that if the dog causes the instructor to stumble, he or she can instantly correct the dog.

At the 50th Anniversary celebration Laurie Sandow, puppy-raiser, said, "Puppy-raising taught me much about giving, about humanity, about partnership, about love. The love of all my dogs remains with me, and I am connected with those who now share a unique partnership with each."

Blind men and women come from all walks of life to The Seeing Eye to be matched with a guide dog. The match between the student and the dog is critical. The instructors and the director of training put a great deal of thought into selecting an appropriate dog. The students are observed during a "Juno" walk, a session with the instructor acting as an imaginary dog, named for the Roman goddess of guidance. The instructor observes the student's strength, agility, coordination, and comfortable walking speed. The blind person must be able to walk two to four miles a day to keep the dog in training. The dog will lose its skills if they are not reinforced on a regular basis.

The blind students live at The Seeing Eye for a 27-day instruction period (20 days if it is not their first dog). Their dogs are with them around the clock. The dogs accompany their blind owners to all meals in The Seeing Eye dining room and have additional practice in Morristown restaurants. Despite the presence of tempting food and tantalizing aromas, the dogs rest quietly under the table, and lead their masters in and out silently and efficiently.

Students are taught to groom their dogs daily to keep the coats clean and shiny and free from doggy odor. Heated buildings and a lack of humidity in colder weather can cause discomfort for dogs, resulting in dry skin that may cause the dog to scratch. In the winter months students are taught to spray the dog's coats with a misting solution made up of two teaspoons of Avon Skin So Soft or one teaspoon of Alpha Keri bath oil in one quart of water. This is mixed in a spray bottle, misted lightly over the dog's coat, and then brushed in to alleviate winter dry skin conditions.

The teams learn to master the elements of daily life, such as going in and out of stores, commuting to work, and eating in restaurants. An instructor may take a city-dweller to New York City to learn to use the subway with his dog. A country-dweller would be taught to walk along curbless roadways.

Seeing Eye dogs technically are not pets. They are highly trained canines that are legally protected and permitted in restaurants throughout the United States and Canada. They are also permitted on all forms of public transportation and in buildings or places open to the public.

Imagine that you are a Labrador puppy in this program. You are full of life and energy and as a puppy, apt to get into mischief. Step by step your young "owner" guides you through lessons that will make you a dependable dog. You are taught to behave with simple commands and corrections that reinforce good behavior. You learn not to fight with other dogs you see when visiting parks, and not to chase squirrels or rabbits.

Later you graduate to training at the school. Leaving your loving family is sad except for the fact that you sense an important mission with the guidance of an adult trainer. The harness is serious business, and you are praised lavishly for doing the job correctly. What seems to be a game is really a serious endeavor. You learn to guide your trainer around obstacles and how to signal him and to keep him from danger, especially watching his right side.

When you progress in one exercise, another is added. You learn about the hazards and flow of traffic. You aren't a machine; you are allowed to develop your own initiative so you can handle situations as they occur. You learn not to be distracted by well-meaning people who want to talk to you or pet you.

The most difficult day comes when you are placed with your new master. You have to stay with him or her all the time, and you sense the uncertainty and natural nervousness of this new person. You have to work with this person, but you would rather have the familiarity of your former teacher. The bonding process is slow, but you soon discover that this new person really needs you. You would like a devoted master whom you can serve, and as every day goes by your team becomes stronger. The strangeness goes away as you go through the days under the watchful eye of your old teacher as you work with your blind owner.

Before long you realize you are the teacher as you guide your owner along the same streets that used to be your classrooms. You show your new master the techniques of working with a guide dog, and in return your new owner becomes more confident and cheerful. You are given lots of praise. You are groomed and loved as your owner becomes rehabilitated to a new way of life. This uncertain person has now become an assured person, and you know it is because of you, the devoted Labrador. You are not only a companion, but your master's eyes and protector. No human being could fill your roles with the same uncomplaining devotion and untiring fidelity.

To the casual observer, you and the blind person look like a man or woman out walking his dog. But dogs on casual walks are easily distracted, while you never allow your attention to wander. You understand your responsibility and maintain a businesslike attitude. Eventually you and your blind owner are as one—a true team thanks to all the people who helped you attain your level of expertise.

"LEADER DOGS FOR THE BLIND"

One of the most dramatic and best known service activities of Lions International is the Leader Dog School, which was founded in 1939 by three Lions from Detroit. They purchased an old farmhouse in Rochester, Michigan, which still stands in the center of a complex now valued at over seven million dollars. At the time there was a need for another guide dog school because there was an 18-month waiting list at The Seeing Eye in New Jersey. For more than 50 years, this has been a major project for the Lions Club, which offers its services through Lions organizations in all states.

Bill Hadden, from Virginia, serves on the Board of Trustees of the school and is also a field representative for Leader Dogs for the Blind. In 1972 when Bill was 44, he became disabled as a result of a cerebral hemorrhage while attending an Adult Scout Leaders meeting. The cerebral hemorrhage caused a brain scar at the optic nerve, which resulted in Bill's blindness and also affected motor nerves to the left arm and leg.

During a period of rehabilitation, Bill learned to walk again with the aid of a cane. Seeking a means of mobility enhancement, Bill was sponsored by the Brookville-Timberlake Lions Club in Lynchburg, Virginia, to attend Leader Dog School for the Blind in Rochester, Michigan. Bill is now with his fourth Leader Dog.

As a field representative for Leader Dogs, Bill and his third Leader Dog, Major, traveled extensively throughout the United States and Canada visiting schools and rehabilitation centers for the blind, in addition to other various public appearances. In 1993 Major was retired at the age of ten, and Bill received a lovely yellow Labrador, Molly. Usually when people get a replacement dog, they go back to Michigan to train with the new dog, but in Bill's case, because of his countless volunteer hours for the school, the trainer went to Virginia. Molly was Bill's fourth dog and came to him at 19 months of age. The trainer chose her for Bill when she was 12 months old. Molly was the 979th dog trained by her instructor in 31 years. To match Molly with Bill, the trainer studied the temperament, character, and habits of each dog that had been trained so that it would be a proper match with the student. The trainer and Bill spent ten days working as Bill "took Molly away from the trainer." Bill said you "have to believe in yourself and your dog as you work away from a protected environment. You have to keep your confidence up and learn to trust the dog, its movements and reactions." Comparing Major and Molly, Bill said, "Major was laid back, always ready to get the job done. All the dogs are different and have their own personalities."

Bill said, "I'm proud of the school I graduated from and the commitment of the trainers. The selection of dogs is vital, with only three of each class of ten being the average number to graduate." The school has a waiting list of people who want to give homes to the dogs who do not make it through the program. The dog has to make its own commitment to the program, and some dogs can't, perhaps because they are afraid of thunder or for some other reason.

When Molly arrived, Bill went to the airport at Lynchburg to practice getting on and off a commuter airplane. The airline serving Lynchburg had a two-hour stop-over, and the pilot agreed to keep the far side engine running for the practice session because in a real-life boarding situation the far engine would not be shut down.

Molly and Bill boarded and reboarded the Dash 8 commuter airplane many times. Molly would find the step and Bill would walk behind on the narrow stairway just using the dog's leash. Bill had to count the steps, at the top tell the dog to go inside, and then he would count the seats. Molly would immediately lie down at the correct spot and check the floor for peanuts. Bill said he always knew where the emergency exit was located, but "I don't sit there because of the greatest good for the most people." Bill Hadden travels over 100,000 miles a year with his Labrador on airlines. "My dog's name is in the airline computer—they know it better than mine."

The majority of dogs in the Leader Dog school's program are Labrador Retrievers. The kennels have housing for 300 dogs in tile stalls with radiant heat and drinking fountains. There is a veterinary hospital with complete facilities including X-ray equipment and a pharmacy. Dogs are checked daily by the staff veterinarian.

The breeding stock is kept out with families. Stud dogs must be OFA excellent for hips, shoulders, and elbows. Most of the bitches whelp with their families. Puppies are weaned at five weeks and socialization starts even

Bill Hadden owes much of his independence to his leader dog, Molly. Molly's eyes and expression have an intensity that make one aware of an intelligence that is beyond one's own comprehension: that of a dog bred and trained for a very special purpose and understanding its responsibilities. *Photos courtesy Bill Hadden*

younger than that. By seven weeks of age, puppies are placed with the puppy walkers. The volunteers study a puppy-raising manual to get prepared for the puppy. A crate is used for the pup's bedroom or sleeping area. A crate solves problems and prevents others, and being den animals, the dogs like their private sleeping quarters. The dogs are trained to relieve themselves outdoors (paper training encourages a dog to go in the house). The volunteers take the puppy outside on a leash to the designated toilet area and praise it for the correct actions. It is much easier to train the dog to have correct habits in the first place than to untrain it later.

The puppies wear leather buckle-type collars to encourage the pup to walk with the person. Puppies in training wear a Leader Dog bandanna to identify their purpose to the public. Handlers have ID cards so the dogs can go into stores and restaurants.

Over 300 bitches are in the program. The puppy program has created stronger stock with the right characteristics for the school. Dogs bred in the school's breeding program graduate at a higher rate than dogs donated by the general public.

The puppies are fed a nutritious complete food with no supplements. They eat puppy food up to five months and then switch over to an adult diet, as this avoids orthopedic problems. (Dogs that grow too fast and get overweight are apt to have joint unsoundness). No tidbits and no feeding at the table are allowed. Nylon bones are offered for chewing as real bones can splinter and puncture the intestines.

There are restrictions on games because the end result of the dog's training is to help a blind person. There can be no fetch games, no frisbees, nothing thrown. Tug-of-war is not allowed as it teaches aggression. The basic rules for raising a puppy must be applied consistently.

When riding in cars, the dogs are taught to ride on the floor. The handlers must not expose the dogs to hazards and must not let the dog ride with its head hanging out the window. The young dogs must learn to walk on all sorts of surfaces and flooring. They must be taken to many new places.

The socialization process is the most important part of the puppy's daily existence. The dog must learn to bond to the human pack. More formal obedience can be taught by the instructor when the dog reports back to the school.

All Leader dogs must be friendly, healthy, willing to lead out, accustomed to people, fairly good-looking, and able to accept responsibility. Sex is not a consideration, and all Leader Dogs are neutered or spayed. Dogs must be at least 20 inches at the shoulder. Unsuitable characteristics would include aggressive, shy or timid, easily distracted, high-strung, inconsistent, nervous, or panicky behavior.

The training program for the dog starts with obedience; dogs are taught the commands come, sit, down, and stay. The trainer learns general characteristics of the dog and studies general habits and temperament. During basic training on the streets of Rochester, Michigan, dogs are taught to observe curbs, pedestrians, parking meters, and low awnings. They begin to check traffic and other hazards. During advanced training on the streets of Royal Oak and Birmingham, Michigan, dogs are placed in confusing situations—heavy traffic, crowded areas, revolving doors, elevators, and noisy construction.

In the beginning the student trains with an imaginary dog called Juno. Using an empty harness, the trainer teaches the student voice commands, footwork, hand gestures, and timing. When the dog comes into this person's life, the dog finds out that the person knows the same commands that the dog has learned over the past four months. The student is introduced to his or her new dog in the student's room so that they can get to know each other in relaxed surroundings. The trainer brings the Labrador in and tells the student the name, age, weight, and sex and acquaints the student with the routine to be followed for feeding and exercising the dog. The students have to learn to put their faith in this dog that will be their lifeline to independence.

The Labrador has proven to be an outstanding choice as a breed to train for this work. Their temperament is such that they can adapt to leaving the family that raised them to go into a training kennel where they may be handled by more than one person. It takes a great deal of willingness and adaptability to leave family life and go into a situation where lessons are demanding,

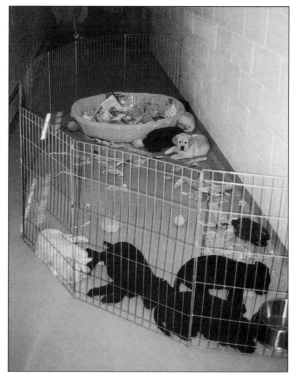

Puppies are socialized at the Guide Dog Foundation for the Blind, Inc., by keeping their pen in a busy hallway. Note that the puppies use the waterproof wading pool for a toilet area. *Maureen Wade*

after which the dog goes into a kennel at the end of the day. There is another complete change when the dog is introduced to the blind person and learns to work with someone who may be very apprehensive and frightened.

Dogs that lead the blind are bred for the characteristics that will make them succeed in their work. The dogs must have a good capacity to develop concentration. They must not have a strong scenting instinct nor be aggressive. Initiative is important. Awareness without fear is important. Responsiveness is essential.

In the school's breeding programs genetic inheritance is important, followed closely by the influence on the puppy of the environment in which it is raised. Puppies need to have an early attachment to people rather than other dogs. Therefore, seven weeks is considered the optimum time to remove a puppy from its littermates.

GUIDE DOG FOUNDATION FOR THE BLIND

At the Guide Dog Foundation for the Blind in Smithtown, New York, all dogs used in the breeding program must complete the same training program as any dog used to guide the blind. There is no breeding farm; breeding dogs are singled out as exceptional, they must pass all the temperament tests, and have hips and eyes certified. If they qualify for the breeding program, they will live with a family, perhaps the family that raised them, or some other family that wants to house a brood bitch. The bitches return to the school only when they are in season, to be bred, or when they come to whelp their puppies. They have only one litter a year and spend the rest of the time with their family, living a wonderful life.

Bitches at the Guide Dog Foundation are bred only five times and then retired. Hopefully some of their daughters will go back into the breeding program. The stud dogs are handled the same way. They come up through the training program and are selected as exceptional and outstanding dogs. None of the breeding animals have to live as kennel dogs.

A stud dog is placed with the family that raised it as a puppy or placed with a family that applied to keep a stud dog. The stud dogs have to report to the kennels several times a year when they are needed for stud duty. It is better for the dog to be a family dog. The family can show him, do obedience work, or do hunt work. In contrast, dogs that are confined to a breeding colony have a really sad life.

The Guide Dog Foundation has its bitches whelp at its own kennel facility under expert supervision. At seven weeks the puppies are placed with the family that will raise them until 14 months of age. During this time they have a preliminary X-ray, and they are also visited by a staff member monthly to make sure they are progressing properly. There are two staff members whose entire work is to oversee the puppy program. They hold a Camp Guide Dog at the school for the puppy walkers, where the dogs go through an extensive obstacle course.

When the Labradors return to the school at 14 months, they are assigned to a trainer. Each trainer at the Guide Dog Foundation has a string of dogs that he or she works with daily. Part of the training is accomplished on the school grounds, but most of it is done in nearby cities. The dogs are transported back and forth in special van-style training vehicles donated by 40 local Lions Clubs in District 20-OK1, with a matching grant from the Lions Club International Foundation. When the school is certain the dog will not enter the breeding program, it is neutered (males and females).

Adoption

If the dog is not going to be kept for either program (breeding or guide dog) because of a health problem or any of a wide range of problems, then they are first offered back to the family that raised them. Ninety-eight percent of those families do take the dog back. The Guide Dog Foundation has a two-year waiting list of people who wish to adopt dogs. Adoption fees cover neutering the dogs and other costs.

Retirement

The dogs stay out working until they are eight to ten years old. Each dog's working life expectancy differs, depending on whether they are city dogs or country dogs. The country dogs usually have a longer working life. The blind person has the option of adopting the dog out to a relative, but not to someone in their household. It is a difficult situation for a young guide dog to come into a new home if the old dog is still there. If the blind person can't arrange a home for the dog, they bring the old dog with them when they go back to the School for a new dog. There is a waiting list of people to adopt the retired guide dogs—they are never put down just because they have finished working. There are many older couples looking for a calm, well-behaved older pet.

Success Rate

The Guide Dog Foundation attributes its especially high success rate to the fact that its program is very thorough. Everything is seen to from the moment the puppies are born. They are socialized early, and the puppy walkers are given very specific guidelines and instructions. The puppy in training wears a little coat identifying it as a Guide Dog trainee. The handlers carry ID cards that let them go everyplace a blind person would go, in stores and on trains and buses. The handlers make an effort to take them everywhere. The more the puppies come in contact with all sorts of sights while they are growing up, the more they will regard strange noises and sights as second nature when they get into formal training.

The families chosen as puppy walkers are screened very carefully. It is better if they have other pets because if the Labrador is their only pet, it is hard to part with it at 14 months. With children in a family, if they have another dog or other animals, the parents can say to their children, "These are our animals, and no one is ever going to take them away. But this is a dog we are helping to teach for a special project, and that specifically is the reason the puppy is going back." With children it is much easier not to take their only dog away.

Frisbee throwing and retrieving are not allowed. These activities are too tempting for a Labrador. The Guide Dog School says, "We don't ask them to do a lot of training per se because we don't want our trainers to have to undo things. We have a very specific kind of training. Their main job is socialization. They teach the basic sit, down, and stay. Never any tight heeling because a Guide Dog has to walk a little in front of the person. We want the puppy walkers to teach the dog to walk comfortably on a leash without dragging. Other than that, just sit, down, and stay."

Stephen Cassell and Second Sight Darcy (Ch. Mardas Brandlesholme Sam Song ex Ch. Lobuff's Tequila Sunrise). Darcy works and lives in New York City. *Lisa Agresta collection*

Training at the School

The trainers spend three years learning what they must know. They start by learning the procedures as if they were blind. They are observed and given a written test. They become qualified as trainers and serve apprenticeships towards becoming instructors. They work with blind people under supervision and observation. Once they qualify as instructors, their real work begins.

The training period for dogs takes from three to six months. The young Labrador starts out slowly and quietly, learning to walk in a straight line. Using an imaginary line down the center of the sidewalk, the dog learns to avoid any obstacles on the right side of the person, which is opposite to the side the dog is on. After avoiding the obstacle, the dog has to bring the person back to the center of the sidewalk again. The dog is taught to stop at curbs. Eventually it is put into harness, and then training becomes more demanding. The dog learns how to walk up and down steps. It learns more about obstacle avoidance with emphasis on always protecting the right side of the blind person. It must also be aware of the height of anything the person walks under.

Students Arrive at the School

In Smithtown, New York, 10 to 12 students live in a dormitory environment where they are introduced to their new dogs. For the first few days, they work with the trainers, without dogs, which gives the trainers a chance to get to know the students, how strong they are, how they walk, and other characteristics that go into matching up a successful team. The matching process is very important. The trainers usually have a class of about 20 trained dogs from which to select the best dog for the student. It is necessary to have more trained dogs than students to give the instructors some leeway in their choices. Some newly blind people (especially diabetics) are heavy-footed, so they must be matched with a dog that doesn't flinch if they inadvertently knock against it.

The first three days are spent with the trainer pretending to be the dog and showing the student how the dog will react to changes in the pavement, to curbs, and when crossing the street. The dog is taught to stop at changes in the pavement and at down curbs and up curbs. They even learn to stop at icy spots, which the blind person investigates with a foot. All students have already had mobility training through a state agency or social services, a prerequisite for guide dog school. Because dogs can't read traffic lights, the blind person has to know, when standing on a street corner, which way the traffic is coming. The person listens to traffic and learns from sound which direction it is coming from. When the person hears the traffic stop, he or she asks

Molly and Bill Hadden prepare to cross the street as Bill listens for the traffic. *Courtesy Bill Hadden*

Two stud dogs for Guiding Eyes for the Blind, Yorktown Heights, New York: on the left, GEB Boomer (Ch. Coalcreek's Gimme A Break ex Tanker Bambi) and right, GEB Marsden (Ch. Coalcreek's Gimme A Break ex Tanker Jaz). *Mary Bloom*

the dog to go forward. If it is safe, the dog will cross the street and stop at the up curb. A dog will also stop at a wheelchair ramp, as this is a pavement change.

Returning students can skip the initial training. The school has always kept in touch with them and already knows their needs (city or country) and habits.

Once training with the dogs begins, the days are very full. The students get up and feed and exercise their dogs. They have breakfast and by 8:30 A.M. are loaded into the vans to go into town. They return for lunch and load up again at 1:00 P.M. It can take from six months to a year for a team to become a really good working unit.

Once they leave the Guide Dog Foundation, there is an aftercare program in which the staff go out to visit the students. The human aspect of the school is very impressive. The guide dogs are given free of charge to every student, while the costs, which include buildings, vehicles, maintenance, clerical, trainers, staff, feed, medicine, utilities, and much more, are provided through private donations.

chapter 18

Labrador Activities

CANINE GOOD CITIZEN

The American Kennel Club launched the Canine Good Citizen (CGC) program in 1989[1] as a response to the anti-canine sentiment that had been gaining momentum in certain public sectors. This test is not an obedience drill, but rather, it is a program of certification that can easily be accomplished by almost any dog and handler. It seeks to identify and officially recognize those dogs that have the necessary attributes to serve as reliable and pleasant personal companions.

The purpose of the Canine Good Citizen Test[2] is to demonstrate that the dog, as a companion to man, can be a respected member of the community and can be trained to behave in the home or in public places, in the presence of other dogs, in a manner that will reflect credit on the dog. Responsible dog owners want well-mannered dogs. They can get this certificate without even attending an obedience class by simply teaching their pet very basic commands.

A handsome certificate is awarded to dogs that pass. CGC is not a title of record so it will not appear on official AKC papers, but it may be included after a dog's name on unofficial pedigrees and in advertising.

Irresponsible dog owners cause 90 percent of the problems with dogs by letting them run loose through a neighborhood or allowing them to bark at all hours, jump all over people, or lunge at others when they are being walked.

---

[1]*The CGC Program was conceived and designed by AKC Secretary James Dearinger.*

[2]*To put on a Test, write for a presentation kit from the American Kennel Club, ATT: CGC, 5580 Centerview Drive, Suite 200, Raleigh, NC 27606.*

Walking on a loose lead:
Ch. Lobuff's Seafaring
Banner (Ch. Spenrock
Heatheredge Mariner ex
Ch. Spenrock's Cognac)
with Lisa Agresta's
daughter, Kyra.

A well-mannered dog is a happier pet. Dogs want to please their owners and to do so must have sensible limits set for them.

The Canine Good Citizen Test is not competitive. To qualify for an award, a dog must pass (on a pass-fail basis) each of the ten test categories. The dog need only pass the test once to receive a Canine Good Citizenship certificate. It must pass each of the ten test categories. Any dog that relieves itself during testing will be marked as failed. Owners should leave ample time for this prior to the testing—know your dog's habits and plan accordingly.

Any dog that growls, snaps, bites, attacks, or attempts to attack any person or other dog shall be dismissed from the test. Any handler who displays unsportsmanlike conduct or who is seen to strike, kick, or otherwise manhandle his or her dog roughly during a test shall be dismissed from the test.

All the tests are performed on leash. Special training collars such as "pinch" or "spike" collars are not acceptable.

Your Labrador is eligible to compete, as are all dogs, even non-purebreds. Local dog and obedience clubs administer the events for which AKC provides direction, evaluator's forms, and certificates.

Matinenda Micki, of field trial lines, has three CDXs (AKC, UKC, and CKC), FDX (Flyball Dog Excellent), WCX (Working Certificate Excellent), and JH (Junior Hunter). Owned by Lynn deBeauclair, a member of the Huron River LRC in Michigan.

The ten tasks to be demonstrated are easy for a Labrador, and since it is a noncompetitive situation, those who don't enjoy competition will find this a pleasant way to spend time with their dog. The tasks are simple and easily taught.

During the Canine Good Citizen test, commands may be given more than once and talking to the dog is encouraged. Harsh commands and the exactitude of obedience tests are not appropriate. The test is simply evaluating a well-mannered dog.

This is a great project for children who belong to 4H Clubs. The tasks for the dog and handler lend themselves well to the 4H philosophy to "learn by doing." The goal is attainable after seven or eight weeks of training with the test given as graduation. There are no entry fees, as would be the case in pursuing an obedience degree, which involves entering a number of dog shows.

While any person can be an evaluator, it should be someone who has considerable knowledge of dogs with lots of experience in working and training them as well as a keen awareness of the public's attitude toward dogs. Items the evaluator will consider before passing the dog would be as follows:

Barbaree Highgate Honour, CD (Ch. Dickendall's Gowdy CD ex Barbarees Island in the Sky, CDX), owned by Nancy Beach, shown completing her USDAA Agility Dog title. *T. Saskor*

Is this the kind of dog you would like to own? Is this the kind of dog that would be safe with children? Would you welcome this dog as a stranger? Is this dog making its owner happy and not making anyone else unhappy?

The dog will be expected to demonstrate confidence and control, and must complete all ten steps comprising the CGC.

Complete details on the CGC program and tests are available from AKC at the address given earlier in this chapter. Also, a very helpful book on Canine Good Citizen activity is *The Canine Good Citizen: Step by Step* (1994, Howell Book House) by Joachim J. Volhard and Wendy Volhard.

The requirements for a Canine Good Citizenship title can be completed by any well-trained and properly socialized dog. Training can be more demanding according to what you plan for your dog, but basically your dog should be a "good citizen."

Marietta Huber encourages
one of her Labradors
through the weave poles
in an Agility course.

AGILITY

The United States Dog Agility Association (USDAA) is the leading organization for a competition that is open to purebreds as well as mixed breeds. The sport originated in England as a challenging way for dog owners to interact and play with their pets. Training seminars are offered around the country. There are demonstrations at dog shows, regional competitions, and international contests.

Any dog owner who enjoys playing with his or her dog can easily train it to perform agility. When a dog works well with its handler, learning to perform the various obstacle tests comes naturally, and so does the fun. The dogs seem to realize that this is great fun, as opposed to the more serious atmosphere of obedience tests.

Agility obstacles are fashioned in part after horse show jumping fences. Other tests include crawling through tunnels, balancing on see-saws, winding back and forth through obstacles, and various other challenging situations. The winners are the dogs that complete the course in the fastest time with the fewest faults. Dogs compete on two levels: open class for dogs 16 to 30 inches tall and a mini class for smaller dogs.

The dogs are coached through the obstacles by their handlers, who can use hand and voice signals, but can never touch the dogs while they are competing on the course. Teamwork between dog and handler is essential. The dogs need some athletic ability to negotiate all the obstacles quickly.

Chilbrook Casablanca,
Therapy Dog, owned by
Kathy Besser.

While a Labrador's natural instincts are in the hunting and detecting (by nose) arenas, there are many instances where field sports are not convenient. A Labrador is very intelligent and likes to be challenged. The breed can do very well in agility tests.

SCENT HURDLE RELAY RACING

This spinoff from obedience began in 1970. The purpose of the races is to demonstrate obedience training control of dogs in competition. Teams of four dogs (not necessarily of the same breed) each wear similar jackets. Each dog has its own handler and two dumbbells, which are painted with the team color. Four white hurdles 18" tall are placed in a straight row ten feet apart with the dumbbell platform, which has four compartments on top, 12 feet beyond the fourth hurdle.

The starting line is about four feet from the first hurdle. The handlers sit their dogs each behind the other in a line. Upon a command from the line judge, the handlers take both dumbbells, which now have scent from their hands, to the far end, placing one in a compartment of the box, and the other upon the traffic judge's table; then all return to their dogs.

When the starter blows a whistle, the handler in front of the line sends his dog over the hurdles after its dumbbell. The dog locates his dumbbell by scent and quickly takes it back over the four hurdles to its handler. The next dog in line is sent immediately to do the same as the first dog, and so on until all four dogs have brought back their dumbbells. As each dog goes to find "its" dumbbell, there are always four to choose from because the traffic judge places a substitute dumbbell in the compartment box as soon as a dog removes a dumbbell.

Handlers must remain behind the starting line at all times. However, they can correct or encourage the dog with voice commands and hand signals.

Timing begins the second the first dog leaves the starting line and ends when the last dog has presented its handler with the correct dumbbell. When a dog brings back the wrong dumbbell, it is sent again after the fourth dog has completed its run. Two teams run simultaneously over two identical set-ups that are fairly close together, thus adding to the challenge and excitement.

The first team to win two out of three heats is declared the winner. The dogs become quite excited because cheering and applauding is allowed from the sidelines. This makes the event exciting for the spectators because dogs become so excited, they may make a mistake and have to be sent for an extra try. A maximum of three or four runs per dog may be allowed.

Scent hurdle racing is another way to enjoy your Labrador's versatility. Labradors are eager, fast, and reliable. This sport is not like anything else they may be trained to do, so it shouldn't affect their performance in other areas.

LABRADOR ASSISTANTS HELP
PEOPLE FIND INDEPENDENCE

Assistance Dogs International is a nonprofit coalition of organizations that train assistance dogs, including guide dogs for the blind, hearing dogs, and service dogs. This organization educates the public about the service dog concept, and public access for service dog teams.

Support Dogs, Inc., in St. Louis, Missouri, is one example of a group dedicated to helping others through dogs. It accepts applications from individuals who have mobility impairments resulting from various disabilities, such as muscular dystrophy, multiple sclerosis, cerebral palsy, post-polio, spinal cord injuries, spina bifida, certain birth defects, arthritis, post-traumatic injuries, post-stroke, and certain other less common conditions. Dogs are trained in various categories, such as street certified service dogs, home certified service dogs, therapy division, and touch teams. Innovative advanced training techniques make it possible to use special skills of the service dogs to assist people with difficult advanced progressive illness. The Support Dogs breeding program specifically selects dogs that are very highly motivated to work and are extremely responsive to verbal commands.

Amer, Can OT Ch. U-CDX Tara Tess JH, WC, TT, TDI, CGC (Lone Oak's Mikes Magic ex Georgia Tess), owned by Allen C. Cappuccio and Kathleen C. Hetfield, loves Fly Ball. *Pam & Sherry Pet Portraits*

Puppies in the Support Dogs breeding program are raised by volunteer canine foster care providers. The "puppy parents" provide socialization and lots of love for the puppies from about six weeks of age until the puppies are about 18 months old. At that time the young dogs enter the training kennel for advanced training. During the foster care phase the pups also learn basic obedience and have fun with fly-ball and agility. Puppy-trainers attend weekly classes to learn basic obedience and socialization skills.

Support Dogs, Inc. has developed a program known as Touch Teams. These teams provide pet-assisted therapy in many different settings. These dogs not only visit nursing homes, but they also provide pet-assisted therapy in conjunction with hospital physical therapists to young patients recovering from significant physical injuries. Patients with head injuries respond very well to dogs.

Special teams, such as Claudia Orf and her yellow Labrador Dusty, are pet-facilitated communication therapy teams, which help to treat children with severe communication and behavior disorders such as autism. Claudia is a certified speech-language pathologist and Dusty is a trained social/ therapeutic Support Dog.

Hearing and assistance dog training centers are working with Labradors, as well as other breeds, to train canine assistants for deaf people as well as those with other handicaps. Labradors love to bond with a person and have a definite sense of purpose when they learn that the human depends on them for assistance.

Dogs for the Deaf, an organization that was established in 1977, rescues dogs from shelters (often just before being put to sleep), trains them, and delivers them throughout the United States, absolutely free. The "Hearing Dogs" are taught to listen for sounds from a baby crying to a smoke alarm. The dog then gently touches the deaf person with its paw and leads him or her to the sound. A hearing canine companion will let its owner know when a car door closes outside the house or if someone enters the house unannounced.

Hearing dogs are allowed the same rights to transportation, buildings, restaurants, markets, schools, and other public buildings as guide dogs. Dogs for the Deaf hearing dogs are identified by a blaze orange collar and leash, and the owner carries a photo I.D.

Canine Companions for Independence is an organization training Labradors to assist people in wheelchairs.

THERAPY DOGS INTERNATIONAL

This organization, known as TDI, was founded in 1980 by Elaine Smith and Milt Winn. As a nurse in England Ms. Smith had noted the benefits to patients when dogs were brought to visit them in nursing homes. Mr. Winn is a blind person, assisted by a guide dog.

Nugget works as a volunteer pet therapy dog. Owned by Joanie Shugar.

TDI sets standards for dogs which enable them to wear "Registered Therapy Dog TDI" tags on their collars. The dogs wear these yellow tags when they are working and adhere to the regulations of TDI. When in public, therapy dogs may wear a red leather or nylon harness with the TDI patch on top as a visible sign they are Therapy Dogs.

A therapy dog brings joy to people. The dogs love the work and Labradors excel at visiting the folks in nursing homes, county homes, places for handicapped people, and emotionally disturbed children. A certified international therapy dog, in addition to having current health inoculations and being well groomed, has had obedience training and is an AKC Canine Good Citizen that goes on to pass the TDI test. TDI has a special requirement that wheelchairs, walkers, crutches, and other equipment routinely used in nursing homes and hospitals are used in the test. The evaluator must be certified by TDI on the basis of previous training experience.

K-9 Bogart and K-9 Chance having fun with carting. *Debby Kay*

Owners of TDI dogs promise to make at least one visit a month, and many do more, to nursing homes. Joanie Shugar of Ventura, California, says:

> Once you are approved, you can visit any place that will have pet therapy visits. The dogs love it. I have one that plays dead when I shoot her with a squirt gun. Another dog smiles while I demonstrate flossing her teeth. These dogs howl when I tell them to sing. Most of the work we do is a full novice show routine, as well as open dumbbell work, off-leash work, and long sits and downs out-of-sight. My group is all in CDX training, so we enjoy the distractions at the various places we visit. Our hardest problem is getting owners to make a commitment to do volunteer work around the elderly and ill children. However, when we leave we feel great. It's so worthwhile to see the smiles on the patients' faces, and the dogs love it.

The effect of the dogs on a sick person is phenomenal. Some dogs are "up" and do tricks while others are extremely calm. Most therapy dogs are privately owned and trained, although a trainer may take the dog for a visitation while the owner is working.

Service dogs are also used to help people who have seizures. The dog can predict when the seizure will occur and warn the person to get to a safe place. The devotion of these dogs and their incredible bond with their owners is heartwarming.

PET PARTNERS

The Pet Partners program is a nationwide registration system for pets that have passed the CGC Test and their handlers to visit lonely and disabled people whose well-being is promoted by interaction with a well-trained pet and understanding handler.

chapter 19

Labrador Retriever Rescue

The popularity of the Labrador Retriever has increased the need for rescue groups to place unwanted Labradors in suitable homes. The Labrador Retriever Club has a committee for "Information on Labrador Retriever Rescue Programs (CILRRP)." Members of area clubs around the country serve on this committee.

Area clubs organize rescue programs which include educational programs to teach the public responsible Labrador Retriever ownership. Education will help reduce the number of young Labs placed by their owners in rescue situations because the dog was too active for the family. Many families find themselves unable to meet the needs of a growing Labrador. Labradors are wonderful dogs but they need to be trained and socialized no matter what their role in life. Most pet owners need to take classes so they can learn to train their dogs.

Puppy kindergarten is a good place to start, followed by obedience classes, canine good citizen courses, and tracking and/or field clinics. Labradors are very intelligent and will respond well to training; in fact, they are easily bored and can get into mischief if they aren't challenged mentally. In most cases, when a dog gets into "trouble" it is the owner's fault. Educational courses help people learn reasonable expectations for their dogs and what standard of behavior to expect.

The majority of dogs that end up in a rescue program have been undersocialized, underexercised, and undertrained. None of this is the dog's fault. It takes time and understanding on the part of family members to raise a wonderful dog. The first year is the most critical, starting the day the puppy enters your home. Everything you say and do with your Labrador helps to develop a nice dog. Conversely, if you don't know what you are doing, or neglect something, problems can develop.

The yellow Labrador, sitting, was rescued from the pound, where he had only two days to live. Although a little oversized, he is well proportioned and is now Lord Galahad of Graystone CD, CDX. One of the dog's favorite crowd-pleasers at fund-raising events is jumping over a broad jump using kids from the audience acting as broad jump boards on the floor. Also pictured is a chocolate Lab, U-CD Lady Chelsea of Graystone CD, CDX. The dog on the left is a Golden Retriever, also rescued by owner Cindy Rice.

Cute little cuddly puppies can turn into boisterous nuisances unless the puppy is trained intelligently. By the same token, if a family can't keep the small puppy, it's usually easy to place it in another home. However, adolescent males from the age of one to two years can be a problem. Firm and sympathetic handling can transform these dogs into useful citizens. Once trained, they often do well in specialized situations, such as drug detecting.

The rescue leagues also lend assistance to people looking for an adult dog. An appealing puppy is not for everyone, especially the elderly, the handicapped, or two-career couples.

Rescue organizations are staffed by members of area breed clubs, who donate their time and services. Adoption fees are usually charged as clubs depend on contributions and fund-raising events to cover expenses.

The LRC distributes an information packet to clubs wishing to begin or expand their rescue. The LRC also provides a broad "standard" to help personnel in animal shelters and dog control officers identify Labradors.

Rescue clubs provide training information and advice to help owners solve problems that will allow them to keep their dogs. Breeders are advised to screen their puppy buyers carefully for suitability and willingness to train the puppy. Breeders are encouraged to keep in touch with the new owner and offer training advice. Breeders should tell the new owners how to use a crate for training. The advantages of spaying and neutering should be discussed. The new owners should be aware of canine problems in their community. Is there a leash law? Are there laws regarding barking? Labradors like to roam and unless supervised may take off to visit places where they aren't welcome. Furthermore, it is dangerous to allow your dog to run at large—it could become an unfortunate statistic.

Safe confinement for rescued dogs is a must. Ideally the adopting family will have a fenced yard or run area. Invisible fencing can be used in yards where other dogs are not in the neighborhood (as they can cross the "fence" at will). Also, it is not a good idea to go off and leave the dog confined only by an invisible fence.

If you plan to adopt a Labrador, remember that the dog may have been through a stressful time. Take it to an obedience class. The dog will enjoy learning your "rules," and with proper praise it will bond to you quickly as you and your pet learn together. Rescued dogs usually respond very well, as they are placed by volunteers who screen the families carefully, checking facilities and the families' attitude toward dogs.

Labrador Retriever Rescue, Inc., began in 1986 and was followed by a number of satellite rescue groups that are now independent. Volunteers man hotlines, do home studies, and transport and evaluate dogs. Dogs accepted into the program must be purebred Labradors in reasonably good health, and with no history of biting. Before being placed every dog is spayed or neutered and its vaccinations are updated. Most dogs placed are between one and five years of age. The majority are happy, willing, and totally undertrained and underexercised. The most common reason for people giving up a Labrador is because they have no idea how active a Labrador is. By the time they are three or four years old, Labradors usually settle down and are dependable dogs. Those trained and exercised properly will reach this stage sooner.

Older dogs are also placed successfully with adopting families who understand the need for modified exercise and certain other considerations. The gentle nature of an older Labrador is well appreciated in some situations.

chapter 20

Establish a Wellness Protocol for Your Labrador

Preventive care for your Labrador is important. A complete, well-thought-out puppy program is important, as is a wellness protocol for the adult dog. Your veterinarian will keep a complete history of your dog's health. This may prove invaluable if problems develop later in the dog's life.

Labradors should be protected from fleas, ticks, and heartworms as well as the usual dog diseases. Internal parasites can cause serious gastrointestinal disturbances if not properly treated. A veterinarian should recommend a vaccination schedule for the dog's lifetime.

Between the ages of six to eight weeks puppies should have an intestinal worm exam and start on heartworm preventative, preferably one with an intestinal wormer (ivermectin or milbermycin). An inoculation should be given for distemper, parainfluenza, parvovirus, adenovirus type 2, coronavirus hepatitis, and leptospirosis. Follow-up inoculations will be given and then annual boosters. Rabies vaccinations must be given at the recommended time. The veterinarian will suggest a schedule for checking for internal parasites.

Dogs that attend shows or are boarded out should receive Bortadella vaccine both nasally and systemically for optimum protection.

Canine distemper is an often fatal viral disease. This neurological disorder can attack adults as well as puppies.

Canine adenovirus type-1 and type-2 cause infectious hepatitis and respiratory infection, respectively. Hepatitis caused by adenovirus type-1 may cause severe kidney damage or death, while adenovirus type-2 may cause kennel cough. Canine bortadella (bronchiseptica) also contributes to kennel

Ch. Agber's Daisy of Campbellcroft CD, WC (Ch. Spenrock's Cardigan Bay ex Ch. Whiskey Creek's Lisa) at 14^1/$_2$ years of age. Owned by Donald and Virginia Campbell. *Fox & Cook*

Am., Can. Ch. Campbellcroft's Angus CD, WC (Ch. Lockerbie Brian Boru WC ex Ch. Campbellcroft's Pede CD, WC) at 10^1/$_2$ years of age. Owned by Donald and Virginia Campbell. *Fox & Cook*

cough and can occur in combination with distemper, adenovirus type-2, parainfluenza, and other respiratory problems.

Leptospirosis in dogs is a bacterial infection that may lead to permanent kidney damage. This disease is very contagious and can spread to other pets or humans.

Parainfluenza and parvovirus can both be deadly to puppies. Canine parainfluenza causes kennel cough, which may be mild in older, healthy dogs but quite severe for a puppy. Canine parvovirus causes severe dehydrating diarrhea in dogs of various ages, but is especially debilitating for puppies.

Puppies may also experience dehydration from canine coronavirus, which is a highly infectious intestinal disease causing vomiting and diarrhea in dogs of all ages. It is especially life-threatening to puppies.

Lyme disease is caused by the *Borrelia burgdorferi* bacterium and may be spread by direct contact by insects, especially ticks, but also flies and fleas. Several species of ticks are associated with Lyme disease: the lone star tick (*Amblyomma americanum*), the American dog tick (*Dermacentor variabilis*), the deer tick (*Ixodes dammini*), the Pacific Coast tick (*D. occidentalis*), the Western black-legged tick (*I. pacificus*), and the black-legged tick (*I. scapularis*).

The American dog tick also carries Rocky Mountain spotted fever and canine ehrlichiosis.

Dogs can pick up ticks easily. The ticks associated with Lyme disease are very small and hard to find when they are burrowed in a dog's coat. Daily inspection of your pet is mandatory. The disease has been reported in every state.

Lyme disease has a broad spectrum of symptoms, many of which are also characteristic of other diseases. Affected dogs will experience lameness, joint pain and/or swelling, fatigue, and fever. The lameness may be present in one leg for a while and then shift to another leg. Lyme is hard to diagnose when there is shifting lameness because in the early stages of the disease, radiography of the joints will appear normal. The migratory and episodic lameness is similar to the symptoms of eosinophilic panosteitis and rheumatoid arthritis. Blood tests are useful but not always accurate in making a diagnosis. More than one blood test may be necessary.

If a dog tests positive for Lyme disease, it can be treated with antibiotics. If there is joint swelling, it must be treated promptly so that the swelling will not calcify and become permanent. Aftereffects for dogs may include kidney damage as well as neurological problems. The heart and other organs may be affected. Antibiotics work well when used in the early stages of the disease. Diagnosis at a later stage means a longer treatment which may not be successful.

Brain damage, which may manifest itself in aggressiveness, increased appetite, or seizures, may develop when the antibiotics used for treatment do not penetrate the blood-brain barrier. It is important that the antibiotic chosen is capable of achieving a high concentration in the cerebrospinal fluid. Serum and cerebrospinal fluid titers should be performed as part of the diagnosis.

There are many products on the market to help eliminate ticks. A vaccine for Lyme disease is available. Various collars and dips may help to keep ticks off your dog. If your dog swims regularly, you will want to use a product that is appropriate for your dog's lifestyle. Veterinarians in your locality are best qualified to help you decide if you should vaccinate your dog.

Heartworms are a hazard to all dogs, but especially dogs that spend time outdoors because the disease is transmitted by mosquitos. Heartworm infection has been identified in all 50 states. Prior to starting a heartworm preventive program in dogs over six months of age, the dog must be tested for heartworm infection. The earliest that either a microfilarial concentration test or an antigen test can detect an infection is six to eight months after the infective larvae have entered the dog.

Heartworms actually settle primarily in a dog's pulmonary arteries, where they can obstruct blood flow and cause pulmonary hypertension, formulation of granulomas in the lung parenchyma, and congestive heart failure. Infected dogs lose weight, cough, and are fatigued or listless. Fluid may accumulate in the abdomen as heart failure develops. Kidneys and lungs are also at risk.

Treatment for a dog with heartworm is difficult, risky, and expensive. The decision to treat a dog with a positive antigen test should be based on clinical signs, the dog's expected activity level, success in clearing microfilaria, and the ease in starting a preventive program. There are many considerations to be discussed with your veterinarian, such as the option of delay in treatment to allow the heartworms to age so that they will be more susceptible to a higher dosage of thiacetarsamide sodium, an organic arsenical compound. Thorough evaluation is essential for an effective treatment. Initial measures for prevention are extremely essential so that one may avoid treatment of advanced infections.

Am., Can. OT Ch. Millgrove's Special Amie, UD, WC, was not only the first (and only) Labrador to be #1 obedience dog (all breeds in the United States), she was also the first dog to be awarded a Working Certificate by the LRC without being a bench champion of record.

Mrs. E. P. Taylor (wife of E.P. Taylor, owner of Windfields Farm, then the top breeder of Thoroughbred race horses in the world) with her Labrador puppy who became Ch. Spenrock Tweed of Windfields. *J. Churchill*

Ambleside Wheel Watcher (Killingworth Kelt O'Hanover ex Ch. Killingworth Bonny of Dimeo CD, CGC). Bred and owned by Julie Sturman, photographed with friend Brooke Huttner.

Any adult dog that has not been on a preventive program must have a microfilaria and an antigen test before starting a preventive. Some owners only give the preventives during the warm months. If this is discontinued during the winter (assuming no mosquitos are present), then the dog must be retested each spring prior to giving the preventive. It is recommended that dogs on the daily preventive medication receive an annual antigen test. Any break in the administration of the daily preventive can cause a loss of protection. Noncompliance with the monthly routine is not as likely to lead to problems as noncompliance with the daily products.

Preventive care will save a dog owner money in the long run. Year 'round protection is the treatment of choice. Eight years of preventive treatment equals approximately the cost of one treatment if the dog gets the disease. You can spare yourself grief, not to mention the medical effects on the dog.

Dogs can be given a daily preventive (diethylcarbamazine) or a monthly tablet. Monthly dose tablets are available which use ivermectin in a formulation that also treats and controls ascarids and hookworms. These tablets work to prevent heartworm by eliminating the tissue stage of heartworm larvae (*Dirofilaria immitis*) for 30 days after infection. Tables are available for dosages based on body weight.

A veterinarian with a "wellness" program can help owners take better care of their dogs. There are many new medications available, and research provides better treatments all the time for all sorts of animal problems. Specialists should be consulted for difficult situations.

chapter 21

Official Standards of the Labrador Retriever

General Description

The general appearance of the Labrador should be that of a strongly-built, short-coupled, very active dog. Compared with the Wavy or Flat-coated Retriever he should be wider in the head, wider through the chest and ribs, wider and stronger over the loins and hindquarters. The coat should be close, short, dense, and free from feather.

Detailed Description

HEAD

The skull should be wide, giving brain room; there should be a slight "stop," i.e. the brow should be slightly pronounced so that the skull is not absolutely in a straight line with the nose. The head should be clean cut and free from fleshy cheeks. The jaws should be long and powerful and quite free from snipiness or exaggeration in length; the nose should be wide and the nostrils well developed. The ears should hang moderately close to the head, rather far back, and should be set somewhat low and not be large and heavy. The eyes should be of medium size, expressing great intelligence and good temper, and can be brown, yellow, or black.

NECK AND CHEST

The neck should be long and powerful and the shoulders long and sloping. The chest must be of good width and depth, the ribs well sprung and the loin wide and strong, stifles well turned and the hindquarters well developed and of great power.

LEGS AND FEET

The legs must be straight from the shoulder to ground, and the feet compact with toes well arched and pads well developed; the hocks should be well bent and the dog must neither be cow-hocked nor move too wide behind; in fact, he must stand and move true all round on legs and feet.

TAIL

The tail is a distinctive feature of the breed; it should be very thick towards the base, gradually tapering towards the tip, of medium length, should be practically free from any feathering, but should be clothed thickly all around with the Labrador's short, dense, thick coat, thus giving that peculiar "rounded" appearance which has been described as the "otter" tail. The tail may be carried gaily, but should not curl too far over the back.

COAT

The coat is another very distinctive feature; it should be short, very dense, and without wave and should give a fairly hard feeling to the hand.

COLOUR

The colour is generally black, free from any rustiness and any white markings except possibly a small spot on the chest. Other whole colours are permissible.

In 1986 The Labrador Club (England) adopted the following Standard:

BRITISH LABRADOR RETRIEVER STANDARD (1986)

GENERAL APPEARANCE

The general appearance of the Labrador should be that of a strongly-built, short-coupled, very active dog, broad in the skull, broad and deep through the chest and ribs, broad and strong over the loins and hindquarters. The coat close, short with dense undercoat and free from feather. The dog must move neither too wide nor too close in front or behind; he must stand and move true all round on legs and feet.

HEAD AND SKULL

The skull should be broad with pronounced stop so that the skull is not in a straight line with the nose. The head should be clean cut without fleshy cheeks. The jaws should be of medium length and powerful and free from snipiness. The nose wide and nostrils well developed.

MOUTH

Teeth should be sound and strong. The lower teeth just behind, but touching the upper.

EYES

The eyes, of medium size, expressing intelligence and good temper, should be brown or hazel.

EARS

Should not be large and heavy and should hang close to the head and set rather far back.

NECK

Should be clean, strong, and powerful and set into well-placed shoulders.

FOREQUARTERS

The shoulders should be long and sloping. The forelegs well boned and straight from the shoulder to the ground when viewed from either the front or side. The dog must move neither too wide nor too close in front.

BODY

The chest must be of good width and depth with well-sprung ribs. The back should be short-coupled.

HINDQUARTERS

The loins must be wide and strong, with well-sprung stifles; hindquarters well developed and not sloping to the tail. The hocks should be slightly bent and the dog must neither be cow-hocked nor move too wide or too close behind.

FEET

Should be round and compact with well-arched toes and well-developed pads.

TAIL

The tail is a distinctive feature of the breed; it should be very thick towards the base, gradually tapering towards the tip, of medium length and practically free from any feathering, but clothed thickly all round with the Labrador's thick dense coat, thus giving that peculiar "rounded" appearance that has been described as the "otter" tail. The tail may be carried gaily, but should not curl over the back.

COAT

The coat is another distinctive feature of the breed; it should be short and dense and without wave with a weather-resisting undercoat and should give a fairly hard feeling to hand.

COLOUR

The colour is generally black, chocolate, or yellow—which may vary from fox-red to cream—free from any white markings. A small white spot on the chest is allowed; the coat should be of a whole colour and not of a flecked appearance.

SIZE

Desired height for dogs, 22–22¹/₂ inches; bitches, 21¹/₂–22 inches.

FAULTS

Under- or overshot mouth, no undercoat, bad action, feathering, snipiness on the head, large or heavy ears, cow-hocked, tail curled over back.

The 1988 version added sections on characteristics and temperament. Eye color was limited to brown or hazel, thus eliminating the yellow (bird of prey) and ink black eyes that are so unattractive and detrimental to a kind expression. A description of the teeth was added. The very important undercoat was added and colors now include "wholly black, yellow, or liver/chocolate." Ideal height at the withers was added.

These were minor changes, so basically the Standard remained intact. The extra detail helped the Labrador Standard conform to the Kennel Club's format of uniform standards for all breeds.

BRITISH LABRADOR RETRIEVER STANDARD (1988)*

GENERAL APPEARANCE

Strongly built, short coupled, very active; broad in skull; broad and deep through chest and ribs; broad and strong over loins and hindquarters.

CHARACTERISTICS

Good tempered, very agile. Excellent nose, soft mouth; keen love of water. Adaptable, devoted companion.

TEMPERAMENT

Intelligent, keen, and biddable, with a strong will to please. Kindly nature, with no trace of aggression or undue shyness.

HEAD & SKULL

Skull broad with defined stop; clean cut without fleshy cheeks. Jaws of medium length, powerful, not snipey. Nose wide, nostrils well developed.

EYES

Medium size, expressing intelligence and good temper; brown or hazel.

EARS

Not large or heavy, hanging close to head and set rather far back.

MOUTH

Jaws and teeth strong, with a perfect, regular, and complete scissor bite, i.e. the upper teeth closely overlapping the lower teeth and set square to the jaws.

NECK

Clean, strong, powerful, set into well-placed shoulders.

FOREQUARTERS

Shoulders long and sloping. Forelegs well-boned and straight from elbow to ground when viewed from either front or side.

---

*Reprinted with Kennel Club permission.

BODY

Chest of good width and depth, with well-sprung barrel ribs. Level topline. Loins wide, short coupled and strong.

HINDQUARTERS

Well-developed not sloping to tail; well turned stifle. Hocks well let down, cow-hocks highly undesirable.

FEET

Round, compact; well-arched toes and well-developed pads.

TAIL

Distinctive feature, very thick towards base, gradually tapering towards tip, medium length, free from feathering, but clothed thickly all around with short, thick, dense coat, thus giving "rounded" appearance described as "otter" tail. May be carried gaily, but should not curl over back.

GAIT/MOVEMENT

Free, covering adequate ground; straight and true in front and rear.

COAT

Distinctive feature, short, dense without wave or feathering, giving fairly hard feel to the touch; weather resistant undercoat.

COLOUR

Wholly black, yellow, or liver/chocolate. Yellows range from light cream to red fox. Small white spot on chest permissible.

SIZE

Ideal height at withers: Dogs 56–57 cms (22–22$\frac{1}{2}$ ins). Bitches 54–56 cms (21$\frac{1}{2}$–22 ins).

FAULTS

Any departure from the foregoing points should be considered a fault and the seriousness with which the fault should be regarded in exact proportion to its degree.

NOTE

Male animals should have two apparently normal testicles fully descended into the scrotum.

AMERICAN LABRADOR RETRIEVER STANDARD

GENERAL APPEARANCE

The Labrador Retriever is a strongly built, medium-sized, short-coupled dog possessing a sound, athletic, well-balanced conformation that enables it to function as a retrieving gun dog; the substance and soundness to hunt waterfowl or upland game for long hours under difficult conditions; the character and quality to win in the show ring; and the temperament to be a family companion. Physical features and mental characteristics should denote a dog bred to perform as an efficient retriever of game with a stable temperament suitable for a variety of pursuits beyond the hunting environment.

The most distinguishing characteristics of the Labrador Retriever are its short, dense, weather-resistant coat; an "otter" tail; a clean-cut head with broad back skull and moderate stop; powerful jaws; and its "kind," friendly eyes, expressing character, intelligence, and good temperament.

Above all, a Labrador Retriever must be well balanced, enabling it to move in the show ring or work in the field with little or no effort. The typical Labrador possesses style and quality without over-refinement, and substance without lumber or cloddiness. The Labrador is bred primarily as a working gun dog; structure and soundness are of great importance.

SIZE, PROPORTION AND SUBSTANCE

Size

The height at the withers for a dog is 22½ to 24½ inches; for a bitch is 21½ to 23½ inches. Any variance greater than ½ inch above or below these heights is a disqualification. Approximate weight of dogs and bitches in working condition: dogs, 65 to 80 pounds; bitches, 55 to 70 pounds.

The minimum height ranges set forth in the paragraph above shall not apply to dogs or bitches under twelve months of age.

Proportion

Short-coupled; length from the point of the shoulder to the point of the rump is equal to or slightly longer than the distance from the withers to the ground. Distance from the elbow to the ground should be equal to one half of the height at the withers. The brisket should extend to the elbows, but not perceptibly deeper. The body must be of sufficient length to permit a straight, free, and efficient stride; but the dog should never appear low and long or tall and leggy in outline.

Substance

Substance and bone proportionate to the overall dog. Light, "weedy" individuals are definitely incorrect; equally objectionable are cloddy, lumbering specimens. Labrador Retrievers shall be shown in working condition well-muscled and without excess fat.

HEAD

Skull

The skull should be wide; well developed but without exaggeration. The skull and foreface should be on parallel planes and of approximately equal length. There should be a moderate stop—the brow slightly pronounced so that the skull is not absolutely in a straight line with the nose. The brow ridges aid in defining the stop. The head should be clean cut and free from fleshy cheeks; the bony structure of the skull chiseled beneath the eye with no prominence in the cheek. The skull may show some median line; the occipital bone is not conspicuous in mature dogs. Lips should not be squared off or pendulous, but fall away in a curve toward the throat. A wedge-shaped head, or a head long and narrow in muzzle and back skull is incorrect as are massive, cheeky heads. The jaws are powerful and free from snippiness—the muzzle neither long and narrow nor short and stubby.

Nose

The nose should be wide and the nostrils well-developed. The nose should be black on black or yellow dogs, and brown on chocolates. Nose color fading to a lighter shade is not a fault. A thoroughly pink nose or one lacking in any pigment is a disqualification.

Teeth

The teeth should be strong and regular with a scissors bite; the lower teeth just behind, but touching the inner side of the upper incisors. A level bite is acceptable, but not desirable. Undershot, overshot, or misaligned teeth are serious faults. Full dentition is preferred. Missing molars or premolars are serious faults.

Ears

The ears should hang moderately close to the head, set rather far back, and somewhat low on the skull; slightly above eye level. Ears should not be large and heavy, but in proportion with the skull and reach to the inside of the eye when pulled forward.

Eyes

Kind, friendly eyes imparting good temperament, intelligence, and alertness are a hallmark of the breed. They should be of medium size, set well apart, and neither protruding nor deep set. Eye color should be brown in black and yellow Labradors, and brown or hazel in chocolates. Black or yellow eyes give a harsh expression and are undesirable. Small eyes set close together or round prominent eyes are not typical of the breed. Eye rims are black in black and yellow Labradors and brown in chocolates. Eye rims without pigmentation is a disqualification.

NECK, TOPLINE, AND BODY

Neck

The neck should be of proper length to allow the dog to retrieve game easily. It should be muscular and free from throatiness. The neck should rise strongly from the shoulders with a moderate arch. A short, thick neck or a "ewe" neck is incorrect.

Topline

The back is strong and the topline is level from the withers to the croup when standing or moving. However, the loin should show evidence of flexibility for athletic endeavor.

Body

The Labrador should be short-coupled, with good spring of ribs tapering to a moderately wide chest. The Labrador should not be narrow-chested, giving the appearance of hollowness between the front legs, nor should it have a wide-spreading, bulldog-like front. Correct chest conformation will result in tapering between the front legs that allows unrestricted forelimb movement. Chest breadth that is either too wide or too narrow for efficient movement and stamina is incorrect. Slab-sided individuals are not typical of the breed; equally objectionable are rotund or barrel-chested specimens. The underline is almost straight, with little or no tuck-up in mature animals. Loins should be short, wide, and strong, extending to well-developed, powerful hindquarters. When viewed from the side, the Labrador Retriever shows a well-developed but not exaggerated forechest.

Tail

The tail is a distinguishing feature of the breed. It should be very thick at the base, gradually tapering toward the tip, of medium length, and extending no longer than to the hock. The tail should be free from feathering and clothed thickly all around with the Labrador's short, dense coat, thus having that peculiar rounded appearance that has been described as the "otter" tail. The tail should follow the topline in repose or when in motion. It may be carried gaily, but should not curl over the back. Extremely short tails or long thin tails are serious faults. The tail completes the balance of the Labrador by giving it a flowing line from the top of the head to the tip of the tail. Docking or otherwise altering the length or natural carriage of the tail is a disqualification.

FOREQUARTERS

Forequarters should be muscular, well coordinated, and balanced with the hindquarters.

Shoulders

The shoulders are well laid back, long and sloping, forming an angle with the upper arm of approximately 90 degrees that permits the dog to move his forelegs in an easy manner with strong forward reach. Ideally, the length of the shoulder blade should equal the length of the upper arm. Straight shoulder blades, short upper arms, or heavily muscled or loaded shoulders, all restricting free movement, are incorrect.

Front Legs

When viewed from the front, the legs should be straight with good strong bone. Too much bone is as undesirable as too little bone, and short-legged, heavy-boned individuals are not typical of the breed. Viewed from the side, the elbows should be directly under the withers, and the front legs should be perpendicular to the ground and well under the body. The elbows should be close to the ribs without looseness. Tied-in elbows or being "out at the elbows" interfere with free movement and are serious faults. Pasterns should be strong and short and should slope slightly from the perpendicular line of the leg. Feet are strong and compact, with well-arched toes and well-developed pads. Dew claws may be removed. Splayed feet, hare feet, knuckling over, or feet turning in or out are serious faults.

HINDQUARTERS

The Labrador's hindquarters are broad, muscular and well-developed from the hip to the hock with well-turned stifles and strong short hocks. Viewed from the rear, the hind legs are straight and parallel. Viewed from the side, the angulation of the rear legs is in balance with the front. The hind legs are strongly boned, muscled with moderate angulation at the stifle, and with powerful, clearly defined thighs. The stifle is strong, and there is no slippage of the patellae while in motion or when standing. The hock joints are strong, well let down, and do not slip or hyperextend while in motion or when standing. Angulation of both stifle and hock joint is such as to achieve the optimal balance of drive and traction. When standing, the rear toes are only slightly behind the point of the rump. Over-angulation produces a sloping topline not typical of the breed. Feet are strong and compact, with well-arched toes and well-developed pads. Cow-hocks, spread hocks, sickle hocks, and over-angulation are serious structural defects and are to be faulted.

COAT

The coat is a distinctive feature of the Labrador Retriever. It should be short, straight and very dense, giving a fairly hard feeling to the hand. The Labrador should have a soft, weather-resistant undercoat that provides protection from water, cold, and all types of ground cover. A slight wave down the back is permissible. Woolly coats, soft silky coats, and sparse slick coats are not typical of the breed, and should be severely penalized.

COLOR

The Labrador Retriever coat colors are black, yellow, and chocolate. Any other color or a combination of colors is a disqualification. A small white spot on the chest is permissible, but not desirable. White hairs from aging or scarring are not to be misinterpreted as brindling.

Black

Blacks are all black. A black with brindle markings or a black with tan markings is a disqualification.

Yellow

Yellows may range in color from fox-red to light cream, with variations in shading on the ears, back, and underparts of the dog.

Chocolate

Chocolates can vary in shade from light to dark chocolate. Chocolate with brindle or tan markings is a disqualification.

MOVEMENT

Movement of the Labrador Retriever should be free and effortless. When watching a dog move toward oneself, there should be no sign of elbows out.

Rather, the elbows should be held neatly to the body with the legs not too close together. Moving straight forward without pacing or weaving, the legs should form straight lines, with all parts moving in the same plane. Upon viewing the dog from the rear, one should have the impression that the hind legs move as nearly as possible in a parallel line with the front legs. The hocks should do their full share of the work, flexing well, giving the appearance of power and strength. When viewed from the side, the shoulders should move freely and effortlessly, and the foreleg should reach forward close to the ground with extension. A short, choppy movement or high knee action indicates a straight shoulder; paddling indicates long, weak pasterns; and a short, stilted rear gait indicates a straight rear assembly; all are serious faults. Movement faults interfering with performance, including weaving, side-winding, crossing over, high knee action, paddling, and short choppy movement, should be severely penalized.

TEMPERAMENT

True Labrador Retriever temperament is as much a hallmark of the breed as the "otter" tail. The ideal disposition is one of a kindly, outgoing, tractable nature; eager to please and non-aggressive towards man or animal. The Labrador has much that appeals to people; his gentle ways, intelligence, and adaptability make him an ideal dog. Aggressiveness towards humans or other animals or any evidence of shyness in an adult should be severely penalized.

Disqualifications

1. Any deviation from the height prescribed in the Standard.
2. A thoroughly pink nose or one lacking in any pigment.
3. Eye rims without pigment.
4. Docking or otherwise altering the length or natural carriage of the tail.
5. Any other color or a combination of colors other than black, yellow, or chocolate as described in the Standard.

Approval Date: February 12, 1994
Effective Date: March 31, 1994

---

chapter 22

The Wind-Morgan Program for Diagnosis of Heritable Joint Disorders in the Labrador Retriever

The Labrador Retriever recently became the most popular purebred dog in the United States, as evidenced by records of the American Kennel Club. The Labrador Retriever is a breed renowned for its versatility, working enthusiastically in the field, excelling at obedience trials, providing assistance to the disabled, and giving active companionship to many. Veterinarians readily recommend the breed as appropriate for families and active individuals. The Labrador is the most common and most successful breed used by Guide Dogs for the Blind, and has found enthusiastic acceptance in other service-oriented groups as well (Canine Companions for Independence, search and rescue, contraband detection). Basic to this popularity is the breed's benevolent personality and athletic ability. The recent increase in potentially crippling orthopedic disorders in the breed is therefore of great concern to its fanciers.

Labrador Retriever fanciers have been aware of the problem of hip dysplasia in the breed for many years. Evaluating hip joint structure prior to breeding an individual has become commonplace, largely due to the guidance and education provided by the Orthopedic Foundation for Animals (OFA). During the last 15 years it has become apparent that disorders in the shoulder, elbow, hock and, less commonly, stifle joints also exist. These disorders include elbow dysplasia (ED), a malformation of the elbow joint resulting in incongruent weight-bearing surfaces, and osteochondroses (OCD), a disturbance in the maturation of cartilage in growing joints, occurring in the shoulder, elbow, hock, and stifle. Review of the veterinary literature supports the heritable nature of these disorders.

The Wind-Morgan program was initiated at the University of California, Davis' School of Veterinary Medicine in August of 1990, in response to pleas from Labrador breeders to gain more understanding and reduce the increasing incidence of lameness in puppies attributed to a diagnosis of elbow dysplasia and/or osteochondritis dissecans. The program was established by Dr. Alida Wind, a renowned orthopedic surgeon credited with the elucidation of elbow dysplasia in Bernese Mountain Dogs, and Dr. Joe Morgan, a well-known orthopedic radiologist. The program is administered, and data computer banked by the Institute of Genetic Disease Control (GDC), also in Davis, California. The program provides an organized mechanism by which breeders can pursue orthopedic improvement of the Labrador Retriever. Great frustration results from the discovery that an inherited orthopedic disorder exists in puppies produced from dogs and bitches selected as breeding stock after seemingly careful evaluation of their conformation, soundness, and personality. The Wind-Morgan program offers a route by which fanciers of the breed can make a more educated scrutiny of potential breeding stock, while at the same time collecting data for the genetic analysis of these disorders. The Wind-Morgan Program is based upon the establishment of an *open* registry emphasizing sibling and progeny evaluation, and encouraging the registry of both normal and affected individuals.

The first step in reducing the presence of any defective trait in a breed is to accurately recognize its existence in individuals and subsequently, the trait's incidence in the breed. Once breeders are aware of the nature of a phenotypic problem, steps can be taken in breeding programs to reduce its incidence. This program has drawn attention to the multiplicity of inherited bone and joint abnormalities in the Labrador Retriever. Feelings of security when a single anatomic site (commonly the hip joint) is evaluated as radiographically normal during pre-breeding evaluation have diminished. The breeder's code of ethics has been changed in several regional California Labrador Retriever clubs to encourage evaluation of the shoulder, elbow, and hock joints in addition to the hip joints, as a result of the Wind-Morgan Program.

In addition to providing a mechanism by which breeders can assess an individual dog's phenotypic soundness, the program illustrates the importance of progeny evaluation. Stud dogs' and brood bitches' value should be based on their ability to produce offspring with desirable traits and lacking undesirable traits such as joint dysplasias. Affected individuals are more likely to produce affected offspring than known normal individuals. Individuals with unknown orthopedic status produce affected offspring at a rate intermediate to that from known affected and known normal individuals. However, because affected individuals were found to be produced by the matings of known normal individuals, the great value of progeny and sibling evaluation became apparent. Pedigree evaluation permitted by the open registry utilized in this program will allow selection of breeding stock less likely to produce affected offspring.

The presence of these disorders may not always be obvious because the lameness may be subtle, or actually present in both limbs. One reason these disorders may have become so common in the Labrador is that affected individuals without obvious lameness have been used unknowingly in breeding programs. Just as has been learned from the evaluation of the pelvis for hip dysplasia, the best current method to diagnose the presence of elbow dysplasia and osteochondroses is radiography (X-rays). The absence of these disorders in the elbows, shoulders, and hocks can usually be accurately determined at 12 months of age. An evaluation of the hip joint for dysplasia can be made at the same time. Preliminary evaluations of the elbows, shoulders, hocks, and hips can be made as early as six months of age, if desired. Dogs showing signs of lameness can be evaluated at any age. The inclusion of older dogs in the program is highly encouraged. Age-related "wear and tear" arthritic changes in joints are distinctly different from those changes caused by developmental disorders such as dysplasias and OCD. To date, several veteran Labrador Retrievers have successfully passed the Wind-Morgan evaluation.

The radiographs necessary for participation in the Wind-Morgan Program can be made by any veterinary practitioner or animal health technician. Radiographic views should be made as follows: a single lateral view of each shoulder; two lateral views of each elbow, one tightly flexed and one at 120 degrees; two conventional ventrodorsal views of the hips; and a plantardorsal (PD) and lateral, slightly flexed view of each hock. These radiographs can be taken without anesthesia; however, in the exuberant Labrador, mild tranquilization often facilitates positioning. Films should be submitted to the Wind-Morgan program for evaluation with a completed application form and a copy of the dog's three-generation pedigree. Although evaluation of all four joint sites is encouraged, the Wind-Morgan Program will evaluate any single joint if desired.

A fee of $35.00 is charged, covering a one-time $10.00 registration fee for an individual dog, and a $25.00 fee for the evaluation of all four joint sites. If an individual is found to be normal in all four joints at or beyond the age of 12 months, a Wind-Morgan number is issued. If the individual is found to be affected in any joint by heritable disease, the $35.00 fee is refunded, thus encouraging the inclusion of affected individuals in the study. Reevaluation of an individual examined previously before the age of 12 months does not require repayment of the $10.00 registration fee. If a diagnosis of normalcy cannot be made due to inadequate X-ray positioning or exposure, or because of the presence of suspicious but not diagnostic changes, repeat x-rays will be requested within a specified time frame. No additional charge will be made for evaluation of these subsequent films.

Copies of the evaluations will be mailed to both the dog's owner and to the veterinarian responsible for taking the films. Additionally, results of the study will be entered into the computer base at the Institute for Genetic Disease Control (GDC), for inclusion in their open registry for genetic and statistical analysis. The x-rays will be archived at the GDC in Davis, California, with copies available to owners for a nominal charge. Interested individuals can obtain information from GDC concerning an individual dog or its relatives, to determine more about the genotype that a prospective sire or dam may pass on to its offspring, by telephoning GDC at (916)756-6773. The Wind-Morgan Program provides assistance to fanciers of Labrador Retrievers through educational seminars for breeders and their veterinarians, as well as individual counseling concerning the treatment of these disorders in affected individuals. As data accumulates, genetic counseling will become available through the GDC. To facilitate the inclusion of numerous dogs in the study, the University of California sponsors weekend X-ray clinics to provide radiography at a minimal expense. Interested veterinarians or breeders may contact the program concerning organization of X-ray clinics in other parts of the country. To obtain further information concerning the Wind-Morgan Program, contact Dr. Autumn Davidson at the Small Animal Clinic. VMTH, University of California, Davis, CA, 95616, telephone (916) 752-1393, fax (916) 756-6773, or telephone GDC at (916) 756-6773. Films should be mailed to Drs. Joe Morgan, Alida Wind, or Autumn Davidson, c/o GDC, P.O. Box 222, Davis, CA 95617.

About the Author

Janet I. Churchill selected Labrador Retrievers as the most desirable hunting breed when she moved to Maryland's Eastern Shore in the mid-1960s. Her first Labrador, Int. Ch. Spenrock Banner, WC, turned out to be a great foundation bitch as well as an excellent gun dog, as was her littermate, Ch. Spenrock Ballot. Banner's first litter produced a National Specialty winner, Ch. Spenrock Sans Souci.

Janet Churchill became an approved Labrador Retriever judge in 1972. She has judged at some of America's most important shows, including Westminster, Philadelphia, Boston, Detroit, Trenton, and in Canada and at numerous Labrador Specialties in both countries from coast to coast.

She wrote the Labrador Column for *Pure-Bred Dogs—American Kennel Club Gazette* for 20 years. She is a Life Member of the Labrador Retriever Club of America, and was for many years a member of the Labrador Retriever Club (England). Her kennel prefix "Spenrock" is registered in England and the United States.

Janet Churchill wrote the chapter on "Standards for the Labrador Retriever" and "Obedience, Gun Dogs and Working Certificates" for *The Book of The Labrador Retriever* by Anna Katherine Nicholas.

Miss Churchill has also bred and shown champion Rottweilers, Pembroke Welsh Corgis, German Shepherd Dogs, and Airedale Terriers. For many years she was Master of Foxhounds of the Groton Hunt Club (Massachusetts), where the excellent working pack that she bred won many honors on the bench at hound shows.

Miss Churchill is a graduate of Sweet Briar College and has a Master's Degree from the University of Virginia in International Law. She holds a Paralegal Certificate from Widener University.

Miss Churchill has published a book about a woman who flew for the military in World War II, *On Wings to War*. Janet Churchill is a pilot with an airline transport license and a certificated flight instructor for instruments and multi-engine. She has written numerous articles for aviation publications and lectures on women military pilots in World War II. Miss Churchill is one of the editors for *Warbirds of America* magazine. She is President of the Delaware Aviation Memorial Foundation and the Delaware chapter of EAA (Experimental Aircraft Association).

Bibliography

Retriever Training

Cofield, Thomas R. *Training and Hunting Retriever, Labrador, Chesapeake and Golden.* D. Van Nostrand, 1959.

Deeley, Martin. *Working Gundogs: An Introduction to Training and Handling.* Crowood Press, UK, 1989.

Deeley, Martin. *Advanced Gundog Training.* Crowood Press, UK, 1990.

Free, James Lamb. *Training Your Retriever* (7th rev. edition). New York: G. P. Putnam's Sons, 1980.

Hutt, Frederick B. *Genetics for Dog Breeders.* W. H. Freeman & Co., 1979. (Basic principles of genetics in dogs).

Little, Clarence C. *The Inheritance of Coat Color in Dogs.* Cornell University Press, 1957.

Milner, Robert. *Retriever Training for the Duck Hunter.* Princeton, N.J.: Nassau Press, 1983.

Quinn, Tom. *The Working Retriever.* New York: Dutton, 1983.

Robinson, Roy. *Genetics for Dog Breeders.* Elmsford, N.Y.: Pergamon Press, 1990.

Rutherford, Clarice, Barbara Branstad, and Sandra Whicker. *Retriever Working Certificate Training*. Loveland, Colorado: Alpine Publications,1986.

Spencer, James B. *Retriever Training Tests*. New York: Arco Publishing, 1983.

Wolters, Richard A. *Duck Dogs*. New York: Dutton, 1990.

Wolters, Richard A. *The Labrador Retriever*. Los Angeles: Petersen, 1981.

Wolters, Richard A. *The Labrador Retriever*. New Yok: Dutton, 1982.

Wolters, Richard A. *Water Dog*. New York: Dutton, 1984.

General Information

Julie Brown's Directory to Labrador Retriever Pedigrees. Melrose Park, Pennsylvania, 1971–1994.

Brown, Julie. *The Judge's Opinion*. Melrose Park, Pennsylvania, 1993.

Labrador Retriever Club Yearbooks: 1931–1956; 1956–1961; 1962–1966.

Hill, F. Warner. *Labradors*. New York: Arco Publishing, 1966.

Howe, Dorothy. *This Is the Labrador Retiever*. Neptune City, N.J.: T.F.H. Publications, 1972.

Martin, Nancy. *Legends in Labradors*. Spring House, PA, 1980.

Nicholas, Anna Katherine. *The Book of the Labrador Retriever*. Neptune City, N.J.: T.F.H. Publications, 1983.

Retriever Field Trials 1967–1972. Retriever Field Trial News and Labrador Retriever Club, 1973.

Roslin–Williams, Mary. *All About the Labrador*. London, England: Pelham Books, 1975.

Roslin–Williams, Mary. *Advanced Labrador Breeding*. London, England: Witherby, Ltd., 1988.

Sanderson, C. Mackay. *The Labrador Retriever Club Stud Book and Record of Field Trials.* Dumfries. Courier Press, 1949.

Warwick, Helen. *The New Complete Labrador Retriever.* New York: Howell Book House, 1986, 1965, 1964.

Health and Genetics

Canine Hip Dysplasia. OFA Symposium, 1972.

GPRA Report. Vols. I, II, III, IV. Woodinville, Washington: PRA Data, Inc. 1991–1994.

Lanting, Riser, and Sten–Eric Olson. *Canine Hip Dysplasia and Other Orthopedic Problems.* Loveland, Colorado: Alpine Publications, 1981.

Little, Clarence C. *The Inheritance of Coat Color in Dogs.* New York: Howell Book House, 1956.

Macan, Joan. *Hips.* Hempstead, England.

Ocular Disorders Proven or Suspected to Be Hereditary in Dogs. Indiana: Purdue University, 1994.

Pritchard, Janice. *Inheritance of Coat Colour in the Labrador Retriever.* Labradors of Australia and New Zealand, 1981.

Stewart, A.P., Templeton, J.W., and Fletcher, W.S. *Coat Color Genetics in the Labrador Retriever.* The Journal of Hereditary, 68: 134–136, 1977.

Willis, Malcolm B. *Genetics of the Dog.* New York: Howell Book House, 1989. (Extremely comprehensive and easy to read).